# RESOLVING STRUCTURAL CONFLICTS

This book analyses how certain types of social systems generate violent conflict and discusses how these systems can be transformed in order to create the conditions for positive peace.

*Resolving Structural Conflicts* addresses a key issue in the field of conflict studies: what to do about violent conflicts that are not the results of misunderstanding, prejudice, or malice, but the products of a social system that generates violent conflict as part of its normal operations. This question poses enormous challenges to those interested in conflict resolution, since the solution to this problem involves restructuring social, political, and cultural systems rather than just calling in a mediator to help people arrive at an agreement. This study breaks new ground in showing how local conflicts involving crime, police, and prisons; transnational conflicts involving religious terrorism by groups like ISIS; and international conflicts involving Great Power clashes are all produced in large part by elite-driven, exploitative or oppressive social structures. It also presents new ideas about the implications of this 'structural turn' for the practice of conflict resolution, emphasizing the need for conflict resolvers to embrace a new politics and to broaden their methods far beyond traditional forms of facilitation.

Written by a leading scholar, this book will be of much interest to students of conflict resolution, peace studies, war and conflict studies, sociology, political science and international relations in general.

**Richard E. Rubenstein** is University Professor of Conflict Resolution and Public Affairs at the School for Conflict Analysis and Resolution, George Mason University, and the author of eight books, including most recently *Reasons to Kill: Why Americans Choose War* (2010).

# Routledge Studies in Peace and Conflict Resolution

Series Editors: Tom Woodhouse and Oliver Ramsbotham
*University of Bradford*

# RESOLVING STRUCTURAL CONFLICTS

## How Violent Systems Can Be Transformed

*Richard E. Rubenstein*

**Routledge**
Taylor & Francis Group

LONDON AND NEW YORK

First published 2017
by Routledge
2 Park Square, Milton Park, Abingdon, Oxon OX14 4RN

and by Routledge
711 Third Avenue, New York, NY 10017

*Routledge is an imprint of the Taylor & Francis Group, an informa business*

*British Library Cataloguing-in-Publication Data*
A catalogue record for this book is available from the British Library

*Library of Congress Cataloging-in-Publication Data*
Names: Rubenstein, Richard E.
Title: Resolving structural conflicts : how violent systems can be
   transformed / Richard E. Rubenstein.
Description: Abingdon, Oxon : New York, NY : Routledge, 2017. |
   Series: Routledge studies in peace and conflict resolution |
   Includes bibliographical references and index.
Identifiers: LCCN 2016035099 | ISBN 9781138956322
   (hardback) | ISBN 9781138956339 (pbk.) | ISBN
   9781315665764 (ebook)
Subjects: LCSH: Conflict management—Social aspects. |
   Social conflict. | Culture conflict. | Social change.
Classification: LCC HM1126 .R83 2017 | DDC 303.6/9—dc23
LC record available at https://lccn.loc.gov/2016035099


ISBN: 978-1-138-95632-2 (hbk)
ISBN: 978-1-138-95633-9 (pbk)
ISBN: 978-1-315-66576-4 (ebk)


Typeset in Bembo
by Swales & Willis Ltd, Exeter, Devon, UK

**For My Students**

'Rubenstein actually does two jobs in *Resolving Structural Conflicts*. He not only shows how vertical, exploitative class structures, pitting high against low domestically and protecting class all over through global hegemony can be broken down. He also paves the way intellectually for breaking the taboos on class in US thinking about conflict without falling into the many Marxist traps. I strongly endorse the book as a major contribution to US conflict studies.'

*Johan Galtung, Founder of Transcend International*

'Richard Rubenstein has done it again! In an accessible, wide-ranging, and brilliant set of discussions he places a mirror before all of us engaged in peace and conflict studies and practice. We have for too long relied on simple explanations about change strategies when we face *direct* and *structural violence*, a field-wide habit that attends to the first but rarely the second. Rubenstein's comprehensive and constructive engagement suggests our platitudes and frameworks must evolve in ways that more seriously address the challenge of how we pursue systemic and structural change. Filled with practical examples, theoretically sophisticated interaction with key authors in both conflict resolution and the wider social sciences, and groundbreaking critique and ideas, this book deepens and expands our scholarship and practice alike. A must-read for which we should all be grateful!'

*John Paul Lederach, Kroc Institute, University of Notre Dame, USA*

'In this provocative book Richard Rubenstein sets out to answer two basic questions: How does the socioeconomic system generate violence? And what can conflict specialists do about it? In response, he returns us to two of the formative ideas in peace and conflict studies – unfulfilled human needs and structural violence – and elaborates them through theorizing and practice in the first two "waves" of conflict and conflict resolution, focused on interests and identity. Rubenstein argues for a "third wave," which demands a critical engagement with the socioeconomic system, the *structure*, within which all the other dynamical, symbolic, and political systems are embedded. This entails "breaking the silence about social class," and about class struggle as the "conflict that dare not speak its name." In returning conflict resolution to structure and class, he argues for recognizing that poverty, inequality, and indelible harm to human dignity, generate and reproduce conflict and violence as normal or naturalized, thus invisible or taken-for-granted. He rejects a vision of conflict resolution as "pallid reform," or an acquiescent "abstentionism" that believes profound structural change is unlikely or impossible. Deeply analytical, infused with passion and powerfully written, I read this book as a provocation, a challenge to conflict studies and conflict resolution practice.'

*Kevin Avruch, George Mason University, USA*

'Over the years Richard Rubenstein has demonstrated an unusual talent for tackling the toughest societal challenges, provocatively combining lucid analysis with humane prescriptive wisdom. Rubenstein does it here once more, daring to consider how the social structures associated with neo-imperial capitalism generate acute violent conflict, yet can and should be transformed. A major intellectual contribution, this book should excite progressives and make liberals tremble.'

*Richard Falk, University of California, Santa Barbara, USA*

# CONTENTS

# ACKNOWLEDGMENTS

Heartfelt thanks, to begin with, to my academic home, George Mason University, which kindly granted me a sabbatical term to provide the time and permit the single-minded attention needed to complete this book. Thanks to Provost S. David Wu and his staff and to my long-time colleague and dear friend, now Dean of the School for Conflict Analysis and Resolution, Kevin Avruch, for making this possible.

*Resolving Structural Conflicts* is dedicated to my students, to whom I owe an unpayable debt of gratitude. Their verve and spirit, creative ideas, love of dissent, and dedication to building a better world are what make my job worth doing.

Certain students, in particular, engaged actively in helping me think through the problems discussed in this book, locating research sources, commenting on my work, and sharing their own insights and suggestions. Dr. Michael English was a constant source of help and inspiration. Thank you, Michael! I am also grateful to other students concerned with these issues who remain valued colleagues and friends. A partial list includes Jarle P. Crocker, Lewis Dabney, Adina Friedman, Melanie Hartmann, Oded Adomi Leshem, Michael Loadenthal, Kate Romanova, Michael Shank, Derek Sweetman, and Hussein Ali Yusuf.

I am most grateful to my dear colleagues at the School for Conflict Analysis and Resolution for giving me the chance to present these ideas and to receive feedback on them in-house. Special thanks to the S-CAR staff, including Jay Moon, Paul Snodgrass, Molly Tepper, Cassie Ammen, Charisse Cardenas, and r.j. nickels for providing help with much-needed office, technical, and library services.

I very much appreciate the kind assistance provided by Andrew Humphrys of Routledge Publishers in helping to get this book launched and providing sage advice during the production process. Thanks also to Hannah Ferguson of Routledge for her skilled assistance in producing the final work, and to Gary Blogg of GSB Editorial for his meticulous and tasteful copyediting.

As always, my family provided the moral and emotional support that one needs (at least, I do) to undertake and complete a project as challenging as this. Thank you, Hannah and Noel, Shana and Danielle, Matt and Alex, Jill and Dave, and Jamie and Deena. Thank you, Elissa and Joe. Most of all, thank you, dearest Susan, for providing, as always, the *sine qua non*.

# INTRODUCTION

This study grows out of my relationships with two pioneers in the field of conflict analysis and resolution, John Burton and Johan Galtung.

In 1987, I began teaching at George Mason University's Center for Conflict Analysis and Resolution, where John Burton was a distinguished visiting professor and an irrepressible source of energy, ideas, and controversy. Burton's theory and practice were largely based on the concept of basic human needs, an approach to conflict resolution that I found challenging and useful. The following year, he convened a consultative conference at Airlie House in Airlie, Virgina, to discuss how best to critique and develop the theory, and there I met Johan Galtung. It was an encounter that I still remember vividly.

The twenty or so scholars in attendance constituted a who's who of leaders in conflict studies. Many later rewrote their conference presentations for inclusion in a compilation of essays edited by Burton and published a year or so later.[1] The overall atmosphere was serious but friendly, with a mixture of intellectual camaraderie and competitiveness reminiscent of a faculty club. When it came to his turn to speak, Johan Galtung rose from his seat and addressed the participants in a tone that seemed surprisingly intense.

Studying human needs was clearly a good idea, Galtung said, promising to offer his own typology of needs, in the context of human development, a bit later.

> But, [here his voice became impassioned] you *must* keep in mind that, although human needs are universal, humanity remains divided into

two great classes: the *herren* [masters] and *knechte* [servants]. The 'top dogs' still lord it over the 'bottom dogs,' and this vast inequality generates misery and violence. Let us, by all means, develop the theory of basic needs. But if we do not incorporate that theory into a theory of society that reflects the relationship of top dogs to bottom dogs, we will not be able to explain or resolve violent conflicts.[2]

That statement resonated strongly with me, since I had come to the field of conflict resolution from a background of teaching law and politics while participating actively in movements for peace, justice, and social change. Influenced by figures like Burton and Galtung, Elise Boulding, and other founders of the field, I assumed that resolving serious social conflicts meant assisting parties in conflict to discover the underlying social and psychological causes of their struggle, to envision methods of eliminating or mitigating these causes, and to agree on new policies designed to make these visions practicable. The basic idea, which I found entirely congenial, was that conflict resolution was based on the sort of in-depth analysis that would naturally generate in-depth solutions to the problems generating violent conflicts. If, as Galtung argued, certain social arrangements had the effect of generating violent conflicts, our job was to discover what those arrangements were and how to transform them.

What I did not understand very well, however, was that the field itself was in a process of evolving from an earlier stage of development, in which social conflicts were conceived of primarily as clashes of *interest*, through a second period defining them as struggles based on threats to *identity*, toward a third stage recognizing the key role of *structures* in generating intergroup violence. This progression, discussed in some detail in Chapter 2, was bound to generate conflicts within the field, over its proper ambit, analytical methodology, and forms of practice. In fact, I discovered that when I spoke or wrote about violent conflicts from a structuralist perspective, others in the field would frequently find it necessary to remind me that system transformation was a 'maximal' goal, that achievable reforms were better than utopian visions, and that the systems requiring change might well be changed from within. In short, I found myself playing the role of the revolutionary in a classic 'reform or revolution' debate (the debate, as applied to our field, is described more fully in Chapter 3). Yet that dichotomy seemed to me unhelpful in helping our field further develop its theory and practice to reflect the reality of conflict-generating social systems.

Thus, the present book, which explores what it calls the 'structural turn' in our understanding of social conflicts and the possibilities of resolving them peacefully. The fundamental idea animating the study is that certain violent conflicts are not only the result of misunderstandings, prejudice, power-lust, or some other manifestation of evil intent but are also the regular products of social systems that reproduce them as part of their normal operations. These systems, like the prison system described in the book's first chapter, tend to be elite-dominated, inequitable, and exploitative. Without identifying them and exploring their methods of operation, it is impossible to account for conflicts that some analysts deem intractable or irresolvable except by force or threats of force, such as the crime/punishment syndrome, religious terrorism/counterterrorism, the political 'culture wars,' protracted ethnonationalist conflicts, and struggles involving competitive Great Powers. Moreover, without focusing on how they generate violence, it is difficult or impossible to devise methods of resolving such struggles, since the methods appropriate to helping resolve other forms of conflict may not be sufficiently system-oriented to get at the roots of structural conflict.

This study is divided into two parts. The first three chapters focus on developing a general understanding of structural conflicts and the problems of resolving them, while the last three discuss specific cases and methods of dealing with them from the perspective of conflict resolution practice. Chapter 1 examines the prison system as an example of a conflict-generating social structure and goes on to discuss 'partisan moralism,' a characteristic response to conflict that signals the absence of a structural perspective. The chapter then explores the issues raised by partisan moralism in the context of the Israel-Gaza War of 2014. The antidote to this mode of thinking, a structuralist viewpoint recognizing the role of social systems in generating violence, is introduced by Chapter 2. This discussion begins by showing how 'objectivist' and 'subjectivist' schools think about social systems, proceeds to outline the three waves of development of the field of conflict studies (interest-based, identity-based, and structural), and concludes with the challenge posed by new forms of conflict that require structural analysis and a broadened range of conflict resolution practices.

An important idea here is that theories of conflict and approaches to resolution are strongly shaped by the types of conflict that conflict specialists are trying to understand and resolve. Especially since the turn of the twenty-first century, conflicts involving crime and intergenerational poverty, religiously motivated violence, a globalizing socioeconomic order, and increasingly dangerous ecological crises have made it clearer that new ideas are needed to advance structural analysis and enable system transformation. Chapter 3 focuses on specific ideas developed by students of conflict in response to these challenges, starting with Johan Galtung's pathbreaking articles on 'structural violence' and 'cultural violence' and developing their implication for conflict resolution practice. Here we deal with fundamental structuralist concepts, like the crossbreeding of types of violence and the existence of interlocked or nested structures, before going on to explore the relation between culture and class and the existence of cultural systems or systems of discourse. Finally, this chapter outlines some of the implications of a structuralist perspective for conflict resolution practice, laying strong emphasis on the need for an expansion of the modes of practice beyond traditional 'third-party' models.

The fourth chapter of the study is devoted to 'breaking the silence about social class.' Here we consider the role of the capitalist class system in generating violent conflicts and discuss the reasons that this form of violence-generating structure has been largely excluded from consideration by conflict specialists (among others). As a vivid example of class-based violence, the chapter then examines the crime/punishment syndrome in its relationship to hierarchical systems of class and race, concluding with an 'anatomy of nonviolent transformation' that points toward the need for new forms of social-constitutional dialogue and social action to break the links between poverty, inequality, and crime. Chapter 5 then extends the analysis globally by discussing 'the mysterious renaissance of religious violence.' It argues that phenomena like religiously motivated insurgencies and the West's 'war on terror' cannot be understood (except in the mode of partisan moralism) without taking into account the neo-imperialist system that generates them. The chapter discusses neo-imperialist structures in their relationship to religious violence before suggesting how the field of conflict studies can further develop its understanding of that system and turn more consciously toward methods of altering or abolishing it.

The book's final chapter focuses on the specific problems of attempting to resolve structural conflicts 'in the shadow of the state,' paying particular attention to the issues that arise when the state is a party to conflict, and when it seeks to use the language and, to some extent, the methods of conflict resolution in achieving its own Great Power aims. The chapter argues that the challenge of resolving structural conflicts dramatizes the distinction between conflict resolution as a *replacement* for state power and as a *supplement* used to strengthen the state and neo-imperial systems. Structural conflict resolution, in the end, means transforming violent systems, a task that requires new social theory which takes us beyond the old revolution/reform dichotomy and a new politics that influences our practice.

*Resolving Structural Conflicts* stops short of describing that new politics in detail. Nor does it analyze or prescribe methods of resolving a number of conflicts of enormous consequence, such as intensifying struggles over scarce resources in an age of climate change, and conflicts caused by the rise of new technologies and the decay of traditional political institutions. My fondest hope is that others will find the arguments made here provocative and substantial enough to refine and correct them, expand them, and go on to help the field of conflict studies finally meet the challenge of transforming violent social systems.

Even so, especially when political violence at home and abroad persisted or worsened and deeper sources of popular discontent started to make themselves known, many students were hungry for ideas about conflict that offered a more critical perspective on established social institutions and ideologies. About ten years ago, I began teaching a course on Critical Theory and System Transformation for doctoral students and later added a course on Structural Conflict Resolution for undergraduates. Several of my former students offered undergraduate and master's courses in Critical Conflict Resolution, and one created a student-edited journal called *Unrest* that presented structuralist perspectives on major issues in the field. With other students and faculty colleagues, we organized workshops and conferences, appeared at academic colloquies, and wrote articles on themes like poverty, inequality, and violence; alternatives to the war on terror; social class and gender conflict; and reconstructing the U.S. political system.

The work continues. This book is part of it. Although the best work on structural conflict and its resolution remains to be done, I am confident that others will bring our profession nearer to its goal of ridding the world of system-generated violence.

## Notes

1 John Burton, Ed. *Conflict: Human Needs Theory* (London and New York: Palgrave Macmillan, 1990). The conference was held at Airlie House in Airlie, Virginia, in July 1988.
2 Quote reconstructed from my detailed notes of the conference.

# 1

# PARTISAN MORALISM AND THE NEED FOR STRUCTURAL THOUGHT

## The mediator goes to prison

Aeschylus is supposed to have said, "In war, the first casualty is truth," but it might be more accurate to say that the first casualty in intense conflicts is moral ambiguity. Especially when one's own group or nation is involved in violence, there is a strong tendency to silence moral doubts by raging at the enemy. The more we wonder secretly whether our own side's actions are necessary and just, the more we feel compelled to emphasize our adversaries' willfulness and malice, their unprincipled, atrocious behavior, and their irrational refusal to make peace. The relevant mantras are these:

- They choose war; we have no choice but to fight.
- We are reasonable; they are fanatics.
- We limit collateral damage; they deliberately put civilians in harm's way.
- We are trustworthy and well meaning; they are malicious and deceitful.

In short, if our violent behavior is to be considered justifiable, theirs must be totally blameworthy.

Standing outside the conflict arena, one can easily criticize such blatantly partisan moralism, but its appearance is understandable. We know that people have a propensity to personalize struggles that frighten or anger them by classifying warring parties either as innocent or culpable, 'good guys' or 'bad guys.' Parties who earn the positive label are thought of as well-intentioned, rational actors defending themselves against unjustified aggression, while those branded wrongdoers are considered malicious or deluded fanatics with a natural bent toward cruelty and violence.

How people embroiled in conflict arrive at these characterizations is a process still not very well understood, but they seem strongly influenced by desires for protection, vindication, and revenge; the need to keep faith with ethnic, national, religious, or political brethren; deeply held beliefs and prejudices; consciousness of past historical traumas; and manipulation of their fears and insecurities by leaders and media propagandists.[1] As the struggle escalates and becomes more violent, the stories that people tell about themselves and their conflict become ever more partisan, simplified, and impoverished. The result is a stark good/evil dualism that some commentators have called 'Manichaean.' A party to conflict is deemed to be either on the side of the angels or under the sway of some Dark Lord.[2]

Conflict resolution specialists generally try to counter this dualism by helping disputants to develop a more complex and nuanced understanding of their conflict, one that admits 'shades of gray' and points toward more deep-rooted causes of strife. These efforts sometimes prove useful, especially when they awaken parties to the existence of needs, desires, or biases of which they were not previously aware. But one major omission often limits their effectiveness. By fixing their attention primarily on the parties' ideas, emotions, and psychosocial interactions – what one might call the subjective factors in conflict – analysts can end occupying the same essential terrain as the partisans. They may paint with considerably more finesse, but they use the same palette. As a result, despite their own preference for shades of gray, they can unwittingly lay the groundwork for the sort of black-and-white dualism that emerges when people become intensely engaged in violent struggle.

Suppose, for example, that a mediator or other outside facilitator is called upon to help resolve an ongoing violent conflict between guards and inmates in a particular prison. The inmates are unruly; the guards treat them roughly; violent incidents are reported by both sides; and the conflict seems to be building toward a riot or some other large-scale explosion. State officials ask the specialist to investigate the situation and to make suggestions that might head off further violence, and she agrees to do so. Now what?

Following normal procedures in such cases, the mediator would begin by collecting relevant data about the dispute – conditions of life in the prison, the makeup of the competing groups, their prior relationship, recent instances of violence, and so forth – from public sources and the parties in conflict. She would almost certainly meet with representatives of the guards and the inmates or facilitate discussions between them in order to explore each group's underlying motivations, map their interactions, and try to pinpoint the sources of their mutual hostility.[3] Depending upon her expertise and theoretical leanings, she might analyze the parties' attitudes using the tools of social psychology, sociology, anthropology, or depth psychology, or explore each group's collective identity, including its self- and enemy-images, modes of discourse, organizational culture, and ethical traditions. She might try to construct the conflict system that the parties had unwittingly created through their social interactions and positioning. And she would probably seek to discover how specific conditions in the prison environment – for example, overcrowding, ethnic and racial diversity, and the presence of gangs – affected relations between the guards and inmates. In the end, the specialist would determine if specific changes in the parties' attitudes and behavior, or in prison policies held promise of ameliorating the dispute. If so, she would recommend these changes to the authorities.

Could this sort of intervention prove useful? Certainly! The literature on conflict resolution is replete with stories of similar third-party activities that have helped soften the impact of violent conflicts and even saved lives.[4] Our conflict specialist's work might well produce useful suggestions for reducing the incidence or intensity of violent confrontations.[5] Yet, to the extent that the institution itself continues to function as a generator of frustration, anger, and despair, the recommended changes will likely provide temporary relief rather than enacting a sustainable resolution of the conflict. If one wants to resolve that conflict on a long-term basis, a different sort of analysis and recommendation is needed. This is because the struggle is not generated and sustained by the guards' and inmates' ideas, attitudes, modes of discourse, or social interactions alone. It is also a product of a structured system that by its very nature disposes people to behave violently toward each other.

The crucial element missing from the mediator's analytical toolbox is the existence of a *conflict-generating system* whose structure and dynamics have a major impact on how disputes within the system are initiated and fought out, how parties and nonparties think about them, and how they can be managed or resolved. I chose the prison to illustrate this point because prisons are akin to factories that manufacture violence. They are highly structured social institutions organized to isolate prisoners, punish them, and (at least in theory) rehabilitate them. But these are long-term goals. The immediate goal is to prevent inmates from satisfying certain basic needs, including the needs for liberty, personal autonomy, love, and, given the endemic dangers of prison life, physical security. As a result, the prison's ordinary operations, not just its cruel excesses, generate very high levels of insecurity, frustration, and anger – conditions that render violent encounters of several types predictable.

Residents of the typical prison threaten and assault each other at a rate vastly in excess of the civilian norm. Guards abuse and intimidate inmates, inmates threaten guards, and riots against the prison authorities erupt periodically.[6] The atmosphere is saturated with violence, creating a 'continuous crisis' that engenders subsystems designed to maintain control by the authorities. These structures include a code of repressive rules, a cadre of officials authorized to interpret them, a corps of police and guards authorized to enforce them violently, and an unofficial, extra-legal apparatus empowering some influential inmates (gang leaders, in many cases) to dispense rewards and inflict punishments in order to maintain institutional order. Since these measures intensify the pressures on prisoners, by making the environment more punitive and less predictable, they produce cycles of violence with a tendency to escalate toward some large-scale explosion, like a gang war or prison riot.[7]

Violent encounters in prisons, therefore, are *not* simply the result of the inmates' violent tendencies or the brutality of prison officials. They are the norm rather than aberrations. Of course, this violence has other causes, too. Inmates and guards bring within the institution's walls attitudes and behavior patterns, including inclinations to use or tolerate physical force, that they acquired outside.[8] ('Outside,' we will shortly see, does not mean outside conflict-generating systems, since the prison itself is a subsystem forming part of a larger structure of inequality and coercion.) Furthermore, even though profoundly influenced by institutional structures and prior inclinations, people in prison still have some degree of autonomy in deciding whether or not to behave violently. Whether the individual source of violence is understood to be deprivation, importation, or choice, however, the prison as a whole must be considered as a conflict-generating system producing internal violence as predictably as the license plates manufactured in the prison shop.

Discovering how to eliminate or greatly reduce this violence and other pathologies of prison life requires not only that the ideas, attitudes, and interactions of the parties be understood, but that they be understood as both products and components of the prison system. Radical reform of the prisons is now a topic on the agenda of more than a few analysts and politicians thanks to a spurt of studies looking at the system from a structural perspective. For example, Michelle Alexander argues in *The New Jim Crow: Mass Incarceration in an Age of Colorblindness* that the imprisonment of very high numbers of African-Americans and other people of color is the result of systematic racism in the U.S. criminal justice system, and that it represents a new form of discriminatory social control. The implication is that inhumane conditions in America's prisons can be remedied by slashing the number of people arrested, prosecuted, and incarcerated for predominantly racial reasons. Critiquing this approach from a somewhat different structuralist angle, James Foreman, Jr. argues that it understates the effect of legal and administrative discrimination based on social class rather than race. Marxist social critics like Angela Davis go even further, maintaining that the prison functions primarily as an instrument of racial, class, and gender oppression, and that the cure for its ills is not reform or downsizing, but abolition. After ending the incarceration of poor people and minorities for minor or victimless offenses, we should replace the prison (and the prison industrial complex) with a radically different form of institution designed to rehabilitate lawbreakers and reintegrate them into society.[9]

One may consider this critique sensible or unrealistic; that is not the question under consideration here. The key point is that failing to think structurally about violent conflict keeps the question of radical system change off the table. For conflict specialists and reform-oriented people who focus exclusively on ameliorating current conditions, considerations of immediate feasibility (defined as going as far as one can within the context of an existing system) tend to trump those of long-term efficacy. The question that remains unasked is whether a conflict that seems intractable, such as that between prison inmates and authorities, is a symptom of a dysfunctional system that requires significant restructuring, and, if so, how to accomplish this task. What changes in the parties' roles and relationships will be sufficient to end or transform their struggle? What alternatives to the current system can be imagined and agreed upon? How can these alternatives be implemented?

Nonsystematic approaches to conflict not only elide these inquiries; they also leave partisan moralists where they found them. Without understanding how structural conflict works, people involved in struggle find it hard to believe that their opponents' attitudes and conduct (not to mention their own) are anything more than the results of mistaken beliefs, peculiar cultural traits, prior hostile interactions, or bad individual choices. Rather than attributing potency to a system embracing all the parties, they blame the other side's bad ideas or bad character for violent behavior. Why disputants and conflict specialists alike find it so difficult to make the turn toward a structural analysis of conflict is the question that must now concern us.

## The persistence of partisan moralism

It is not hard to understand why people embroiled in conflict resist recognizing their own roles as participants in a violence-producing system. To begin with, acknowledging the system's role has the immediate effect of undermining comforting narratives of the totally good Self and the totally evil Other. If it is the prison, not just the prisoners or the guards, that generates violent conflict, or if responsibility for it belongs to some overarching system rather than to rebels or authorities alone, no party is either entirely responsible or entirely free of responsibility for violence. Indeed, many conflict specialists argue that the first step in moving toward peaceful resolution is to admit that neither side has a monopoly on virtue, and that both, to some extent, have employed illegitimate (unnecessary or excessive) force. To partisans, however, the idea of mutual responsibility smacks of heresy. *Are you saying that both sides are equally at fault? Don't you realize how vicious they are? How vulnerable we are?* The heresy has a name; it is known as 'moral equivalency,' and parties to conflict abhor it since it delegitimizes their own actions and sacrifices.

One answer to this invocation of moral equivalency seems obvious. Attributing *some* moral responsibility to all the warring parties does not mean holding them *equally* responsible. It means only that no one's hands are entirely clean. But this sort of reasoning seldom satisfies the partisans, not only because of some neurotic desire for absolute purity, but also because admitting that a violence-generating system is implicated raises uncomfortable questions about how moral responsibility should be allocated. If underlying structural factors play an active role in a conflict, for example, a case can be made that the system's chief beneficiaries have a special obligation to atone for its destructive consequences and to help reconstruct it. This puts a heavy burden of responsibility on the top dogs of the prison or any other hierarchically structured system, and – equally or more important – on those *outside* the formal structure who maintain the system and benefit from its operations. (Who benefits from the current operations of the U.S. prison system?) Note, too, that this allocation does *not* relieve those oppressed by the system – the bottom dogs – of moral responsibility. They, too, are obligated to struggle for system change rather than for mere group supremacy or revenge, a burden that many on the bottom would just as soon not shoulder. Moreover, if they use excessive, indiscriminate, or unnecessary violence, their subordinate structural position will provide no defense.

A fear that acknowledging any responsibility for violence will validate the idea of moral equivalency is one reason that disputing parties may be averse to recognizing the structural aspects of their conflict. A second reason is the common view that if a structured system is generating violence, *nobody* in particular is responsible for it. Call this the doctrine of 'moral irrelevancy.' This idea also rests on a fallacy: the notion that by imposing on people, as it were, from the outside, the system of inequality robs them entirely of agency. Not so, argues the sociologist Anthony Giddens. Social structures don't just restrain and control people; they also enable them. Giddens disagrees with those who think that systemic constraints "operate like forces of nature," as if people were "being driven irresistibly and uncomprehendingly by mechanical pressures." On the contrary, he insists, "all forms of dependence offer some resources whereby those who are subordinate can influence the activities of their superiors." Therefore,

> we should not conceive of the structures of domination built into social institutions as in some way grinding out 'docile bodies' who behave like the automata suggested by objectivist social science.[10]

In this view, system and agency are really opposite sides of the same coin. What Giddens calls the "duality of structure" means that people don't necessarily lose their power to act or become morally irresponsible just because their actions are conditioned by the existence of a structured system. This idea seems generally convincing even though it leaves some questions unanswered. Giddens himself recognizes that there is a great difference between systems that aim at total control of populations and those whose more modest aims and effects can be described as hegemonic. It may be true that the inmates of the Auschwitz death camp had some resources whereby they could "influence the activities of their superiors," but no one would conclude that they exercised effective agency, or that they should be considered jointly responsible with the Nazis for the Holocaust. Some commentators take this a step further, arguing that the totalizing ambitions of modern systems of domination, with their global reach and immense influence over modes of discourse, also deprive agents of resources needed to express themselves effectively.[11] Still, Giddens reminds us, people do not lose their power to think and act, even though social systems empower some groups, oppress or exploit others, and limit the range of allowable choices. If the system's top dogs cannot defend their oppressive actions on the grounds that they were 'just following orders,' neither can the bottom dogs claim moral immunity on the grounds of their victimhood.[12]

A third factor may also prevent parties in conflict from recognizing the impact of a violence-producing system on their thinking and behavior. When people begin to analyze the structural basis for a conflict, they often discover that their own 'side' — and sometimes the other side as well — is not nearly as coherent or unified as they had thought, and that the system itself is responsible for creating and exacerbating social divisions that make a mockery of unity. As World War I descended into the unparalleled slaughter of trench warfare, for example, significant numbers of fighters on both sides became aware that social class divisions were more relevant to their survival than national identity. The excessive sacrifices demanded of lower-class soldiers and sailors by more privileged officers and politicians belied the national unity that had earlier provided a patriotic rationale for the war. The result was a tendency to resist taking orders (called insubordination by those in power) and a series of mutinies that in some cases – the Russian case in particular – ended both the war effort and the war-making regime.[13] Fifty years later, at the time of the U.S.-Vietnam War, a similar social dynamic produced unprecedented dissension both in the military forces and among civilians that contributed to the American withdrawal from Indochina.[14]

For all these reasons, discussions that invite an embattled people to think about the social-structural dimensions of their struggle are often felt to be dangerous and are considered taboo. During the Cold War era, it was *verboten* in the United States to suggest that the anti-Soviet struggle (which was believed to justify military action against a wide variety of groups struggling for national liberation) was motivated by interests other than the West's devotion to freedom and democracy. Partisan moralism made beliefs in the essential goodness of the Free World, the essential evil of 'godless Communism,' and the West's purely defensive motivation mandatory. Critical analyses of, say, the relationship of American capitalism to U.S. military adventures abroad was effectively forbidden.[15] (Soviet leaders, of course, simply reversed the taboo's polarities.) Later on, when the Cold War ended and the so-called war on terror began, the same sort of inhibition made it difficult to recognize that the accepted narrative of virtuous, self-defensive 'us' versus evil, aggressive 'them' was strongly shaped (even if it was not dictated) by the existence of a highly structured sociopolitical system.

We will examine that system more closely a bit later. For the moment, it is worth noting that to assert the existence of a taboo against structural thinking by parties in conflict is not hyperbole. A taboo creates a boundary rendering certain thoughts, as well as their expression, unacceptable – even unthinkable. The classic studies of the phenomenon suggest that these restrictions function as a method of defining and stabilizing certain particularly important social relationships, and family relationships in particular. (The incest taboo is often cited as a primary example.) An implication is that these relationships are somewhat unstable to begin with; they are vulnerable to disruption and require the special support of the taboo either because of people's antiauthoritarian impulses, because they are cultural rules rather than natural creations, or for some other reason.[16] Taboos, in any case, are more than mere opinions. Between people who feel the fear, disgust, and resentment that the violation of a particular taboo provokes and people who don't (or who are themselves subject to other taboos), there exists what the conflict theorist Oliver Ramsbotham calls "radical disagreement."

The distinction between ordinary and radical disagreement provides us with two important clues to the question of how to understand and resolve structurally based conflicts. First, as Ramsbotham suggests, the well-intentioned conflict specialist will rarely succeed in convincing people caught up in a violent struggle to abandon Manichaean narratives by urging them to engage in reasonable dialogue, put themselves in their opponent's shoes, think about their real needs and interests, and other such nostrums. This is because radical disagreements are not ordinary differences of the sort that can be dealt with through 'dialogues for mutual understanding' that try to separate facts, values, and emotions. Rather, they are "conflicts of belief. . . clashes of perspective, horizons and visual fields," whose hallmark is "the *breakdown* of distinctions between facts, values and emotions . . ."[17] The implication is that some form of conflict resolution process other than the usual sort of facilitated dialogue may well be needed.

An example: In 1967, during the U.S.-Vietnam War, heavyweight boxing champion Muhammed Ali refused induction into the U.S. Army, stating, "My conscience won't let me go shoot my brother, or some darker people, or some poor hungry people in the mud for big powerful America. And shoot them for what? They never called me nigger . . ."[18] This statement violated several taboos, particularly the ban on thinking that the American nation itself might, in some important senses, be a fiction – that 'darker people' and 'poor hungry people' on both sides of the U.S./Vietnam divide might have more in common than comfortable white Americans and poor or nonwhite Americans. Ali's insistence on maintaining solidarity with others along lines of class and race rather than of nation was an act of *critical structural dissent* that was bound to provoke ostracism and punishment. Regardless of the facts that the United States had not declared war on Vietnam, that the Vietnamese had not attacked the United States, and that Ali was a member of the Nation of Islam religiously opposed to the war, he was stripped of his boxing title, arrested, and convicted of draft evasion, a conviction that was later overturned by the U.S. Supreme Court. (This radical disagreement, in fact, was never resolved, since in the more than four decades following the war's end, Americans continue to disagree on whether it was justified or unjustified.)

Ramsbotham's work suggests a second insight, although not one that the author himself addresses specifically. Radical disagreement is a characteristic not only of complex conflict systems – that is, difficult-to-resolve or intractable conflicts considered as systems in themselves – but of conflicts generated by certain types of systems that organize and exert social power.[19] Structured social and political systems, as we will see, normally contain substructures that are designed to manage disputes arising in-house. But if the overarching system becomes sufficiently unstable, these local dispute settlement mechanisms weaken, and radical disagreements can emerge. Taboos, representing one form of radical disagreement, are associated with vitally important but vulnerable, potentially unstable social groupings like the family, the ethnic, racial, or religious group, and the nation-state. (As Samuel Huntington's work implies, even the multinational civilization can be considered a family writ large.)[20] Moreover, where violent conflicts are raging, this is precisely how such groups often present themselves both to external enemies and internal dissenters.[21] One can almost suggest this as a law: a social system in trouble attempts to convert itself into a family, thus invoking typical familial narratives and taboos. Little wonder that, in times of conflict, partisan moralism is so well entrenched!

## The costs of partisan moralism: on the Gaza War of 2014

Critical structural thought, I have been arguing, provides the antidote to partisan moralism. Without an understanding that their struggle is shaped and, to some extent, caused by the operations of a structured system, the parties to conflict are left with explanations and images of the conflict based purely on intentions, ideas, and character. They remain trapped, as it were, in the realm of familial thought and its taboos, embracing 'our people's' narrative and arguments and vehemently rejecting 'theirs.' This does not necessarily render the conflict unresolvable, but it makes peace far more difficult to obtain and compels a rethinking of conflict resolution principles and methods.

An illustration may throw additional light on this problem. During the worst days of the Gaza War of 2014, a learned and sensitive rabbi of my acquaintance struggled with the problem of the large number of civilian deaths (the total would grow to be more than 2,100, including more than 400 children) caused by Israeli Defense Force activity against the virtually defenseless Gazan population. The rabbi discussed the prophet Isaiah's vision of the destruction of Judah, a passage containing what he termed "the most painful verse in the Bible" (Isaiah 1:15):

> When you stretch out your hands to Me, I will turn My gaze away from you;
> Even if you multiply your prayers, I will not listen;
> Your hands are full of blood.

"As the conflict in Gaza stretches into its fourth week," he wrote, "I will pray that this verse does not apply to us – not now, not in this war."

> I pray that our cause is just and that our prosecution of that cause just. I pray that I can take refuge in the judgment of Amos Oz, a man of great moral seriousness, who said yesterday that this action is justified, even if 'in some points excessive,' and in the judgment of all those whose moral compass I respect – teachers, rabbis, friends – who assure us that it is necessary. I will pray that I am right to stand with Israel, as I do – because the devastation and suffering caused by this war is almost too much to fathom. And I will be grateful once again for this beautiful tradition of ours, that even in the midst of terrible, necessary wars, forces us to confront these questions, to reconsider our judgments, to consider and reconsider the basis on which we act.[22]

What should we make of this impassioned, self-questioning pronouncement? On the one hand, the speaker is a morally aware person who understands that the war presents a troubling moral problem – something that needs "considering and reconsidering." On the other hand, he seems to short-circuit the process of reconsideration by accepting the judgment of respected figures who assure him that Israel's actions are necessary. The question then becomes: what does it mean to say that violence is necessary? Deconstructing the notion of military necessity enables us to see that defending a war on these grounds without taking into account the conflict-generating role of a structured system leads one in endless circles that fail to challenge the partisan moralist stance.

We know what the novelist Amos Oz meant by declaring Israel's attack on Gaza excessive but necessary.

> What would you do, [Oz asks,] if your neighbor across the street sits down on the balcony, puts his little boy on his lap and starts shooting machine gun fire into your nursery? What would you do if your neighbor across the street digs a tunnel from his nursery to your nursery in order to blow up your home or in order to kidnap your family?[23]

Oz is referring here to the facts that the Hamas organization, which ruled Gaza, fired more than 4,500 rockets into Israeli territory, with many of the rocket launchers located in the heart of densely populated Gaza, and that it had built an elaborate network of tunnels to supply the community with various goods, including mortars and other military equipment. His parable does not note that these rockets killed only one person, a Bedouin Arab, although they injured several people and terrified many more.[24]

The commonly held definition of necessity implied by Oz's questions encapsulates several elements, of which the first is *self-defense against prior attack: 'they struck first.'* Violence is often said to be necessary in order to defend oneself against an aggressive enemy who was the first to attack. The novelist's narrative begins with the Gazan neighbor who, for discreditable tactical reasons, puts his own child on his lap and begins to shoot at Israeli children. But suppose that we enrich the narrative by beginning the story earlier in time? Imagine that, at an earlier date, the Israeli neighbor had padlocked the Gazan's front and back doors, barred his windows, and refused to allow people or goods to enter or leave his house. (Gaza, where 1.5 million impoverished Palestinians live on 140 square miles of land under severe travel restrictions, has been called "the world's largest open-air prison.")[25] What if, before the Gazan fired his weapon, the Israeli had attacked an adjacent house, killing its innocent occupants? The problem, typical of partisan moralism, is that each party to the conflict had reason to believe that its own stance was defensive and that the enemy had attacked first.

Events prior to the July war further illustrate the pitfalls of a chronologically based 'family narrative.' The *status quo ante* the war was a 'cold peace' between Israel and Hamas, an eighteen-month cease-fire in which Hamas leaders refrained from attacking Israel notwithstanding the latter's refusal to recognize them as the legally elected rulers of Gaza, and their own refusal to recognize the existence of the Jewish State. In June 2014, the members of a dissident West Bank Palestinian clan kidnapped and murdered three Israeli settler teenagers near Hebron, probably without prior Hamas approval, although the organization later approved of their act. The Israeli government responded by concealing its knowledge of the teenagers' deaths and mounting a month-long military operation that killed 11 West Bank Palestinians, wounded 51, and jailed more than 350, including virtually the entire Hamas leadership outside Gaza. Israel's Air Force also conducted air strikes on Hamas facilities in Gaza. Although the Gazan leaders initially refrained from retaliating, competing Palestinian groups fired rockets of their own into Israel. Israel then launched more air strikes and threatened a ground invasion. Attempts to negotiate a cease-fire failed, and Hamas finally began firing rockets of its own, as well as using mortars to shell nearby Israeli military outposts. The large-scale Israeli invasion of Gaza began on July 16, accompanied by devastating air and artillery attacks.[26]

A partisan of the Palestinians would argue that this scenario demonstrates, contrary to Amos Oz's story, that the people of Gaza were defenders, not aggressors, and that it was the Israelis who used an isolated incident of kidnapping and murder to break the cease-fire with Hamas and begin an aggressive war. As soon as he made this argument, of course, Israeli partisans would reply that if one goes back a few years further in time, one discovers that the Israelis were forced to respond to repeated acts of aggression by Hamas, including that organization's uncompromising rejectionism, virulent anti-Semitic propaganda, and multiple suicide attacks directed against Israeli civilians. This assertion would very likely provoke a Palestinian rejoinder based on Israel's seizure of Gaza during the preemptive Six Day War and subsequent isolation of the territory, which would provoke an Israeli response based on the Arab nations' refusal to accept the UN Partition Plan and their attempt to crush the nascent State of Israel, which would provoke a Palestinian condemnation of the Partition Plan and the mass expulsion of their people from Israel during the 1948 war . . . In this way, the 'they struck first' narrative leads to an endless dance in which aggressors and defenders change identities with each new modulation of the historical tune. The argument based on chronology forces one back in time step by step, until one actually finds partisans contending that the pre-Exodus Canaanites were or were not predecessors of the Ottoman Palestinians!

Perhaps for this reason, the argument is almost always supplemented, and in some cases even replaced, by a second rationale: *self-defense against an implacable, irremediably vicious enemy.* The core idea here is that, regardless of chronological priority, 'our' side can be identified as the innocent victim or defender because 'their' side is aggressive *by nature.* Driven by fanatically held beliefs and a callous disregard for human life, they choose to fight. Motivated by respect for life and a dedication to reason, we have no choice but to resist. Attributing violence to the other side's aggressive nature renders chronology irrelevant, since, threatened by such an enemy, the only sensible thing to do is to hit him before he becomes strong enough to launch the inevitable attack. In a sense, this is what happened in the Gaza War. Discovering that Hamas was building tunnels to import military equipment (as well as civilian goods) into the territory, the Israelis concluded that, despite the cease-fire, the organization would attack when it was ready. The possibility that these weapons were intended to be deterrents against another Israeli invasion like the highly destructive Operation Cast Lead campaign of 2008–09 was discounted. The kidnappings near Hebron thus provided a pretext for a preemptive strike.

The aggressive-by-nature approach presents several obvious problems, which we can summarize very briefly. First, the hypothesis is self-fulfilling, since it sanctions preemptive attacks that, in turn, generate predictably violent responses. Assuming, even for purposes of experiment, that one's adversary is *not* implacably aggressive opens the door to the possibility that evidence may show him to be capable of acting cooperatively and peaceably. But hostile action based on the assumption of implacability assures that such evidence will never be presented. Second, the assumption is self-justifying, since one can always interpret an enemy's violence as long-planned aggression. Was Hamas's stockpile of weapons intended to deter an Israeli breach of the cease-fire or was it evidence of an implacable will to violence? The answer may well be neither of the above, since the Hamas armory was too weak and inefficient to serve as a deterrent, and the inclination of Gazans to resort to violence was not based so much on malicious intent as on the existence of a violence-producing system. (More of this in a moment.) Finally, it seems clear that military action based on a radical distinction between a naturally aggressive 'them' and a naturally peaceful 'us' obliterates that distinction in practice. As in the case of arguments based on chronology, the attempt to distinguish aggressors from defenders becomes a virtually meaningless exercise in partisan moralism.

Much the same may be said of a third rationale for 'necessary' war: *self-defense as a right and requirement of national sovereignty*. Repeatedly, during the Gaza War, one heard Israeli officials and their supporters state that no nation can be expected to live under conditions of being subject to attack by missiles or insurgent fighters. The Palestinian rejoinder, of course, was that they are a people who deserve their own state, and that no people can be expected to live under conditions of prison-like subjection and apparently endless siege. Once again, witnessing such radical disagreements, one cannot help feeling that each side, mired in its own truth, is unable to find a language or means of communication that the other will understand. What is missing, in my view, is a *framework* that might permit them to share responsibility for the conflict and begin to analyze its hidden or denied structural dimensions.

When things seem hopeless, one searches for signs of hope. Even in cases of violent conflict in which the great majority of group members support their own side, some, although partisan, are able to recognize that neither side is guiltless. During the Gaza War, for example, the American social critic Leon Wieseltier, a strong sympathizer with Israel, called Hamas's strategy of provoking Israeli attacks on Gaza civilians immoral and labeled its leaders "monsters." "But," he added,

> the population of Gaza are not monsters and the Palestinian people are not monsters; and I will confess that I have found myself unable to be satisfied, in the analysis of responsibility in this war, by the assertion, which is incontrovertible, that the killing of non-combatant

Palestinians by Israel in Gaza is one of Hamas's war aims, and so Israel is completely absolved if it obliges. A provocation does not relieve one of accountability for how one responds to it. For this reason, the war has filled me with disquiet, which my sympathetic understanding of Israel's position has failed to stifle.[27]

What makes these remarks unusual is Wieseltier's refusal, at a time of intense denunciatory moralism, to let enmity toward the adversary or communal taboos silence his own moral qualms. What his brave statement lacks, however, is any sense of the existence of a structured *system* conditioning the moral choices made by both sides. If Hamas is to be called a provocateur for resisting Israeli domination, what should Prime Minister Netanyahu be called for attacking that organization physically rather than recognizing its electoral victory in Gaza and negotiating with it as part of a Palestinian unity government? If inciting Israel to attack Palestinian civilians was a Hamas war aim, what sort of relationship might have provoked that provocation?[28]

The rhetoric of provocation misses the point that bellicose behaviors by both sides (not just by Palestinians) were, to a large extent, the products of a system that generates violent conflict as part of its normal operations. We have already discussed prison violence, and, as noted earlier, analysts have compared the conditions of life for Palestinians in Gaza with the situation of inmates in a prison. But Gaza is part of a larger social system which includes the West Bank and Israel proper, and which arguably extends beyond Israel/Palestine to include other nations within and outside the Middle Eastern region. What is the nature of this system? How does it produce (or tempt partisan groups to use) collective violence? What changes in it need to be made to eliminate or greatly reduce that violence?

Two points seem crucial. First, answering these questions is not optional; it seems to me to be a prerequisite to any meaningful, potentially successful peace process. If there is a structured social system generating violent conflict, transforming it so as to make peace possible has to be at the top of one's agenda. To move beyond adversarial moralizing in the Middle East, both sides need to understand that violence is not simply an expression of the other side's malice or intransigence; it is also a product of the result of the way the current system operates. With respect to Israel/Palestine, this is where I part company not only with Leon Wieseltier, but also with Palestinian commentators who believe that all will be well if Israel agrees to lift the siege of Gaza, restrict new Jewish settlements in the West Bank, and negotiate with the Palestinian Authority. All these reforms may be needed. None, in my view, has the capacity to transform the current violence-generating structure.

Second, the nature of that system is almost never self-evident. As soon as one begins to discuss it, it becomes obvious that its structure, dynamics, and consequences are likely to be contested by the conflicting parties as well as by interested observers and third parties. In the case of Israel/Palestine, for example, some analysts believe that the system requiring recognition and analysis is a type of *colonial-settler society* in which settlers representing an industrially developed, politically sophisticated, militarily aggressive metropolis migrate to a less-developed peripheral region and either displace the native inhabitants or reduce them to some sort of servitude. Others disagree.[29] I find this idea persuasive and potentially useful, although the analogy between Israelis and European settlers in places like the Americas, Algeria, and South Africa needs to be qualified and the role of the United States in the system clarified. Among other things, the colonial-settler framework suggests why a 'two-state' solution or any other proposed solution that does not recognize these structural issues will not command mass support.

Even so, the nature of the operative system is a matter requiring analysis not only by academics and would-be peacemakers, but also by the parties in conflict themselves. The system's organization and dynamics, the roles of various groups within and without the zone of conflict in maintaining it, and its impact on local populations are issues that are crucial in assisting the parties to understand what is generating the struggle and how to transform violent social structures. The essential point is for a dialogue to take place — a sustained conversation in which each conflicting party and the conflicting elements within each party are freed to raise questions and engage in speculations heretofore considered taboo. How this can happen, given the obstacles to overcoming radical disagreement pointed out by Oliver Ramsbotham and others, is a topic that will occupy us in the course of this study. The immediate tasks at hand are to define more precisely what 'structured system' means, and to begin to suggest how such systems generate violent conflict.

To summarize: Intellectually and ethically, claims that a violent struggle is justified by necessity most often turn out to be little more than self-serving propaganda. If one's ultimate aim is peace, such arguments lead in precisely the wrong direction: toward more fixed ideological positions and more intense violence, rather than toward conflict resolution. This is not just because of internal deficiencies in argument (for example, the interchangeability of 'aggressor' and 'defender' categories), but because of vital issues that partisan moralism excludes from discussion. The most important exclusion, perhaps, is the existence of national, regional, and global structures of power and meaning — sociopolitical systems and cultural epistemes —

that condition each party's social roles and political expectations. When the existence of these conflict-generating systems goes unrecognized, their relationship to each party's cultural norms and ideological commitments is similarly occluded. And since social and cultural structures appear, change, and disappear over the course of history, history tends to vanish as well, except in the form of carefully selected, highly 'edited' partisan memories. Bringing social structures into focus may be the most effective way to combat this one-dimensional mythmaking, and to recapture history's potential role as a handmaiden of peace.

## Notes

1 For a wide range of approaches to identity issues in conflict, see Daniel Rothbart and Karina V. Korostelina, Eds., *Identity, Morality, and Threat* (Lanham, MD and Plymouth, UK: Lexington Books, 2006). Identity as an irrepressible human need is explored by John W. Burton and others in *Conflict: Human Needs Theory* (London and New York: Palgrave Macmillan, 1990). Ethnic identity and historical traumas are discussed by Vamik Volkan in *Bloodlines: From Ethnic Pride to Ethnic Terrorism* (New York: Basic Books, 1998). See also David Berreby, *Us and Them: The Science of Identity* (Chicago: University of Chicago Press, 2008).

2 According to some analysts the tendency toward "Manichaean" thinking about conflicts is particularly pronounced in cultures strongly influenced by Abrahamic religious traditions. See, for example, Johan Galtung, *Peace by Peaceful Means: Peace and Conflict, Development, and Civilization* (London: Sage Publications, 1996), 271. I have argued elsewhere that the "bad guy" image in Western thinking is strongly influenced by traditional Christian concepts of Satan. See *Reasons to Kill: Why Americans Choose War* (New York: Bloomsbury, 2010), 60–74. On narrative impoverishment, see Sara Cobb, *Speaking of Violence: The Politics and Poetics of Narrative in Conflict Resolution* (Oxford: Oxford University Press, 2013).

3 What follows represents a short summary, necessarily incomplete, of typical conflict resolution techniques currently in use. There are many handbooks of conflict resolution theories and practices in print, but the most comprehensive (certainly the longest) is Peter T. Coleman, et al., Eds., *Handbook of Conflict Resolution: Theory and Practice*, 3rd Edn. (San Francisco, CA: Jossey-Bass, 2014). See also Christopher W. Moore, *The Mediation Process: Practical Strategies for Resolving Conflict*, 4th Edn. (San Francisco, CA: 2014); Jay Rothman, *Resolving Identity-Based Conflicts in Nations, Organizations, and Communities* (San Francisco, CA: Jossey-Bass, 1997); John Winslade and Gerald D. Monk, *Narrative Mediation: A New Approach to Conflict Resolution* (San Francisco, CA: Jossey-Bass, 2000).

4 See the stories of successful conflict interventions collected in Ronald Fisher, *Interactive Conflict Resolution* (Syracuse, NY: Syracuse University Press, 1997); George J. Mitchell, *Making Peace* (Berkeley, CA: University of California Press, 2001); Ronald Fisher and Andrea Bartoli, *Paving the Way: Contributions of*

*Interactive Conflict Resolution to Peacemaking* (Lanham, MD: Lexington Books, 2004); Harold H. Saunders, *Sustained Dialogue in Conflicts: Transformation and Change* (London and New York: Palgrave Macmillan, 2011), and Louis Kriesberg and Bruce W. Dayton, *Constructive Conflicts: From Escalation to Resolution*, 4th Edn. (Lanham, MD: Rowman & Littlefield, 2011).

5 Some sensible suggestions for reform are to be found, for example, in Ross Homel and Carleen Thompson, "Causes and Prevention of Violence in Prisons" (Griffiths University, 2005), 6–10 (longer version), https://www.griffith.edu. au/__data/assets/pdf_file/0007/82618/causes.pdf. The authors note, however, that the effectiveness of treatment programs ("anger management," etc.) has not been proven, while structural changes in prisons providing for less coercive, more consensual forms of social organization have sometimes reduced prison violence.

6 See Nancy Wolff, et al., "Physical Violence in Prisons: Rates of Victimization." *Criminal Justice and Behavior*, 34:5 (May 2007), 588–599. See also Human Rights Watch, *Conditions In United States Prisons: A Human Rights Watch Report* (November 1991).

7 Rosemary Ricciardelli and Victoria Sit, "Practicing Social (Dis)Order in Prison: The Effect of Administrative Controls on Prisoner-on-Prisoner Violence." *The Prison Journal*, 96:2 (March 2016), 210–231. http://tpj.sagepub.com/content/96/2/210.abstract.

8 For discussion of the "deprivation" and "importation" theories of prison violence, see Ross Homel and Carleen Thompson, "Causes and Prevention of Violence in Prisons," in Ross Homel, et al., Eds., *Corrections Criminology* (Sydney: Hawkins Press, 2005), 101–108 (longer version available at https://www. griffith.edu.au/__data/assets/pdf_file/0003/188706/causes2.pdf). A study that effectively links the "inside" and "outside" causes of personal violence is that by prison psychiatrist James Gilligan, *Violence: Reflections on a National Epidemic* (New York: Vintage, 1997).

9 Michelle Alexander, *The New Jim Crow: Mass Incarceration in an Age of Colorblindness* (New York: New Press, 2012). James Foreman, Jr., "Racial Incarceration: Beyond the New Jim Crow." Faculty Scholarship Series, Paper 3599 (2012). http://digitalcommons.law.yale.edu/fss_papers/3599. Angela Y. Davis, *Are Prisons Obsolete?* (New York: Seven Stories Press, 2002). See also United Nations Office on Drugs and Crime, *Handbook of Basic Principles and Promising Practices on Alternatives to Imprisonment* (New York: United Nations, 2007); Marie Gottschalk, *Caught: The Prison State and the Lockdown of American Politics* (Princeton, NJ: Princeton University Press, 2016). http://www.unodc. org/pdf/criminal_justice/Handbook_of_Basic_Principles_and_Promising_ Practices_on_Alternatives_to_Imprisonment.pdf.

10 In Giddens's view, social systems can be defined as "rules and resources recursively implicated in social reproduction." Anthony Giddens, *The Constitution of Society: Outline of the Theory of Structuration* (Berkeley and Los Angeles: University of California Press, 1984), xxxi, 15–16. See also Jolle Demmers,

*Theories of Violent Conflict: An Introduction* (London and New York: Routledge, 2012), 116–138.

11 Some Critical Theorists like Herbert Marcuse offer a critique of "one-dimensional thought" alleging that consumer consciousness in modern industrial societies has become almost a "second nature," depriving working people of effective agency. See Marcuse's *One-Dimensional Man: Studies in the Ideology of Advanced Industrial Society*, 2nd Rev. Edn. (London and New York: Routledge, 2012).

12 For a provocative study of the relationship of victimhood to violence, see Diane Enns, *The Violence of Victimhood* (University Park, PA: Pennsylvania State University Press, 2012).

13 Although the French army mutinied several times in 1917, the German fleet (at Kiel) mutinied in 1918, and the British army (in Southampton) in 1919, there is no general history of European mutinies in World War I. As to Russia, see Leon Trotsky, *History of the Russian Revolution*, Vol. II (1932), 26 *et seq.* https://www.marxists.org/ebooks/trotsky/history-of-the-russian-revolution/ebook-history-of-the-russian-revolution-v1.pdf.

14 See Richard Moser, *The New Winter Soldiers: GI and Veteran Dissent During the Vietnam Era* (New Brunswick, NJ: Rutgers University Press, 1996); David Cortright, *Soldiers in Revolt: GI Resistance During the Vietnam War* (Chicago: Haymarket Books, 2005).

15 It is hard to overstate the impact of such taboo-smashing works as C. Wright Mills's *Listen, Yankee: The Revolution in Cuba* (New York: Ballantine Books, 1960) and I.F. Stone's *Hidden History of the Korean War, 1950–51* (New York: Monthly Review Press, 1969) on young scholars such as I during the years of strict conformity.

16 The classic works on taboo are Sigmund Freud, *Totem and Taboo*, Std. Edn. (New York: W.W. Norton, 1990), Claude Lévi-Strauss, *The Elementary Structures of Kinship*, Rev. Edn. (Boston: Beacon Press, 1969), and Franz Baermann Steiner, *Taboo, Truth, and Religion* (New York: Berghahn Books, 1999). Focusing on the incest and pollution taboos, they remain controversial long after their original publication.

17 Oliver Ramsbotham, "Radical Disagreement and Systemic Conflict Transformation," in Daniela Korppen, et al., Eds., *The Non-Linearity of Peace Processes: Theory and Practice of Systemic Conflict Transformation* (Opladen, Germany and Farmington Hills, MI: Verlag Barbara Budrich, 2011), 57, 61.

18 The televised interview at which Muhammed Ali made this statement can be viewed at http://listenonrepeat.com/watch/?v=HeFMyrWlZ68#Muhammad_Ali_on_the_Vietnam_War-Draft.

19 "Systemic conflict" and "systemic conflict transformation" are terms adopted to describe conflicts as "self-organizing and complex adaptive systems" (Ramsbotham, *op. cit.*, 58, and especially the other chapters of Korppen, et al., *op. cit.*). This type of system-analysis, which seems to me overly detached from structures of power, is discussed further in Chapter 2, *infra*.

20 Samuel P. Huntington, *The Clash of Civilizations and the Remaking of World Order* (New York: Simon & Schuster, 1998). See also Richard E. Rubenstein and Jarle Crocker, "Challenging Huntington." *Foreign Policy* 96 (Autumn 1994), 113–128.

21 This is Vamik Volkan's argument in *Bloodlines: From Ethnic Pride to Ethnic Terrorism* (New York: Basic Books, 1998).

22 Private communication to the author, August 3, 2014.

23 Dennis Stute, "Oz: Lose-Lose situation for Israel." *DW*, July 30, 2014. http://www.dw.de/oz-lose-lose-situation-for-israel/a-17822511.

24 Mortar attacks from Gaza accounted for four more civilian deaths, while sixty-six IDF fighters died in the subsequent invasion. "2014 Israel-Gaza conflict." *Wikipedia, op. cit.*

25 See, e.g., Noam Chomsky, "My Visit to Gaza, the World's Largest Open-Air Prison." *Truthout* (May 16, 2016). http://www.truth-out.org/opinion/item/12635-noam-chomsky-my-visit-to-gaza-the-worlds-largest-open-air-prison.

26 Amos Harel and Yaniv Kubovich, "Revealed: Behind the scenes on the hunt to find the kidnapped teens." *Haaretz* (July 1, 2014); Jonathan Freedland, "Liberal Zionism After Gaza," *New York Review of Books* (July 26, 2014). The Hamas leadership did, however, accept and ratify the attack after the fact. See also the carefully documented description of events by *Wikipedia* entitled "2014 Israel-Gaza conflict." https://en.wikipedia.org/wiki/2014_Israel%E2%80%93Gaza_conflict#Immediate_events.

27 Leon Wieseltier, "Israel and Gaza: A Just and Unjust War." *The New Republic* (August 7, 2014).

28 See, e.g, John B. Judis, "Who Bears More Responsibility for the War in Gaza?" *The New Republic* (July 25, 2014). http://www.newrepublic.com/article/118846/israel-palestine-history-behind-their-new-war.

29 The *locus classicus* for application of this framework to Israel is Maxime Rodinson, *Israel: A Colonial-Settler State?* (New York: Pathfinder Press, 1973). See also Lorenzo Veracini, *Israel and Settler Society* (London: Pluto Press, 2006). For an opposing view, see S. Ilan Troen, "De-Judaizing the Homeland: Academic Politics in Rewriting the History of Palestine." *Israel Affairs*, 13:4 (2007). On the colonial-settler state in general see Lorenzo Veracini, *Settler Colonialism: A Theoretical Overview* (London and New York: Palgrave Macmillan, 2010) and *The Settler Colonial Present* (London and New York: Palgrave Macmillan, 2015). See also Julia Amalia Heyer, "Gaza Crisis: The Real Danger to Israel Comes from Within." *Der Spiegel* (August 5, 2014). http://www.spiegel.de/international/world/interview-with-sociologist-eva-illouz-about-gaza-and-israeli-society-a-984536.html.

## Bibliography

Alexander, Michelle, *The New Jim Crow: Mass Incarceration in an Age of Colorblindness* (New York: New Press, 2012).

Berreby, David, *Us and Them: The Science of Identity* (Chicago: University of Chicago Press, 2008).

Burton, John W., Ed., *Conflict: Human Needs Theory* (London and New York: Palgrave Macmillan, 1990).

Chomsky, Noam, "My Visit to Gaza, the World's Largest Open-Air Prison." *Truthout* (May 16, 2016). http://www.truth-out.org/opinion/item/12635-noam-chomsky-my-visit-to-gaza-the-worlds-largest-open-air-prison.

Cobb, Sara, *Speaking of Violence: The Politics and Poetics of Narrative in Conflict Resolution* (Oxford: Oxford University Press, 2013).

Coleman, Peter T. et al., Eds., *Handbook of Conflict Resolution: Theory and Practice*, 3rd Edn. (San Francisco, CA: Jossey-Bass, 2014).

Cortright, David, *Soldiers in Revolt: GI Resistance During the Vietnam War* (Chicago: Haymarket Books, 2005).

Davis, Angela Y., *Are Prisons Obsolete?* (New York: Seven Stories Press, 2002).

Demmers, Jolle, *Theories of Violent Conflict: An Introduction* (London and New York: Routledge, 2012).

Enns, Diane, *The Violence of Victimhood* (University Park, PA: Pennsylvania State University Press, 2012).

Fisher, Ronald, *Interactive Conflict Resolution* (Syracuse, NY: Syracuse University Press, 1997).

——and Andrea Bartoli, *Paving the Way: Contributions of Interactive Conflict Resolution to Peacemaking* (Lanham, MD: Lexington Books, 2004).

Foreman, James Jr., "Racial Incarceration: Beyond the New Jim Crow." Faculty Scholarship Series, Paper 3599 (2012). http://digitalcommons.law.yale.edu/fss_papers/3599.

Freedland, Jonathan, "Liberal Zionism After Gaza," *New York Review of Books* (July 26, 2014).

Freud, Sigmund, *Totem and Taboo*, Std. Edn. (New York: W.W. Norton, 1990).

Galtung, Johan, *Peace by Peaceful Means: Peace and Conflict, Development, and Civilization* (London: Sage Publications, 1996).

Giddens, Anthony, *The Constitution of Society: Outline of the Theory of Structuration* (Berkeley and Los Angeles: University of California Press, 1984).

Gilligan, James, *Violence: Reflections on a National Epidemic* (New York: Vintage, 1997).

Gottschalk, Marie, *Caught: The Prison State and the Lockdown of American Politics* (Princeton, NJ: Princeton University Press, 2016).

Harel, Amos and Yaniv Kubovich, "Revealed: Behind the scenes on the hunt to find the kidnapped teens." *Haaretz* (July 1, 2014).

Heyer, Julia Amalia, "Gaza Crisis: The Real Danger to Israel Comes from Within." *Der Spiegel* (August 5, 2014). http://www.spiegel.de/international/world/interview-with-sociologist-eva-illouz-about-gaza-and-israeli-society-a-984536.html.

Homel, Ross and Carleen Thompson, "Causes and Prevention of Violence in Prisons," in Ross Homel, et al., Eds., *Corrections Criminology* (Sydney: Hawkins Press, 2005).

Human Rights Watch, *Conditions In United States Prisons: A Human Rights Watch Report* (November, 1991).

Huntington, Samuel P., *The Clash of Civilizations and the Remaking of World Order* (New York: Simon & Schuster, 1998).

Judis, John B., "Who Bears More Responsibility for the War in Gaza?" *The New Republic* (July 25, 2014). http://www.newrepublic.com/article/118846/israel-palestine-history-behind-their-new-war.

Kriesberg, Louis and Bruce W. Dayton, *Constructive Conflicts: From Escalation to Resolution*, 4th Edn. (Lanham, MD: Rowman & Littlefield, 2011).

Lévi-Strauss, Claude, *The Elementary Structures of Kinship*, Rev. Edn. (Boston: Beacon Press, 1969).

Marcuse, Herbert, *One-Dimensional Man: Studies in the Ideology of Advanced Industrial Society*, 2nd Rev. Edn. (London and New York: Routledge, 2012).

Mills, C. Wright, *Listen, Yankee: The Revolution in Cuba* (New York: Ballantine Books, 1960).

Mitchell, George J., *Making Peace* (Berkeley, CA: University of California Press, 2001).

Moore, Christopher W., *The Mediation Process: Practical Strategies for Resolving Conflict*, 4th Edn. (San Francisco, CA: 2014).

Moser, Richard, *The New Winter Soldiers: GI and Veteran Dissent During the Vietnam Era* (New Brunswick, NJ: Rutgers University Press, 1996).

Ramsbotham, Oliver, "Radical Disagreement and Systemic Conflict Transformation," in Daniela Korppen, et al., Eds., *The Non-Linearity of Peace Processes: Theory and Practice of Systemic Conflict Transformation* (Opladen, Germany and Farmington Hills, MI: Verlag Barbara Budrich, 2011).

Ricciardelli, Rosemary and Victoria Sit, "Practicing Social (Dis)Order in Prison: The Effect of Administrative Controls on Prisoner-on-Prisoner Violence." *The Prison Journal, 96:2* (March 2016). http://tpj.sagepub.com/content/96/2/210.abstract.

Rodinson, Maxime, *Israel: A Colonial-Settler State?* (New York: Pathfinder Press, 1973).

Rothbart, Daniel and Karina V. Korostelina, Eds., *Identity, Morality, and Threat* (Lanham, MD and Plymouth, UK: Lexington Books, 2006).

Rothman, Jay, *Resolving Identity-Based Conflicts in Nations, Organizations, and Communities* (San Francisco, CA: Jossey-Bass, 1997).

Rubenstein, Richard E., *Reasons to Kill: Why Americans Choose War* (New York: Bloomsbury, 2010).

——and Jarle Crocker, "Challenging Huntington," *Foreign Policy* 96 (Autumn 1994).

Saunders, Harold H., *Sustained Dialogue in Conflicts: Transformation and Change* (London and New York: Palgrave Macmillan, 2011).

Steiner, Franz Baermann, *Taboo, Truth, and Religion* (New York: Berghahn Books, 1999).

Stone, I.F., *Hidden History of the Korean War, 1950–51* (New York: Monthly Review Press, 1969).

Stute, Dennis, "Oz: Lose-Lose situation for Israel." *DW*, July 30, 2014. http://www.dw.de/oz-lose-lose-situation-for-israel/a-17822511.

Troen, S. Ilan, "De-Judaizing the Homeland: Academic Politics in Rewriting the History of Palestine." *Israel Affairs*, 13:4 (2007).

Trotsky, Leon, *History of the Russian Revolution*, Vol. II (1932). https://www.marxists.org/ebooks/trotsky/history-of-the-russian-revolution/ebook-history-of-the-russian-revolution-v1.pdf.

United Nations Office on Drugs and Crime, *Handbook of Basic Principles and Promising Practices on Alternatives to Imprisonment* (New York: United Nations, 2007).

Veracini, Lorenzo, *Israel and Settler Society* (London: Pluto Press, 2006).

——*Settler Colonialism: A Theoretical Overview* (London and New York: Palgrave Macmillan, 2010).

——*The Settler Colonial Present* (London and New York: Palgrave Macmillan, 2015).

Volkan, Vamik, *Bloodlines: From Ethnic Pride to Ethnic Terrorism* (New York: Basic Books, 1998).

Wieseltier, Leon, "Israel and Gaza: A Just and Unjust War." *The New Republic* (August 7, 2014).

Winslade, John and Gerald D. Monk, *Narrative Mediation: A New Approach to Conflict Resolution* (San Francisco, CA: Jossey-Bass, 2000).

Wolff, Nancy et al., "Physical Violence in Prisons: Rates of Victimization." *Criminal Justice and Behavior*, 34:5 (May 2007).

# 2

# HOW DO SOCIAL SYSTEMS GENERATE VIOLENCE?

## Thinking about social systems

It may seem odd, at least at first glance, to talk about social or political systems that produce violent conflict. It is often said that the main purpose of organizing society systematically, of recognizing individuals and groups publicly, ordering their affairs, and regularizing their relations, is to do away with serious conflicts, or else to manage them in accordance with commonly accepted legal, moral, and political norms. Especially in the West, a structured social and legal order is commonly identified with civilization, in contrast to weak or failing states where violence is the norm, as in some Hobbesian state of nature. As a result, if violent social conflict erupts in almost any ordered society, people immediately want to know how the relevant conflict management systems failed, or why they became dysfunctional. In certain cases, however – the prison and the colonial-settler state are two examples – not only do structured systems fail to produce peace, they succeed very well in producing violence. Violent social conflicts need not be the result of system dysfunction. Depending upon the type of structure in play and other factors we will shortly discuss, they may be entirely 'functional.'

Social analysts, of course, are not the only scholars interested in systems. The concept has become influential in fields ranging from biochemistry and quantum physics to engineering, information science, psychiatry, and business management. At the most general level, the idea of the system is highly abstract. Natural and applied scientists speak about systems as Xs – things – consisting of interdependent parts or functions that interact over time in patterned ways, creating some stable (or at least describable) whole that is more than the sum of its parts. As soon as they begin to analyze specific systems, however, the experts find themselves focusing on their subject's unique characteristics: the existence of causal loops in closed systems, the indeterminacy of certain complex systems, and so forth.[1] Social analysts also examine patterned relationships, but their focus on human beings and their differing views on the 'goodness of fit' between people and social structures tend to divide them roughly into two groups that we can call objectivist and subjectivist.

Most objectivists do not think that the fit between humans and structures is very good. They conceive of social systems as hierarchically organized, 'vertical' relationships whose primary thrust is to empower, enrich, and confer status on some individuals and groups while keeping others subordinate. These analysts tend to emphasize the external and compulsory elements of the system, which many compare to a machine or other inhuman device operating according to laws of its own and imposing itself on people with or without – but mostly without – their consent.[2] For example, my discussion of the prison in the previous chapter used the metaphor of the factory to describe that system's regular and inhumane production of violence. The other piece of this theoretical picture is a decidedly nonmechanistic view of human beings. The objectivists tend to portray humans as vital, willful, impassioned, decidedly not malleable, and stubbornly determined to resist being forced to play the demeaning roles dictated by an inequitable system. The theologian Reinhold Niebuhr once wrote a book called *Moral Man and Immoral Society*.[3] Objectivist thinkers might entitle their own perspective *Vital Humans and Mechanistic Systems*.

This view of social structure, while manifestly critical of oppressive systems, has been embraced by critics representing a variety of political perspectives. To leftists like Karl Marx, Herbert Marcuse, and C. Wright Mills, as well as conservatives like Friedrich Hayek, Ayn Rand, and Milton Friedman, certain structures of domination and subordination are a primary source of alienation and violence.[4] Where competing schools differ is on the primary source and social basis of this alienation. For the left analysts, the chief problem, located in civil society but heavily reliant on the state, is the capitalist order. The rightists, on the other hand, see the state dedicated to social engineering as the primary structural source of oppression – an external force said to exercise a deforming and corrupting influence on the business community in particular, as well as on civil society in general.

Whatever their political stances, however, objectivist thinkers are not surprised to discover that the systems they analyze generate discontent, anger, and, at times, violent behavior on the part of both high-ranking and low-ranking groups. This perspective has deep historical roots going back at least as far as Jean-Jacques Rousseau, who opened his famous pamphlet on "The Social Contract" (1762) by declaring "Man is born free, and everywhere he is in chains."[5]

Subjectivists, by contrast, tend to emphasize the relative *absence* of discontent and violence even in highly structured social and political systems. For social analysts like Max Weber and Talcott Parsons, the question is not 'why men rebel' (the title of Ted Gurr's well-known study of political violence), but why, most of the time, there is so *little* serious antisystem violence.[6] The answer that they offer is that social systems are not externally imposed on unwilling subjects; they are the result of deep correspondences and subtle accommodations between structured institutions and human needs and desires. From a subjectivist viewpoint, the people enmeshed in systems are its components and creators – willing collaborators, to a significant extent, and not just its coerced, bribed, or brainwashed victims.

This primary reliance on consent (in Weberian terms, legitimacy) rather than on force is what gives structured institutions their relative stability and longevity, even when they instantiate inequality. The subjectivists' more sanguine view of the relationship between system and agent is reflected in their language. Rather than use mechanical metaphors to describe social systems, many of them are drawn to organic metaphors, the most famous of which, perhaps, is Edmund Burke's description of the British state as a great oak tree, growing naturally over the centuries to shelter a grateful people.[7] Furthermore, while objectivists looking at human psychology tend to stress the psychic basis for resistance to systematized authority – irrepressible individual needs, say, or rising group expectations – subjectivists emphasize the extent to which individuals *internalize* such authority, accepting ideas, attitudes, emotions, and bodily practices inculcated or sanctioned by the system as their own. They, too, disagree among themselves politically, depending upon whether they consider the system-agent relationship just and efficacious or exploitative and dehumanizing. Even so, most modern subjectivists consider the structured system as "a construction of reality rather than *the actual* reality" – a relational network that can be analyzed primarily in terms of "processes, communication, relationships and network structures."[8]

Really? One wonders what a current inmate of, say, the maximum security prison operated by the U.S. Army in Guantanamo Bay, Cuba, would make of the assertion that his place of residence is a construction of reality rather than reality itself. To be sure, one can (and should) analyze any social institution, including a torture chamber, as a situs and agglomeration of rules, processes, communication networks, and other intersubjective relations and activities. Stopping there, however, leaves one feeling that something essential has been omitted. The subjectivized prison is an abstraction, but it is an abstraction organized to perform concrete acts of violence. To someone at the bottom of this sort of hierarchy, intersubjectivity is not a comforting concept. Having said this, one must also recognize that Guantanamo is a creation of the law, defined by and operated in accordance with written and nonwritten rules. In addition, as Michel Foucault said of prisons in general, it is an institution which interacts with inmates psychosocially as well as a physically, incorporating them in the system not just as inert objects but as active (if relatively powerless) components.[9] If the objectivists' main insight is that there is something in human beings that resists being subjected to domination by social and political hierarchies, subjectivists understand that these systems are within us as well as without, and that there is also something human about adapting to the social environment.

In short, both schools have important things to say about people's relationship to social structures, but integrating these perspectives has proven to be far more difficult than it may seem. Many contemporary analysts have concluded that the road forward in understanding structured systems lies in incorporating the insights of both schools in a synthesis that recognizes their coercive, elite-dominated aspects as well as their more internal and participatory aspects. The French sociologist Pierre Bourdieu put the matter very well in his discussion of the state, which could also serve as a discussion of almost any structured system. The state, he remarked, "incarnates itself simultaneously in objectivity, in the form of specific organizational structures and mechanisms, and in subjectivity, in the form of mental structures and categories of perception and thought." He went on to say:

> By realizing itself in the form of social structures and the mental structures adapted to them, the instituted institution makes us forget that it issues out of a long series of acts of *institution* (in the active sense) and hence has all the appearance of the *natural*.[10]

These last lines illustrate that it is one thing to declare one's intention to transcend the subjectivist/objectivist divide and another thing to actually do it. By insisting that social institutions are "instituted" – that is, created by particular people for particular purposes of their own – the left-leaning Bourdieu takes issue with those conservative commentators, from Thomas Aquinas and Edmund Burke to the present, who believe that structured institutions with staying power (marriage, for example, courts of law, or organized religions) *are* in a sense natural, and not just the creations of some groups hoping to dominate others. Although Bourdieu recognizes many forms of subjective 'capital' not considered by the materialist Karl Marx (including cultural, social, and symbolic capital), he continues to view most institutions as power-based systems serving to perpetuate class domination.[11] On the other hand, his own theories, which describe the extent to which people internalize social relations, even to the extent of making them part of their bodily functions, portray a *more* stable and powerful subjectivized social order than that described by Marx, and suggest that Bourdieu is haunted by the subjectivists' favorite question: why, considering the persistence of inequality and deprivation, is there so *little* rebellion?

Analysts attempting to discover a new basis for understanding social structure have largely abandoned both the mechanical imagery of the objectivists and the organic metaphors of the subjectivists in favor of more abstract (and more up-to-date) metaphors. Bourdieu himself discussed "fields of power," implicitly comparing the positions and movements of individuals and groups subject to the power of social hierarchies, but possessing various forms of capital, to the behavior of particles (with charges of their own) subject to an electromagnetic or gravitational field.[12] Others have moved even further toward abstraction by discussing social relations in terms of 'networks' (multiple interrelated lines representing relationships connected by nodes), or 'dynamical systems' (a mathematical concept now used by some social analysts to discover patterns in highly complex, chaotic systems, including systems of conflict).[13] Again, many of these conceptions seem to fall either on one side or the other of the old divide. Bourdieu's field of power, while more complex than any machine, still focuses primarily on asymmetric power relations and the dominant role of elites, while in the network and dynamical systems approaches, structured asymmetrical power virtually disappears in the welter of complex interdependent relationships.

Researchers and practitioners in the field of conflict studies also find themselves attempting to move beyond this same divide in order to deal with a problem that now seems unavoidable, although it throws many of the field's earlier assumptions and predilections into question: the utility of mediation in helping to resolve structural conflicts. The existence (and, some would say, proliferation) of violence-generating systems presents a serious challenge to the conflict specialists' long-established preference for resolving or managing conflicts through mediation and other forms of third-party practice rather than through legislation, political mobilization, or social action. During the past three decades, as the field of conflict studies became professionalized and of increasing interest to powerful public and private agencies, working to transform social systems seemed an activity smacking unacceptably of partisan politics.[14] Partly as a result, structured social systems were seldom recognized, even in theory, as a problem to be solved by conflict resolvers. A brief overview of the field may help us discover why this recognition took so long and how it finally occurred.

## Social systems and conflict resolution: from avoidance to recognition

In the discipline of peace and conflict studies, the present study and related writings and practices represent a *structure-based* wave of theory and practice, following a first wave that one can term *interest-based* and a second that might be called *identity-based*.[15] We can review this development briefly, understanding that the wave metaphor has its limits. These movements of praxis do not all crash on some shore and dissipate. Since every approach to social conflict, no matter how generally stated, represents a response to some particular type of struggle, the older waves persist as long as the older forms of conflict do. This multiplicity of approaches can, of course, produce conflict within the field of conflict studies. If, as some believe, a new 'Cold War' between the Western powers and Russia or China is now brewing, should this sort of conflict be understood in 'first wave' (interest-based) or 'second wave' (identity-based) terms? Or is the better alternative the 'third wave' (structure-based) approach? Explanations of each of these movements follow, with particular emphasis on their views of social structure and the relation between social or political systems and their human subjects.

### The first wave: conflict as the pursuit of competing interests

During much of the Cold War period, thinking about conflict and its resolution hinged on three related concepts: interests, rationality, and power. A guiding assumption was that rational actors pursuing individual or group interests would use their power to strike an acceptable bargain if they could, or take up arms where bargaining failed. Self-proclaimed Realists interpreted international conflicts as power struggles between states pursuing their national interests. For them, war was 'the continuation of politics by other means,' and the chief alternative to military force was 'negotiation from strength,' a form of strategic, power-based bargaining that reached its acme, perhaps, in negotiations over nuclear weapons between the Soviet Union and the United States.[16]

With regard to social systems, the Realists made two additional assumptions. First, the relevant unit of conflict was the nation, which was considered a stable system united, at least in relation to other nations, by common interests. The nation as a hierarchically structured system manifesting or incubating serious internal conflicts did not play a significant role in their thinking. (This same assumption, we will see, colored the views of analysts who defined political competition *within* the nation as the pursuit of competing group interests.) Internationally, the overarching reality embracing the parties was defined as 'no-system,' or global anarchy. Nations could form alliances, of course, and some alliances, like the competing power blocs of the Cold War, seemed relatively stable. But, Realist thinkers insisted, these were arrangements of convenience whose continued existence was always contingent upon the consent of states pursuing their own interests. Although there were Great Powers whose influence exceeded that of small powers most of the time, the international system *lacked* structure in the sense of a stable, rule-governed hierarchy. The somewhat ironic result, from the point of view of conflict resolution, was that many heads of state and diplomats considered themselves free to create new international systems – the United Nations, for example, at the end of World War II, and the European Union a generation later. The notion that because some Great Powers were actually empires, the international order was never quite as anarchic as it seemed, was not much considered by the Realists, although their 'neo-Realist' successors are clearly aware of the problem.[17]

Second, a similar approach to local conflicts interpreted them primarily as struggles for power, economic advantage, and social status between competing economic and political 'interest groups.' Unlike international conflicts, however, these struggles took place in the context of a system that was thought to have tamed and civilized them. One and only one overarching system was recognized. This was the nation, which, according to the prevailing liberal theory, maintained a political, legal, and cultural consensus permitting domestic interest groups to pursue their interests competitively, but nonviolently.[18] Specialists interested in developing less competitive alternatives to purely adversary procedures accepted the same interest-based definition of disputes, portraying them as clashes analogous to commercial disputes that could be settled, with the assistance of mediators or other trained facilitators, by various methods of alternative dispute resolution (ADR) or "principled negotiation."[19] To the assumption that people in conflict were rational cost–benefit calculators who would use whatever power they could mobilize to advance their interests, those flying ADR banners added an additional hopeful proviso: local disputants could be assisted by expert facilitators to define their interests and interact in ways conducive to peaceful conflict management.[20]

Particularly after dispute resolution was incorporated into law school curricula throughout the United States and recognized in many other nations, its practitioners had considerable success in developing alternatives to litigation as methods of settling a wide variety of local disputes. At the same time, analogous techniques were used by foreign affairs agencies to mitigate some international disputes under the label of 'second-track' diplomacy.[21] Nevertheless, neither 'hard power' Realists nor 'soft power' negotiators were much inclined to recognize the existence of violence-producing systems outside the immediate context of the conflict itself. (The immediate conflict, of course, could be considered a system in itself, as the game theorists well understood.)[22] Their almost universal belief was that the same state performing as a unit of conflict in international affairs was a conflict managing system domestically.

The key to the state's successful operation in this regard was continuous interest group bargaining, which was made possible by the willingness of organized groups to accept two implicit rules. First, they must accept the limitations on appropriate subjects for negotiation imposed by an alleged national consensus. (The existence of the capitalist market and management rights within that context, for example, were *not* considered appropriate subjects for interest group bargaining.)[23] Second, they must express their differences and demands either quantitatively, as in labor-management and intercorporate disputes, or in other terms conducive to compromises that 'split the difference,' as in disputes over budgetary allocations, jurisdictional boundaries, and regulatory policies. A famous example of what might be called quasi-quantitative bargaining in the United States involved disputes between Protestant, Catholic, and Jewish organizations in locales like New York which were settled by granting the leaders of each group certain powers and privileges. It was said, only half-jokingly, that when a Jew served as governor of New York State, a Roman Catholic would be mayor of New York City, and vice versa.[24]

The decision to play the bargaining game according to these systemic rules was sometimes made consciously, as when leaders of the African-American civil rights movement openly appealed to northern business and political leaders to vindicate their legal and constitutional rights against white southern racists.[25] More often than not, however, the parties in dispute simply ignored the existence of a hierarchical, power-based social system outside the immediate arena of conflict. It was not that they were ignorant of the fact that existing social structures privileged a wealthy elite over the middle class and both of these groups over the poor; white people over people of color; men over women; straights over gays, and so forth. But why raise the issue of large-scale inequalities when one could make some progress for oneself or one's group in immediate bargaining, when the broader system was considered unchangeable, and when the national consensus was thought to reflect a cultural, political, and spiritual unity that transcended social divisions?

This last point was crucial. The alleged consensus that was believed to override power-based hierarchies was asserted and inculcated during the Cold War by nationalist ideologues both liberal and conservative, and elaborated by scholars celebrating America's unique freedom from serious social conflict, the Western-ness of the West, liberal capitalism as "the end of history," and similar hopeful topics.[26] Consensus thinking, as a handful of maverick analysts pointed out, was an intellectual potion designed to serve as a comforting antidote to the perception of radical social inequality and large-scale deprivation. The fact that it was so heavily consumed may explain, in part, the shock that greeted outbreaks of two new types of conflict, one involving domestic groups making demands and participating in activities outside the conventional modes of interest-based bargaining, compromise, and conflict management, and the other involving international rebels who could not be suppressed by superior force or threats of force. The second wave of conflict studies theories and practices was largely a response to these newer manifestations of violence.

## The second wave: conflict as a nonnegotiable struggle for group identity

What exposed the limitations of the interest-based approach was the appearance and persistence of a number of intensely violent, apparently intractable conflicts fought out by groups that were not necessarily recognized nation-states or conventional interest groups, and whose members did not act like rational cost–benefit calculators. Among these struggles were anti-imperial revolts and wars of national liberation, ethnonationalist conflicts pitting secessionists against unionists, racial and ethnic riots and pogroms, tribal wars, and religiously motivated interstate and civil wars. Faced with the incapacity of interest-based negotiations to resolve many of these conflicts, specialists sought to discover the psychosocial and cultural factors that made them especially violent and hard to resolve.

The analysts of the second wave challenged the mechanistic, utilitarian psychology implicit in many Realist theories, and questioned the related behaviorist notion that people could be conditioned or educated to think and act as the authorities wished them to. Their ideas about enemy images, social identities, frustration–aggression, and basic psychic needs represented an important advance over the narrowly framed conceptions of conflict that long held sway among many conflict analysts and resolvers. Certain theorists strongly emphasized innate drives or capacities of the mind and left open the question of what would trigger, say, aggressive impulses, culturally ingrained prejudices, or a need to proclaim one's own group superior to all other groups. The most useful approaches, however, attempted to link people's inner states to some extent with outward circumstances, in order to establish a foundation for new techniques of practical conflict resolution. Three examples are especially worth noting: the theory of basic human needs developed by John Burton and others; Ted Robert Gurr's explanation of relative deprivation; and Vamik Volkan's concept of the chosen trauma.[27]

For John Burton, the existence of fundamental, irrepressible human needs for identity, recognition, security, and personal development – needs, as he said, that were "not for trading" – explained why power-based hard bargaining was ineffective to prevent or end certain types of rebellion and antisocial behavior. (The title of his first book on basic needs – *Deviance, Terrorism and War* – suggests how broadly Burton defined these types of conflict.)[28] If their basic needs, and most importantly their identity-based needs, were not satisfied, people would rebel, violently if necessary, notwithstanding promises of reward or threats of punishment by those who considered themselves their betters. In a somewhat similar vein, Ted Gurr maintained that the basis for rebellion was "relative deprivation": a gap between certain key goods and values to which people felt themselves entitled and the goods and values they actually obtained under the operation of current political and economic systems. When the differential became large enough, Gurr asserted, a popular movement driven by frustration and anger would attempt to close it by any means necessary, including violence. Movements motivated mainly by rising expectations would likely aim at radical reform of current systems. Those motivated mainly by declining system capabilities would aim, more conservatively, at restoring some previous status quo. And those driven by a simultaneous rise in expectations and decline in capabilities would be revolutionary in intent.

Into this grievance-based political psychology, the psychoanalyst Vamik Volkan imported a subconscious dimension, suggesting that a propensity for collective violence among identity groups could be stimulated by current events that revived repressed feelings of shame, insecurity, and rage caused by a historical trauma – for example, a humiliating military defeat, violent persecution, or foreign occupation. Members of ethnic or national groups conflating current threats with past traumas, Volkan declared, were easily persuaded by leaders vowing to protect and avenge them to use mass violence against malicious enemies. Such appeals might also awaken the group members' sense of pride and entitlement by invoking memories of historical chosen glories, but the dominant motive of ethnonationalist groups in violent conflict was to defend their existence against real or fancied threats of extermination.

Some of these insights bore practical fruit in the shape of new ideas or programs for conflict resolution. Volkan conducted dialogue-based interventions in the Baltic nations, the former Yugoslav nations, Greece, Turkey, and elsewhere, attempting to assist conflicting groups to recognize and deal with the effects of historical traumas and to reconcile with their enemies.[29] Gurr, a social scientist, utilized his theoretical framework to report on *Violence in America* as a staff director of the National Commission on the Causes and Prevention of Violence and devised a method of predicting possible genocides in his *Minorities at Risk* project.[30] Most important for the field of conflict resolution, perhaps, the former diplomat John Burton, working with Edward Azar, Christopher Mitchell, Herbert Kelman, and others, developed a form of facilitated dialogue known as the analytical problem-solving workshop in order to assist conflicting parties to discover methods of identifying and satisfying the basic needs that, unsatisfied, appeared to be driving their conflict. Facilitated dialogues of this sort achieved some notable successes in helping to resolve or mitigate ethnonationalist conflicts in a number of nations, including Northern Ireland, Liberia, Mozambique, South Africa, Macedonia, Nepal, Colombia, Moldova, Tajikistan, and several other ex-Soviet republics.[31]

The relative success of these efforts (keeping in mind that violent conflicts remain partly unresolved or have revived in a number of these locales) had two sources. First, approaches stressing unsatisfied basic needs and other deep-rooted psychological sources of conflict were better able to account for the parties' behavior in identity-based struggles than the old Realist assumptions. Second, the theorists made some effort to identify the social contextual factors that might explain why needs, anxieties, expectations, prejudices, and other aspects of personality and culture that operate for long periods of time *without* necessarily producing violent conflict would sometimes become apparent generators of violence. John Burton frequently noted that elitist rulers or dominant ethnic or racial groups often acted to prevent less powerful and privileged groups from satisfying their needs for identity and autonomy. Ted Gurr held unresponsive political leaders and institutions responsible for permitting the growth of relative deprivation. (Some conservative critics, on the other hand, preferred to blame government for promising too much, and thus raising have-not expectations to *unrealistic* levels.)[32] Vamik Volkan criticized demagogic ethnonationalist leaders for exploiting the unhealed wounds of historical traumas.

Many second wave approaches reflected a left-liberal political bent owing much to the political upheavals in North America and Europe during the 1960s and 1970s. Declining to condemn rebellious actors for behaving rebelliously, the analysts attributed racial and political uprisings to a mismatch between people's legitimate needs (particularly for identity, recognition, and a 'place at the table' of power) and the political status quo. Once the relevant needs, rights, and expectations were identified, they assumed, and once the costs of continuing to avoid satisfying them were calculated, the parties would agree to reform the political system to the extent necessary to resolve the conflict. The fact that some parties were far more powerful than others in military or financial terms was irrelevant, since the lesson to be learned from protracted identity group struggles was that Realist-style power was irrelevant; only needs-satisfaction could terminate the violence. Once all the parties understood this (as they came to understand it, for example, in Northern Ireland), the sort of rational calculation that second wave theorists had found wanting as the primary basis for conflict psychology would become possible, and successful peace negotiations could take place.

This reasoning, although quite convincing in some respects, left a number of difficult questions unanswered, including the following examples.

*When will dissatisfied people rebel?* Although obviously interested in preventing avoidable violence, the analysts found it difficult to predict the point at which people would become conscious enough of their unsatisfied needs, relatively deprived enough, or fearful enough of a repetition of some historical trauma to mobilize for violent activity. This theoretical blind spot was related to a failure to describe and account for the operations of conflict-generating systems in concrete terms. Most specialists had far more to say about the conflicting parties' states of mind than about the patterned situations that would be likely to turn dissatisfaction into violence. To put the matter too simply, perhaps, this focus on psychological states arose from the tendency of parties embroiled in identity group conflicts to resist rational calculation, consensual bargaining, and "principled negotiation." Compared to their violent passions and rigidities, sociopolitical systems seemed relatively plastic and conformable to agreed-upon changes, at least after all parties had been brought to recognize the primacy of basic needs. But, in many cases, elite-driven systems proved more difficult to transform than had been expected.

*How much change is enough?* Even assuming recognition of basic needs, the concrete question of what it would take to satisfy them was never answered systematically. How much change would be sufficient to reintegrate alienated individuals and groups into a reconstructed consensual order? As Christopher Mitchell pointed out, no theory of satisfiers was ever produced to complement the theory of human needs.[33] What Mitchell did not note specifically, although his approach implied it, was that a useful theory of satisfiers was unlikely to develop without a better understanding

of the social-structural context of the parties' dissatisfaction and the possibilities of altering those structures. True, some second wave theorists
attempted to specify what sorts of change in political systems (e.g., separa-
tion, federation, semiautonomy, consociation, power-sharing) might satisfy
the needs and aspirations of groups seeking to defend their collective identities.[34] But even these discussions tended to concentrate on the constitutional reforms possible in particular cases of ethnonationalist conflict. The
analysts' focus on cultural (mainly ethnic) identities threw other social divisions, including those based on social class, into shadow, and largely limited
the consideration of alternative systems to formal political rearrangements.

*What about socioeconomic systems?* Where the relevant conflict-generating
system was purely political, there existed an ample stock of ideas (going
back at least to Plato's *Republic*) about possible institutional alternatives.
Moreover, where political systems had visibly broken down, it was usually clear to all parties that resolving the conflict would require some new
constitutional arrangement. But what if violent conflict was directly related
to the existence of a particular type or subtype of socioeconomic organization? There, the range of possible alternative systems seemed quite limited.
Furthermore, while, in many cases, old political regimes had given way
to new regimes without violent revolutions taking place, there seemed a
much closer connection between the overthrow of socioeconomic systems
and violent, long-lasting struggles. Most important, while discussing alternative political constitutions was difficult, discussing alternative socioeconomic arrangements was taboo. As a result, second wave conflict specialists
who had little difficulty talking to Palestinians and Israelis, say, about various political alternatives to the conflicted status quo hesitated to facilitate
any discussion of alternatives to Israeli-style capitalism, one of whose effects
has been the economic colonization of Palestine. Yet a case can be made
that the failure to put such issues on the table is a major factor undermining attempts to restart the peace process, since all sides understand (without
necessarily saying so) that, under current conditions, a Palestinian state is
likely to be an economic Bantustan.

One of the events suggesting a need for a third wave of praxis in conflict
studies, in fact, was the failure of the Palestinians and Israelis to implement
the peace process mandated by the Oslo Accords, the 1993 agreement
reached as the result of a classic 'second-track' dialogue in Oslo, Norway.
This disappointment was, at least in part, the result of a misunderstanding
of the systemic framework of the Israeli-Palestinian struggle. The sociopolitical system that embraced the parties (and was itself imbedded in larger
systems) proved far more resistant to change than the negotiators had imagined.[35] Meanwhile, as the 1990s gave way to a new century, other local and

global developments broadened the range of conflicts requiring analysis and resolution beyond the identity group struggles that had earlier dominated the scene. What some called 'the new global disorder' included violent clashes based not only on people's ethnicity and nationality, but also on their membership in social classes, religious organizations, civilizational groups, and regions affected by climate change.[36]

Especially following the attacks by al-Qaeda on U.S. targets in 2001, a so-called 'war on terror' began which, spreading to a large number of nations in Europe, the Middle East, the Sahel, and Africa, shows no signs of abating. Savage civil conflicts triggered by the U.S. invasions of Afghanistan and Iraq and fueled by Sunni-Shia religious hostility have now spread throughout the Muslim world. In Africa, violent struggles reflecting the disruptions of rapid economic development, climate change, religious competition, and foreign intervention have become endemic in certain regions. Mass migrations involving millions fleeing unlivable conflict zones and unviable economic orders have generated political disputes worldwide. Meanwhile, in a worrisome and unexpected revival of Great Power competition, tensions between the Western powers, Russia, and China have risen dramatically, fostering fears of a new world war.

New intellectual and practical tools were required to comprehend and deal with these new forms of conflict. A third wave of praxis was therefore set in motion which we can call the structural turn in conflict studies. Its hallmark is *conflict as a struggle to maintain or overthrow systems of domination*. The third wave's premises, its limitations, and the challenges it offers to the study and practice of conflict resolution are the subjects next on our agenda.

## Notes

1 For a general introduction to system theory, see Ludwig von Bertalanffy's *General System Theory: Foundations, Development, Applications* (New York: George Braziller, 2015). Kenneth Boulding's pioneering article (1956), "General systems theory: the skeleton of science," is reprinted in *E:CO*, 6:1–2 (2004), 127–139.

2 This metaphor is substantiated in Franz Kafka's justly famed story, "In the Penal Colony" (1919), in which the system of punishment becomes a literal machine. See https://records.viu.ca/~Johnstoi/kafka/inthepenalcolony.htm.

3 Reinhold Niebuhr, *Moral Man and Immoral Society: A Study in Ethics and Politics*, 2nd Edn. (Louisville, KY: Westminster John Knox Press, 2013).

4 For Marx on social structure, see Neil J. Smelser, Ed., *Karl Marx on Society and Social Change, With Selections from Friedrich Engels* (Chicago: University of Chicago Press, 1975). For Marcuse, see *One-Dimensional Man: Studies in the Ideology of Advanced Industrial Society*, 2nd Edn. (Boston: Beacon Press, 1991). C.

Wright Mills is best known for *The Power Elite* and *The Sociological Imagination*, both republished by Oxford University Press in 2000. For F.A. Hayek, see *The Road To Serfdom: Texts and Documents, the Definitive Edition* (Chicago: University of Chicago Press, 2007). For Milton Friedman, see *Capitalism and Freedom: The 40th Anniversary Edition* (Chicago: University of Chicago Press, 2002). See also Russell Kirk, *The Conservative Mind: From Burke to Eliot*, 7th Edn. (Washington, D.C.: Regnery Publishing, 2001).

5 Jean-Jacques Rousseau, *The Social Contract, or Principles of Political Right*. Trans. By G.D.H. Cole. (Cork: University College Cork, 2002). https://www.ucc.ie/archive/hdsp/Rousseau_contrat-social.pdf.

6 See Ted Robert Gurr, *Why Men Rebel*, 40th Anniversary Edn. (London and New York: Routledge, 2010). For Max Weber, see *Economy and Society: An Outline of Interpretive Sociology*, 2 Vols. (Berkeley, CA: University of California Press, 1978). Talcott Parsons' *magnum opus* is *The Theory of Social Action,* 2 Vols. (New York: Free Press, 1967).

7 Edmund Burke, *Reflections on the Revolution in France* (1789). (Oxford: Oxford University Press, 2009). See also Jeffrey Hart, "Burke and the English Revolution." *Modern Age* (December 1997), 11–20. http://www.mmisi.org/ma/39_01/hart.pdf.

8 Sirin Bernshausen and Thorsten Bonacker, "A Constructivist Perspective on Systemic Conflict Transformation," in Daniela Korppen, et al., Eds, *The Non-Linearity of Peace Processes: Theory and Practice of Systemic Conflict Transformation* (Opladen, Germany and Farmington Hills, MI: Verlag Barbara Budrich, 2011), 23.

9 Michel Foucault, *Discipline and Punish: The Birth of the Prison*, 4th Edn. (New York: Vintage Books, 2007).

10 Pierre Bourdieu, et al., "Rethinking the State: Genesis and Structure of the Bureaucratic Field." *Sociological Theory*, 12:1 (March 1994), 1–18, 3–4.

11 "So it has to be posited simultaneously that economic capital is at the root of all the other types of capital and that these transformed, disguised forms of economic capital, never entirely reducible to that definition, produce their most specific effects only to the extent that they conceal (not least from their possessors) the fact that economic capital is at their root, in other words – but only in the last analysis – at the root of their effects." Pierre Bourdieu, "The Forms of Capital," in J. Richardson, Ed., *Handbook of Theory and Practice for the Sociology of Education*. (New York: Greenwood Press, 1986), "Conversions," Paragraph 2. https://www.marxists.org/reference/subject/philosophy/works/fr/bourdieu-forms-capital.htm.

12 See, e.g., Pierre Bourdieu, *The State Nobility: Elite Schools in the Field of Power* (Cambridge: Polity Press, 1998), 161 *et seq.* See also John Levi Martin, "What Is Field Theory?" *American Journal of Sociology*, 109:1 (July 2003), 1–49. https://www.csudh.edu/dearhabermas/lewinkurt01.pdf.

13 For network theory, see Charles Kadushin, *Understanding Social Networks: Theories, Concepts, and Findings* (Oxford and New York: Oxford University Press, 2011). For dynamical systems theory as applied to conflict analysis, see Peter T.

Coleman, *The Five Percent: Finding Solutions to Seemingly Impossible Conflicts* (New York: PublicAffairs, 2011). See also Coleman, et al., "Navigating the Landscape of Conflict: Applications of Dynamical Systems Theory to Addressing Protracted Conflict," in Daniela Korppen, et al., *op. cit.*, 39–56.

14 Christopher W. Moore's *The Mediation Process: Practical Strategies for Resolving Conflict*, 4th Edn. (San Francisco, CA: Jossey-Bass, 2014), something of a Bible for students and practitioners in the field, contains no index entries for "politics," "power," "social structure," or "system." An apparent exception to this apoliticality, is James Laue and Gerald Cormick, "The Ethics of Community Intervention," in Gordon Bermant, et al., *The Ethics of Social Intervention* (Washington and London: Hemisphere Publishers, 1978), and will be discussed in Chapter 5, *infra*.

15 Several analysts have attempted to periodize or thematize the development of the conflict studies field – see esp. Oliver Ramsbotham, et al., *Contemporary Conflict Resolution*, 4th Edn. (Cambridge, UK and Malden, MA: Polity Press, 2016), 38–67; Peter Wallensteen, *Understanding Conflict Resolution*, 4th Edn. (London and Los Angeles: Sage, 2015), 37–52. See also the "Parents of the Field" videos produced by Christopher R. Mitchell and Johannes Botes for the School for Conflict Analysis and Resolution at George Mason University, accessible at http://scar.gmu.edu/parents. I am grateful to my S-CAR colleague, Prof. Sara Cobb, for outlining a periodization based on philosophical (especially epistemological) approaches to conflict.

16 The *locus classicus* for Realist thinking is Hans J. Morgenthau, *Politics Among Nations: The Struggle for Power and Peace*, 3rd Edn. (New York: Alfred A. Knopf, 1965). See also the later work of "neo-Realists" like Kenneth N. Waltz, *Theory of International Politics* (New York: McGraw-Hill, 1979) and John J. Mearsheimer, *The Tragedy of Great Power Politics* (New York: W.W. Norton, 2001). On strategic bargaining see Henry A. Kissinger, *Nuclear Weapons and Foreign Policy* (New York: W.W. Norton, 1969).

17 See, e.g., Stephen M. Walt, *Taming American Power: The Global Response to U.S. Primacy* (New York: W.W. Norton, 2006).

18 See, e.g., Louis Hartz, *The Liberal Tradition in America* (New York: Harvest Books, 1991).

19 "Interest group" theory is exemplified by Robert A. Dahl, *Who Governs? Democracy and Power in an American City* (New Haven: Yale University Press, 1961). "Principled negotiation" is a phrase coined by Roger Fisher and William L. Ury in *Getting to Yes: Negotiating Agreement Without Giving In*, Rev. Edn. (London and New York: Penguin Books, 1991). See also William L. Ury, *Getting Past No: Negotiating in Difficult Situations*, Rev. Edn. (New York: Bantam, 1993).

20 Not surprisingly, a number of pioneers in the field of international peace studies were game theorists setting out to discover how rational calculation could produce peace rather than war. See, e.g., Anatol Rapoport, *Fights, Games, and Debates* (Ann Arbor, MI: University of Michigan Press, 1974); *The Origins of*

*Violence: Approaches to the Study of Conflict*, Reprint Edn. (New Brunswick, NJ: Transactions Press, 1995).

21 The techniques collectively known as alternative dispute resolution or ADR, have become part of the standard law school curriculum in the United States. See, e.g., Stephen B. Goldberg, et al., *Dispute Resolution: Negotiation, Mediation, Arbitration and Other Processes*, 6th Edn. (Alphen aan den Rijn, Netherlands: Aspen Publishers, 2012). For second-track diplomacy, see John Paul Lederach, *Building Peace: Sustainable Reconciliation in Divided Societies* (Washington, DC: U.S. Institute of Peace, 1998); I. William Zartman, Ed., *Peacemaking in International Conflict: Methods and Techniques*, Rev. Edn. (Washington, DC: U.S. Institute of Peace, 2007).

22 Probably the best known expression of this view was that of Kenneth N. Waltz in *Man, The State, and War: A Theoretical Analysis*, Rev. Edn. (New York: Columbia University Press, 2001).

23 Class conflict as a feature of the industrial social structure is considered at more length in Chapter 4, *infra*.

24 These compromises are discussed at length in Will Herberg, *Protestant-Catholic-Jew: An Essay in American Religious Sociology*, Reprint Edn. (Chicago: University of Chicago Press, 1983).

25 Civil rights leaders made active use of government-supported ADR services like those administered by the Community Relations Division of the U.S. Department of Justice. See, e.g., Roger Wilkins's *A Man's Life: An Autobiography* (Woodbridge, CT: Ox Bow Press, 1991).

26 The acme of consensus scholarship is probably Francis Fukuyama's *The End of History and the Last Man* (New York: Harper, 1993). See the expose of consensus sociology thirty years earlier by Irving Louis Horowitz, "Consensus, Conflict and Cooperation: A Sociological Inventory," *Social Forces*, 41:2 (December 1962), 177–188.

27 Major works of the "second wave" include Ted Robert Gurr, *Why Men Rebel*, 40th Anniversary Edn. (London and New York: Routledge, 2010); John W. Burton, *Conflict: Resolution and Prevention* (London and New York: Palgrave Macmillan, 1990); Herbert C. Kelman, *International Behavior: A Social-Psychological Analysis* (New York: Holt, Rinehart and Winston, 1996); Sudhir Kakar, *The Colors of Violence: Cultural Identities, Religion and Conflict* (Chicago: University of Chicago Press, 1996); Vamik Volkan, *Bloodlines: From Ethnic Pride to Ethnic Terrorism* (New York: Basic Books, 1998); Dean Pruitt, et al., *Social Conflict: Escalation, Stalemate, and Settlement* (New York: McGraw-Hill, 2003); Louis Kriesberg, *Constructive Conflicts: from Escalation to Resolution*, 3rd Edn. (Lanham, MD: Rowman & Littlefield, 2006).

28 John W. Burton, *Deviance, Terrorism and War: The Process of Solving Unsolved Social and Political Problems* (London and New York: Palgrave Macmillan, 1979).

29 Vamik D. Volkan, *Enemies on the Couch: A Psychopolitical Journey Through War and Peace* (Charlottesville, VA: Pitchstone Press, 2013).

30 See Ted Robert Gurr, *Violence in America: Protest, Rebellion, Reform* (Washington, DC: Sage Publishers, 1989); *Minorities at Risk: A Global View of Ethnopolitical Conflicts* (Washington, DC: U.S. Institute of Peace, 1993).

31 George Mitchell, *Making Peace* (Berkeley, CA: University of California Press, 2001); Christopher Mitchell and Michael Banks, *Handbook of Conflict Resolution: The Analytical Problem-Solving Approach* (London: Pinter, 1996); Kevin Avruch and Christopher Mitchell, Eds., *Conflict Resolution and Human Needs: Linking Theory and Practice* (London and New York: Routledge, 2014). Facilitated processes of this sort were also known as "interactive" and "sustained" dialogues. See Ronald Fisher, *Interactive Conflict Resolution* (Syracuse, NY: Syracuse University Press, 1997); Ronald Fisher and Andrea Bartoli, *Paving the Way: Contributions of Interactive Conflict Resolution to Peacemaking* (Lanham, MD: Lexington Books, 2004); Harold H. Saunders, *Sustained Dialogue in Conflicts: Transformation and Change* (London and New York: Palgrave Macmillan, 2011). See also Christopher Mitchell, *The Nature of Intractable Conflict: Resolution in the Twenty-First Century* (London and New York: Palgrave Macmillan, 2014).

32 See for example, Daniel Patrick Moynihan, *Maximum Feasible Misunderstanding: Community Action in the War on Poverty* (New York: Free Press, 1969). As an official of the Nixon administration, Moynihan famously called for "benign neglect" of America's racial problems.

33 Christopher Mitchell, "Necessitous Man and Conflict Resolution: More Basic Questions About Basic Human Needs," in John Burton, Ed., *Conflict: Human Needs Theory* (London and New York: Palgrave Macmillan, 1990). See also Richard E. Rubenstein, "Basic Human Needs: Steps Toward Further Theory Development." *International Journal of Peace Studies*, 6:1 (September 2001). http://www.gmu.edu/programs/icar/ijps/vol6_1/Rubenstein.htm.

34 See, e.g., Jay Rothman, *Resolving Identity-Based Conflicts in Nations, Organizations, and Communities* (San Francisco, CA: Jossey-Bass, 1997); Stefan Wolff and Christalla Yakinthou, Eds., *Conflict Management in Divided Societies* (London and New York: Routledge, 2011).

35 There is now a fairly large literature on the failure of the Oslo peace process. See, e.g., Robert L. Rothstein, et al., Eds., *The Israel-Palestinian Peace Process: Oslo and the Lessons of Failure* (Sussex, UK: Sussex Academic Press, 2004).

36 See, for example, Richard M. Pearlstein, *Fatal Future? Transnational Terrorism and the New Global Disorder* (Austin, TX: University of Texas Press, 2004).

## Bibliography

Avruch, Kevin, and Christopher Mitchell, Eds., *Conflict Resolution and Human Needs: Linking Theory and Practice* (London and New York: Routledge, 2014).

Bernshausen, Sirin and Thorsten Bonacker, "A Constructivist Perspective on Systemic Conflict Transformation," in Daniela Korppen, et al., Eds, *The Non-Linearity of Peace Processes: Theory and Practice of Systemic Conflict Transformation*

(Opladen, Germany and Farmington Hills, MI: Verlag Barbara Budrich, 2011), 23.

Boulding, Kenneth, "General systems theory: the skeleton of science." *E:CO*, 6:1–2 (2004), 127–139.

Bourdieu, Pierre, "The Forms of Capital," in J. Richardson, Ed., *Handbook of Theory and Practice for the Sociology of Education*. (New York: Greenwood Press, 1986), "Conversions" https://www.marxists.org/reference/subject/philosophy/works/fr/bourdieu-forms-capital.htm.

—— "Rethinking the State: Genesis and Structure of the Bureaucratic Field." *Sociological Theory*, 12:1 (March 1994), 1–18, 3–4.

—— *The State Nobility: Elite Schools in the Field of Power* (Cambridge: Polity Press, 1998).

Burke, Edmund, *Reflections on the Revolution in France* (1789). (Oxford: Oxford University Press, 2009).

Burton, John W., *Deviance, Terrorism and War: The Process of Solving Unsolved Social and Political Problems* (London and New York: Palgrave Macmillan, 1979).

—— *Conflict: Resolution and Provention* (London and New York: Palgrave Macmillan, 1990).

Coleman, Peter T., *The Five Percent: Finding Solutions to Seemingly Impossible Conflicts* (New York: PublicAffairs, 2011).

—— et al., "Navigating the Landscape of Conflict: Applications of Dynamical Systems Theory to Addressing Protracted Conflict," in Daniela Korppen, et al., Eds., *The Non-Linearity of Peace Processes: Theory and Practice of Systemic Conflict Transformation* (Opladen, Germany and Farmington Hills, MI: Verlag Barbara Budrich, 2011), 39–56

Dahl, Robert A., *Who Governs? Democracy and Power in an American City* (New Haven: Yale University Press, 1961).

Fisher, Roger and William L. Ury, *Getting to Yes: Negotiating Agreement Without Giving In*, Rev. Edn. (London and New York: Penguin Books, 1991).

Fisher, Ronald, *Interactive Conflict Resolution* (Syracuse, NY: Syracuse University Press, 1997).

—— and Andrea Bartoli, *Paving the Way: Contributions of Interactive Conflict Resolution to Peacemaking* (Lanham, MD: Lexington Books, 2004).

Foucault, Michel, *Discipline and Punish: The Birth of the Prison*, 4th Edn. (New York: Vintage Books, 2007).

Friedman, Milton, *Capitalism and Freedom: The 40th Anniversary Edition* (Chicago: University of Chicago Press, 2002).

Fukuyama, Francis, *The End of History and the Last Man* (New York: Harper, 1993).

Goldberg, Stephen B., et al., *Dispute Resolution: Negotiation, Mediation, Arbitration and Other Processes*, 6th Edn. (Alphen aan den Rijn, Netherlands: Aspen Publishers, 2012).

Gurr, Ted Robert, *Violence in America: Protest, Rebellion, Reform* (Washington, DC: Sage Publishers, 1989).

——*Minorities at Risk: A Global View of Ethnopolitical Conflicts* (Washington, DC: U.S. Institute of Peace, 1993).

——*Why Men Rebel*, 40th Anniversary Edn. (London and New York: Routledge, 2010).

Hart, Jeffrey, "Burke and the English Revolution." *Modern Age* (December 1997), 11–20. http://www.mmisi.org/ma/39_01/hart.pdf.

Hartz, Louis, *The Liberal Tradition in America* (New York: Harvest Books, 1991).

Hayek, F.A., *The Road To Serfdom: Texts and Documents, the Definitive Edition* (Chicago: University of Chicago Press, 2007).

Herberg, Will, *Protestant-Catholic-Jew: An Essay in American Religious Sociology*, Reprint Edn. (Chicago: University of Chicago Press, 1983).

Horowitz, Irving Louis, "Consensus, Conflict and Cooperation: A Sociological Inventory," *Social Forces*, 41:2 (December 1962), 177–188.

Kadushin, Charles, *Understanding Social Networks: Theories, Concepts, and Findings* (Oxford and New York: Oxford University Press, 2011).

Kafka, Franz, "In the Penal Colony" (1919). https://records.viu.ca/~Johnstoi/kafka/inthepenalcolony.htm.

Kakar, Sudhir, *The Colors of Violence: Cultural Identities, Religion and Conflict* (Chicago: University of Chicago Press, 1996).

Kelman, Herbert C., *International Behavior: A Social-Psychological Analysis* (New York: Holt, Rinehart and Winston, 1996).

Kirk, Russell, *The Conservative Mind: From Burke to Eliot*, 7th Edn. (Washington, D.C.: Regnery Publishing, 2001).

Kissinger, Henry A., *Nuclear Weapons and Foreign Policy* (New York: W.W. Norton, 1969).

Kriesberg, Louis, *Constructive Conflicts: from Escalation to Resolution*, 3rd Edn. (Lanham, MD: Rowman & Littlefield, 2006).

Lederach, John Paul, *Building Peace: Sustainable Reconciliation in Divided Societies* (Washington, DC: U.S. Institute of Peace, 1998).

Laue, James and Gerald Cormick, "The Ethics of Community Intervention," in Gordon Bermant, et al., *The Ethics of Social Intervention* (Washington and London: Hemisphere Publishers, 1978).

Marcuse, Herbert, *One-Dimensional Man: Studies in the Ideology of Advanced Industrial Society*, 2nd Edn. (Boston: Beacon Press, 1991).

Martin, John Levi, "What Is Field Theory?" *American Journal of Sociology*, 109:1 (July 2003), 1–49. https://www.csudh.edu/dearhabermas/lewinkurt01.pdf.

Mearsheimer, John J., *The Tragedy of Great Power Politics* (New York: W.W. Norton, 2001).

Mills, C. Wright, *The Power Elite* (Oxford: Oxford University Press, 2000).

—— *The Sociological Imagination* (Oxford: Oxford University Press, 2000).

Mitchell, Christopher, "Necessitous Man and Conflict Resolution: More Basic Questions About Basic Human Needs," in John Burton, Ed., *Conflict: Human Needs Theory* (London and New York: Palgrave Macmillan, 1990).

—— *The Nature of Intractable Conflict: Resolution in the Twenty-First Century* (London and New York: Palgrave Macmillan, 2014).

——and Michael Banks, *Handbook of Conflict Resolution: The Analytical Problem-Solving Approach* (London: Pinter, 1996).

Mitchell, George J., *Making Peace* (Berkeley, CA: University of California Press, 2001).

Moore, Christopher W., *The Mediation Process: Practical Strategies for Resolving Conflict*, 4th Edn. (San Francisco, CA: Jossey-Bass, 2014).

Morgenthau, Hans J., *Politics Among Nations: The Struggle for Power and Peace*, 3rd Edn. (New York: Alfred A. Knopf, 1965).

Moynihan, Daniel Patrick, *Maximum Feasible Misunderstanding: Community Action in the War on Poverty* (New York: Free Press, 1969).

Niebuhr, Reinhold, *Moral Man and Immoral Society: A Study in Ethics and Politics*, 2nd Edn. (Louisville, KY: Westminster John Knox Press, 2013).

Parsons, Talcott, *The Theory of Social Action*, 2 Vols. (New York: Free Press, 1967).

Pearlstein, Richard M., *Fatal Future? Transnational Terrorism and the New Global Disorder* (Austin, TX: University of Texas Press, 2004).

Pruitt, Dean, et al., *Social Conflict: Escalation, Stalemate, and Settlement* (New York: McGraw-Hill, 2003).

Ramsbotham, Oliver et al., *Contemporary Conflict Resolution*, 4th Edn. (Cambridge, UK and Malden, MA: Polity Press, 2016).

Rapoport, Anatol, *Fights, Games, and Debates* (Ann Arbor, MI: University of Michigan Press, 1974).

——*The Origins of Violence: Approaches to the Study of Conflict*, Reprint Edn. (New Brunswick, NJ: Transactions Press, 1995).

Rothman, Jay, *Resolving Identity-Based Conflicts in Nations, Organizations, and Communities* (San Francisco, CA: Jossey-Bass, 1997).

Rothstein, Robert L. et al., Eds., *The Israel-Palestinian Peace Process: Oslo and the Lessons of Failure* (Sussex, UK: Sussex Academic Press, 2004).

Rousseau, Jean-Jacques, *The Social Contract, or Principles of Political Right*. Trans. By G.D.H. Cole. (Cork: University College Cork, 2002). https://www.ucc.ie/archive/hdsp/Rousseau_contrat-social.pdf.

Rubenstein, Richard E., "Basic Human Needs: Steps Toward Further Theory Development." *International Journal of Peace Studies*, 6:1 (September 2001). http://www.gmu.edu/programs/icar/ijps/vol6_1/Rubenstein.htm.

Saunders, Harold H., *Sustained Dialogue in Conflicts: Transformation and Change* (London and New York: Palgrave Macmillan, 2011).

Smelser, Neil J., Ed., *Karl Marx on Society and Social Change, With Selections from Friedrich Engels* (Chicago: University of Chicago Press, 1975).

Ury, William L., *Getting Past No: Negotiating in Difficult Situations*, Rev. Edn. (New York: Bantam, 1993).

Volkan, Vamik, *Bloodlines: From Ethnic Pride to Ethnic Terrorism* (New York: Basic Books, 1998).

——*Enemies on the Couch: A Psychopolitical Journey Through War and Peace* (Charlottesville, VA: Pitchstone Press, 2013).

von Bertalanffy, Ludwig, *General System Theory: Foundations, Development, Applications* (New York: George Braziller, 2015).

Wallensteen, Peter, *Understanding Conflict Resolution*, 4th Edn. (London and Los Angeles: Sage, 2015).

Walt, Stephen M., *Taming American Power: The Global Response to U.S. Primacy* (New York: W.W. Norton, 2006).

Waltz, Kenneth N., *Theory of International Politics* (New York: McGraw-Hill, 1979).

——*Man, The State, and War: A Theoretical Analysis*, Rev. Edn. (New York: Columbia University Press, 2001).

Weber, Max, *Economy and Society: An Outline of Interpretive Sociology*, 2 Vols. (Berkeley, CA: University of California Press, 1978).

Wilkins, Roger, *A Man's Life: An Autobiography* (Woodbridge, CT: Ox Bow Press, 1991).

Wolff, Stefan and Christalla Yakinthou, Eds., *Conflict Management in Divided Societies* (London and New York: Routledge, 2011).

Zartman, I. William, Ed., *Peacemaking in International Conflict: Methods and Techniques*, Rev. Edn. (Washington, DC: U.S. Institute of Peace, 2007).

# 3
# VIOLENT SYSTEMS AND THEIR TRANSFORMATION

## The theory of structural violence

The idea that social structures often played a role in generating conflict was not foreign to analysts and resolvers of the 'second wave.' Many acute observers saw violent identity group struggles as engendered, in part, by political systems too rigid, authoritarian, or majority-group dominated to satisfy the basic needs of discontented people. Even so, their strong focus on group identities made psychological states and political arrangements seem more germane than socioeconomic factors to an understanding of these conflicts.[1] Moreover, the theorists seldom offered any general account of the relationship of social systems to violent conflict. The introduction of conflict-generating social structures as an idea of critical importance to the field was largely the work of one scholar/activist: the pioneering Norwegian peace theorist and practitioner, Johan Galtung.

I have recounted my first exposure to Galtung's ideas at the conference on human needs theory organized in 1988 by John Burton. The theorist's paper on basic needs reflected his conviction that the distinction between haves and have-nots, 'herren' and 'knechte,' was primary. Rather than focusing primarily on needs related to identity, which many other analysts were inclined to do, his paper put equal emphasis on needs for security ("to avoid violence"), welfare ("to avoid misery"), and freedom ("to avoid repression"). Moreover, he argued strongly that a hierarchy of needs such as that constructed by the psychologist Abraham Maslow could easily be used to further marginalize oppressed out-groups. In Galtung's view, the major weakness of many basic needs approaches (BNAs) was that

> BNAs say nothing about how misery is produced; they do not comprise a social theory. Thus they say nothing about inequity, for these are relations, even abstract ones, and it would be hard to assume that there is a need not to be exploited or not to live in a society with too much inequality.

The danger posed by this lacuna was that satisfying human needs might not end exploitation and human misery, and therefore might not resolve social conflicts. The answer, he concluded,

> should not be to pretend that BNAs can offer what is not within their paradigm, but to call for additional perspectives, theories, paradigms, approaches. Most important would be theories about how misery is produced and reproduced, and such theories exist – they are indispensable to get at the roots of the phenomenon.[2]

Galtung had been thinking about this for a long time. Almost two decades earlier, he had published an article in *The Journal of Peace Research* that introduced the idea of structural violence to the conflict studies field. *Structural violence*, he stated, is force or influence exerted in accordance with patterned social arrangements that prevent people from realizing their human potential and satisfying basic developmental needs.[3] Unlike *direct* personal violence, which involves one person acting to harm another, it is indirect and may or may not involve people acting deliberately. If I withhold food from you, intending to starve you to death, that is direct violence. If the system of food production delivers food only to those who can afford to pay for it, and you starve because you can't afford the price, that violence is structural. In both cases, "individuals may be killed or mutilated . . . hit or hurt . . . and manipulated by means of stick or carrot strategies." But, where structural violence takes place, "The violence is built into the structure and shows up as unequal power and consequently as unequal life chances."[4] Of course, this sort of violence need not take a form as dramatic as the physical starvation of one of the system's bottom dogs. Stressing the difference between human potentiality and actuality means that preventing a child from going to school or a woman from working out of the home should also be considered violent, at least where these restrictions are avoidable.

There are three primary reasons for expanding the usual common sense definition of violence to include structural components. The first is that it renders visible forms of destruction which many people in relatively static societies consider natural, hence invisible:

In a static society, personal violence will be registered, whereas structural violence may be seen as about as natural as the air around us. Conversely, in a highly dynamic society, personal violence may be seen as wrong and harmful, but still somehow congruent with the order of things, whereas structural violence becomes apparent because it stands out like an enormous rock in a creek, impeding the free flow, creating all kinds of eddies and turbulences.[5]

Second, the concept provides a corrective to a common view that the first parties in conflict to resort to direct violence are breakers of the peace, when, as to them, the apparent peace is often *already* violent. (One thinks of terrorist attacks in the West, which seem to Westerners virtually unprovoked breaches of the peace, but which are often done to retaliate for large-scale attacks by Western forces in other regions.) Conflict begins with an "avoidable insult to human needs," not with one's response to the insult. In fact, a reciprocal causal relationship between direct violence and structural violence exists in which each form tends to provoke or generate the other. Finally, "an extended concept of violence leads to an extended concept of peace." If the absence of direct violence, at least for the time being, can be considered peace in a negative sense, the absence of structural violence and the replacement of abusive or exploitative relationships by valued, mutually rewarding relationships should be considered "positive peace."[6]

Although Johan Galtung's detractors joked that the activist scholar had redefined violence to include everything he did not like, his definition of structural violence is coherent enough. His theory makes it clear that the systems which administer and provoke violence can be political and cultural as well as socioeconomic, but it puts considerably more emphasis on the unequal distribution of economic power than do many other approaches. Under capitalism, he notes, the distribution of resources, including income, education, and medical services, is grossly unequal, with "rank dimensions . . . tied together in the social structure." In other words, as Karl Marx had said, society is sharply divided into classes:

> Marxist criticism of capitalist society emphasizes how power to decide over the surplus from the production process is reserved for the owners of the means of production, who then can buy themselves into top positions on all other rank dimensions because money is highly convertible in a capitalist society – if you have money to convert, that is.

Galtung then goes on to cite, apparently with approval, the liberal critique that socialist (i.e., Stalinized) systems also concentrate economic power in a few hands, thus opening the door to structural violence from noncapitalist regimes as well.[7] His dislike of vertically ranked systems clearly extends to those whose advocates declare themselves to be leftists. Even so, his social vision, departing from the generally accepted assumption that the capitalist 'free market' is the final stage of socioeconomic development, owes a great deal to Marxist and post-Marxist traditions of critical analysis.

Galtung's passion for social equality eventually produced a famous exchange of views between the Norwegian polymath and an equally acute and energetic British colleague, Kenneth E. Boulding. In 1977, Boulding produced "Twelve Friendly Quarrels with Johan Galtung," an essay that, as Galtung pointed out in a reply published a decade later ("Only One Quarrel with Kenneth Boulding"), boils down to a single large disagreement over the necessity of transforming elitist social structures.[8] Essentially accusing Galtung of being a Marxist without portfolio, Boulding criticizes his insistence that violence is deeply related to social inequality and cannot be reduced significantly without eliminating exploitation and repression. On the contrary, Boulding maintains, since violence and poverty (or powerlessness) derive from different sources, equalizing social positions will not necessarily have the potent peacemaking effects predicted by Galtung. His own perspective, which he terms "evolutionary," suggests that society is developing autonomously, in accordance with entropic laws, in the direction of "human betterment." The implication (distantly reminiscent of Burke's objections to the French Revolution) is that deliberate attempts to restructure social institutions are likely to interfere with this natural process. In his reply, Galtung insists that greater social and political equality is not just one long-term goal, among many. It is a *sine qua non* for the resolution of structural conflicts and the creation of positive peace.

Of course, this exchange left many questions unanswered. A less sweeping critique of Galtung's approach might have noted that, despite some intriguing speculation about the relationship between structural and direct violence, he does not clearly indicate the conditions under which the former is likely to produce the latter, or vice versa. When (if ever) will an unjust or oppressive social system produce violent rebellion? When (if ever) will the spread of personal violence generate violent repression? Adding the social-structural dimension to psychologically based theories such as human needs, relative deprivation, and historical trauma brings the answers to such questions closer, but still leaves a large area indeterminate and subject to influence by multiple variables. For this reason, some analysts (including Galtung himself in later works) have used psychopolitical notions like Paulo Freire's theory of "conscientization" to explain why passive victims of social injustice sometimes – but far from always – become active resisters or rebels.[9] In addition, Galtung offered two important concepts that help explain how one form of violence can be converted into the other: *nested systems* and *cultural violence.*

To illustrate nested systems, consider the prison, which I described in Chapter 1 as a violence-generating system based on structural inequality and the nonsatisfaction of human needs. Even before going behind bars, most prison inmates-to-be already live in an 'iron cage': a society organized so as to make it difficult, if not impossible, for the poor, people of color, and members of other marginalized groups living in certain communities to get a decent education, hold a remunerative job, feel safe and at peace with others, or enjoy a satisfying family life. We know that poverty and income inequality gestate crime, and that crime gestates prisons.[10] Prisons, in turn, recycle prisoners, sending them impoverished and stigmatized into structurally violent environments that insure that some two-thirds of them will be arrested again within three years.[11] This situation illustrates the fact that social systems almost never exist in isolation; to use Galtung's metaphor, they are nested like "Chinese boxes."[12] Each system may form part of a larger structure, a tendency that becomes more pronounced as the social world (including structures of domination) becomes more interconnected on a global scale. As a result, the inequalities associated with structural violence appear and are aggravated at all levels from the local to the national, regional, and international.

Within these nested systems, Galtung points out, structural violence and direct violence "crossbreed." Repressive structures generate rebellion, crime, and self-destructive behaviors such as suicide and substance abuse, while rebellious acts incubate repressive institutions and punitive norms. To illustrate how this crossbreeding occurs, the theorist introduces a third element of the conflict triangle, cultural violence, defined as "those aspects of culture . . . that can be used to justify or legitimize direct or structural violence."[13] The cultural products that he considers especially potent in this regard are religion, ideology, language, art, science, and cosmology, although he might also have noted the peculiar importance in today's world of narrative forms, including the graphic arts (films, video games, images and stories shared on social media), as well as the subconscious imagery explored by psychoanalysts like Freud, Jung, and Lacan. Like Pierre Bourdieu, who sees 'symbolic violence' as authority's most effective tool, Galtung stresses the extent to which cultural conditioning maintains the oppressive structures that end by provoking and delivering violence:

> The culture preaches, teaches, admonishes, eggs on, and dulls us into seeing exploitation and/or repression as normal and natural, or into

not seeing them (particularly not exploitation) at all. Then come the eruptions, the efforts to use direct violence to get out of the structural iron cage . . . and counter-violence to keep the cage intact.[14]

Other commentators, noting that cultural ideas and practices tend to lag behind changes in the system of production, consider deep-rooted socio-economic shifts the primary causal factor.[15] But the causes can flow in any direction once the triangle – an integrated violent system – has been established. Moreover, Galtung's theory points to the fact that the generation and crossbreeding of violent conflict can take place in a wide variety of systems less circumscribed and more loosely structured than the prison. The family, school, workplace, religious community, nation, and empire – all can become sites and producers of direct, structural, and cultural violence. This is especially likely to happen under certain conditions, which will be described differently, of course, by those challenging the system and those defending it. What are these conditions?

From the perspective of the challengers, violence erupts when (a) social and political systems marked by a seriously unequal and inequitable distribution of wealth, power, and honor, (b) fail to satisfy the basic needs or legitimate expectations of disadvantaged groups at a time when (c) these groups have become sharply aware of the legitimacy of their needs and expectations, and (d) systemic injustice has become manifest despite the ideological and cultural smokescreens usually effective to justify or disguise it.

From the perspective of the defenders, on the other hand, violence is likely to erupt when (a) groups alienated and embittered by their failure to succeed in society and by their self-destructive lifestyles (b) are manipulated by ambitious leaders to believe that their unrealistic expectations are just and reasonable and that (c) relevant social and political systems are rigged to favor others and exploit or oppress them, notwithstanding that (d) these systems (which can never be perfect) are successful in rewarding meritorious individuals and groups and disfavoring those who lack merit.

These conflicting perspectives draw attention to a number of important, still unanswered questions about the resolution of structural conflicts. The theory of structural violence seems to assume that the existence and character of relevant social systems is a matter of common knowledge. But what if the system's role in generating conflict is itself a major subject of contention between the parties? Although all parties to intense conflicts personalize their enemy to some extent, the rebels tend to be determinist vis-à-vis the system. That is, they blame an unjust social order, and those representing or profiting from it, for failing to satisfy the legitimate needs and expectations of less favored groups.[16] The system's defenders, on the other hand, often attribute such groups' misfortunes to their failure to meet legitimate standards. That is, the defenders tend to be voluntarist vis-à-vis disfavored groups. A classic example is their tendency to blame high unemployment on unemployed people's personal or collective failings (laziness, indiscipline, unwillingness to stay in school, disrupted families, etc.), rather than seeing it as a product of late capitalist structural features and a *cause* of personal or cultural problems.[17]

How, indeed, is the conflict-causing system to be identified and defined? The existence and functions of social systems are not self-evident; they are matters of inference to be determined by interpreting events and people's behavior. The parties to a serious social conflict may therefore agree that its sources are to some degree systemic, but still disagree strongly about the nature and dynamics of the system. Such disagreements (a form of what Oliver Ramsbotham calls "radical disagreement") are fairly common. We have already noted that, to some libertarians, the state is the culprit responsible for much human misery, whereas others tend to identify the system socioeconomically (e.g., as oligopoly capitalism) or culturally (e.g., as fundamentalist religion). Many Palestinians, when asked what system is responsible for violence in the Middle East, would immediately respond, "the U.S.-European-Zionist alliance," while many Israelis would name "the Arab-Iranian-Palestinian alliance." How should a putative peacemaker approach radical differences of this sort, which involve conflicting narratives as well as clashes of philosophy and political values?

This query points to an even broader question. What are the implications of structural analysis for conflict resolution practice? Galtung himself has pursued a very active practice that, although unique in many respects, is in broad structural terms fairly traditional among conflict interveners. That is, he offers or is invited to supply services to conflicting parties as a mediator, facilitator, or advisor – a third-party role that permits him to use his analytical, imaginative, and practice skills to help parties transcend their differences and transform the relationships that have been generating violence.[18] The often impressive results of this approach have been described in a small flood of publications. But is third-party practice the sole or most effective method of transforming conflict-generating systems? Galtung's own answer has been to supplement his work as a mediator with programs in training and education, peace journalism, and other forms of public outreach involving the advocacy of system-transforming policies.[19] We will return to this issue after examining another 'third wave' approach to the analysis and resolution of conflict: the theory of discursive systems.

## Culture, discourse, and systemic violence

A fundamental tenet of the theory of structural violence is that elitist, inequitable social systems generate violence first, by failing to satisfy human needs, thus provoking rebellion, and then, by legitimizing the violent repression of rebellious or deviant behavior. This, in turn, incites further acts of rebellion, and so produces a cycle of conflict escalation that continues until the system's destructive role as a generator of conflict is exposed and some sort of restructuring takes place. (The bleak alternative, as Mark Twain pointed out in his description of a backwoods feud in *Huckleberry Finn*, is for the violence to continue, tit for tat, until "everyone is killed off.")[20] But, a skeptical critic might object, *how* people become conscious of the conflict's systemic roots is not at all clear. Furthermore, the development of such an understanding is not inevitable; as Twain suggests, it may never take place at all. Finally, even if parties in conflict decide that an oppressive system is at the core of their problem, restructuring it so as to eliminate violence is far easier to discuss than to accomplish.

These related issues – the development of mass consciousness and the need for radical system change – are not new. Similar questions confronted Marxists more than a century ago as a result of working people's failure to transform the capitalist system in the time, place, and manner predicted by the founders of socialism. When misery fueled by inequality and structural violence reached a tipping point, Marx and his colleagues believed, the workers would rebel, overthrow the capitalist order, and replace it with a socialist system. This was expected to happen in the most industrially advanced societies, because it was there that wage workers were best educated and organized, and there that the contradiction between their current plight and the promise of a glowing future was most painfully obvious.

Nevertheless, with one exception, workers' revolutions did not take place in the West, where a combination of technological abundance and communal sharing might have made a significant reduction in structural violence possible. The exception was France, where rebellious workers created the Commune of Paris in 1870–71, only to have it drowned in blood by a liberal capitalist government wielding hi-tech weaponry.[21] Elsewhere in the industrialized world, most politicized working people opted to support a gradualist 'evolutionary socialism' rather than attempt to change capitalism all at once through a mass upheaval. They based their strategy on the hope of creating a more egalitarian system by following the lead of theorists like Germany's Eduard Bernstein and increasing the influence of trade unions and working class political parties in each nation, while leaving in place capitalism's most advanced institutions: the great financial and industrial corporations, parliaments, court systems, and military establishments.[22]

This reform movement enjoyed considerable success in helping to democratize Western politics and (in conjunction with a period of rapid economic growth) to raise workers' living standards. Unfortunately, the moderate socialists' agreement to function as a loyal opposition in each nation coincided with a sharp rise in nationalism, militarism, and global competition between Western empires, leading to the unparalleled slaughter of World War I. Furthermore, the political and social reforms that working class political parties helped engineer did not alter capitalism's basic structure sufficiently to avoid the disastrous economic collapse of the Great Depression.[23] The period of reform was therefore followed by a holocaust of repression, war, and genocide: the rise of fascism and World War II. Furthermore, in the first nation to experience a radical overthrow of capitalism – the former Russia, renamed the Union of Soviet Socialist Republics – a restructured but beleaguered social system continued to generate intense structural violence. One way to interpret these events was to declare that the theory of structural violence was simply wrong – that there was no causal link between elite-dominated social structures and mass violence. But those convinced that there *was* such a connection discovered several methods of saving the theory by modifying it substantially.

The first was associated with the Critical Theorists of the Institute for Social Research, the so-called Frankfurt School that included such thinkers as Theodor Adorno, Max Horkheimer, Herbert Marcuse, Wilhelm Reich, and Walter Benjamin.[24] These analysts maintained that the earlier Marxists' great error was to assume that working people suffering under capitalist rule would pursue their class interests by using their reason, calculating costs and benefits as business people do, and coming to a recognition that their oppressor was the capitalist class. That is, the Marxists believed that workers would naturally identify themselves as a collectivity with common interests, and, on that basis, would unify their own forces for the struggle to end capitalist rule, and would proceed to reconstruct the social system so as to secure their own power.[25] Instead, most of them, along with farmers, small entrepreneurs, and professional people, ended up either by allying themselves with bellicose nationalists, empire-builders, and even outright fascists in what seemed an orgy of self-destructive violence, or else being destroyed by these same forces.

According to the Critical Theorists, this miscalculation was based on three underlying mistakes. First, the old-line Marxists discounted the importance of irrational desires and drives. The essence of what Freud had discovered about human beings – the existence of the subconscious mind, the mechanism of repression, and the potency of thoughts and emotions linked to primary family relations – needed incorporation into thinking about the politics of social class. Without this sort of understanding, it was impossible to account, for example, for the enormous appeal of paternalistic nationalists who promised to protect their (childlike) subjects from danger in times of threat and crisis. Nor could one appreciate that the drive of disadvantaged groups for emancipation was not an interest-based desire like the quest for material goods, but a psychic need related to the needs for play, love, and erotic pleasure.[26] If the bottom dogs decided to transform existing systems, they would not do so on the basis of a cost–benefit analysis, but because they had decided to enact a realizable dream.

Second, 'economistic' radicals underestimated the power of existing cultural products to condition the understanding and limit the imagination of oppressed classes and groups.[27] Cultural activity, ranging from performances by artistic and intellectual elites to the mass culture produced by the schools, entertainment industries, and media of communication, had become both an industry in itself and a form of ideology inculcating and reinforcing attitudes favorable to maintaining existing systems. These cultural products, for example, made it clear to working people that the nation or race was their proper 'family' to which ultimate loyalty was owed. People outside that family were dangerous or maleficent strangers requiring exclusion or punishment by the state. The culture also reinforced the messages that happiness resided in the consumption of the free market's products, that a failure to rise in society was the result of one's personal defects, and that visions of a more just and egalitarian social system were deceptive and utopian, as well as disloyal.

Finally, earlier Marxists (or at least some of them) misstated the relationship between culture and the socioeconomic system by considering the former a mere 'superstructure' that would be transformed in due course by the 'base' of material production.[28] This was the basis for assuming that workers' ideas and behavior would eventually (sooner rather than later) come to reflect their class interests. Even in Marx's own work, things are not nearly this simple, since the socioeconomic system includes *relations* as well as means of production, and human relations are, in part, the product of cultural history. What was becoming clear, however, especially in light of the rise of fascism, was the high degree of interdependence of socioeconomic and cultural systems. Later socialist theorists like Antonio Gramsci, Herbert Marcuse, and Louis Althusser struggled to make it clear that even an elite-dominated capitalism does not exist outside human culture and personality but becomes, to some extent, part of both.[29] How people define the system, their role in it, and possible alternatives to it will *not* be dictated by purely economic considerations such as income levels or career opportunities – not even when incomes sink dangerously low or career opportunities vanish. In fact, it may be when things are hardest for people in the system's lower reaches that they are most likely to act on the basis of culturally conditioned instincts like the impulse to defend the national family against alleged threats or to seek scapegoats for economic disasters.

The problem with this analysis, at least from the perspective of those seeking to transform violence-generating systems, was that, like some of the subjectivist views discussed earlier, it seemed to make culture the servant of elites and the master of everyone else. It was already understood that cultural relations, like power relations, are structured – a discovery made before Foucault's time by anthropologists like Claude Lévi-Strauss and Clifford Geertz.[30] But, if the power structure and culture structure are *coterminous* – that is, if people are entirely incorporated into a structured system as its products and components – how can they ever develop enough detachment even to describe it accurately, much less overturn and rebuild it? A second group of theorists were determined to grapple with this question without repeating the errors of those who they thought had made too sharp a distinction between thinking 'subjects' and thought-about 'objects.' Language, they declared, was not just a way of communicating about pre-existing things, but also a way of creating the things communicated about. Philosophers like Michel Foucault and Anthony Giddens focused on *discourse* as a communicative activity shaped by the unequal power relations between social groups, but also defining or constituting these groups and relations.

Foucault's key insight was that power and knowledge together form a single field that he called "power/knowledge," meaning that social structure and culture cannot be separated. Every shift in power relations involves a redefinition of what can be known and how to learn it, just as every change in the field of knowledge alters the generation and distribution of power.[31] For example, the Roman Catholic Church in late-medieval Europe spawned the legal profession, which in turn created new rule-based relationships between individuals: a cultural revolution, to be sure. But this change was part of the same transformation that extended Church power (economic and political as well as religious) throughout civil society at the expense of local chieftains and lay leaders.[32] Similarly, the prison appeared in European society a few centuries later as a new type of institution designed to alter lawbreakers by disciplining them to budget their time and use their bodies and minds in approved ways, rather than simply punishing them publicly to demonstrate the glory of the monarch. Again, this was simultaneously an assertion of power by a new ruling class, the creation of a new profession and intellectual discipline (penology), and – because prisoners were undergoing training very much like that administered to schoolchildren, workers, and other bottom dogs outside the prison – an indication of a transformation affecting the whole social system.

Foucault argued that the social structure was not just a system in any case, but an episteme – a sociocultural world whose characteristic forms of organization, knowing, and feeling were now considered normal (meaning ordinary *and* obligatory) although they were all products of a fairly recent transformation.[33] This formulation raised the important question of how such transformations take place. The French theorist's work strongly suggests a complex interplay between structures of power and knowledge, not just a rubber-stamping of either structure by the other. In what the philosopher Nancy Fraser calls "the single most important feature" of his thought, Foucault argued that power in modern society is "capillary," running throughout the entire system like blood through a body, rather than emanating from one high-ranking source and running from top to bottom. Furthermore, power is exercised through 'micropractices,' the small gestures and moves that make up everyday life, and of which we are often unconscious.[34]

For example, when students sit quietly at their seats in a classroom listening to their professor speak, they are participating in a micropractice instantiating the professor's institutionalized power to control classroom discussions. The students accept this situation either because it has become an unconscious habit (part of what Pierre Bourdieu called a "habitus"), because they are fearful of the professor's power to give them a bad grade or to embarrass them publicly, or because they actively consent to the arrangement for other reasons (e.g., they are interested in what the professor is saying; they understand that they will have a chance to speak later; they are happy to have the chance to daydream for a few minutes, etc.) Or, perhaps, all these reasons are operating simultaneously.

Nancy Fraser thinks that Foucault opens the door here to the sort of exercise of power by bottom dogs that Anthony Giddens also refers to when he states that even the weakest groups can "influence the activities of their superiors."[35] If power in the episteme is the result of microprocesses involving some sort of constant negotiation at all levels, this suggests that structures can be altered by people pushing back in small, everyday ways, not only by mobilizing in a larger, more centralized fashion to radically reform or overthrow the whole system. One can hypothesize that this is one way, at least, in which structured systems are transformed. Students start interrupting professors, wives stop obeying husbands, or American colonists stop paying the tea tax to their British overlords. These movements of nonviolent resistance take place at first sporadically, here and there; then they become more widespread and better organized; and, finally, they confront the system's top dogs with a choice: either repress the protest violently or negotiate with the resisters. In either case, some sort of system change is likely, although clearly it is not guaranteed. But whether this vision of ending structural violence through local resistance is realistic or merely wishful thinking is far from clear.

In the field of conflict studies, the postmodernist challenge inspired a number of theorists and practitioners to describe power-based systems in terms of discourse and to seek discourse-related methods of altering them. Vivienne Jabri's *Discourses on Violence* describes how warfare and other forms of state violence are legitimized by a well-developed, long-inculcated nationalist discourse that defines 'us' as entitled to use violence against 'them.'[36] The same discursive system establishes group identities, gives these identities positive and negative charges, justifies the group leader's right to make decisions about the use of violence, and establishes the duty of other group members to support these decisions. Following the more optimistic implications of Foucault's and Giddens's work, Jabri advocates creating "discourses of peace" to counter the inherited discourses of war. More specific suggestions about how this might be accomplished are provided by a new school of critical narrative theorists such as Sara Cobb, who describes how the stories people tell (or fail to tell) about themselves and others shape their perceptions of Self and Other, conflict and its possible resolution, at a deep discursive level. Supported by the experiences of narrative mediators like John Winslade and Gerald Monk, Cobb argues that conflicting parties and conflict survivors can be assisted to develop "better formed stories" that will restore depth, nuance, and complexity to narratives that have become flattened out and brutally oversimplified by conflict. [37]

Critical narrative theory responds directly to the problem of partisan moralism described in Chapter 1 of this study. It offers hope that by dematerializing and decentering social systems previously thought of as material and centralized, a basis for challenging inherited narratives may be established and put to use by marginalized groups. One reacts to this prescription (in any event, this writer reacts to it) with a mixture of appreciation and skepticism. True, counter-discourses have sometimes challenged and altered deeply ingrained narratives instantiating long-established relations of power and privilege. As evidence of this, theorists like Jolle Demmers cite selected historical movements such as the movement to legalize gay and lesbian marriage:

> People engage in the social practice of marriage and reproduce the structure. Powerful agents such as the church and the state manage to sustain structures of signification and legitimation in favour of male-female marriage. However, in the 1960s somewhere in western Europe, a counter-narrative on the normality of homosexuality gained ground, and decades later this narrative became institutionalized in the legal construct of gay marriage. In turn, a number of people engaged in the social practice of gay marriage . . . The social system transformed through interaction.[38]

This argument makes a good point, but its implications are problematical. The "counter-narrative on the normality of homosexuality," which formed part of a much larger movement for sexual liberation and feminism, did not emanate mainly from poor and working class sectors of society, but from rising business and professional groups, students and intellectuals, many of whom had ties to political elites.[39] Gay rights in general and gay marriage in particular were causes embraced by elements of both major political parties in the United States, but especially by the Democratic Party, which saw no inconsistency between this counter-discourse and other narratives embraced by party leaders legitimizing the hegemony of the great business corporations, the military establishment, and the political ruling class. Indeed, a major justification for permitting people to make their own decisions about matters involving their sexuality and gender was that these were private issues in which public authorities should not meddle – a classically bourgeois drawing of the public/private line which, while expanding the area of private decision-making, did not threaten to alter matters left on the public side. (These matters included capitalist market relations, the status of private property, the organization and role of political parties, and the construction of the national security state!)

A key question, then, is whether an alteration in consciousness regarding sexuality and marriage indicates the possibility of transforming common narratives more closely adjoined to socioeconomic and political power structures. If the episteme is entirely decentered, as Foucault sometimes seems to suggest (although at other times he doesn't), distinctions between primary and secondary sources of power, or between a center and a periphery, are washed away, and changes made in one part of the system can spread to others, as the revolutionary theorist Régis Debray once put it, like an "oil stain."[40] To put this a bit differently, it is possible to view discourse not as reflecting or interacting with still existing structures of power but as replacing them. There are reasons to believe, however, that this flattened-out vision of the structural/cultural system understates the centrality of vital socioeconomic and political structures, and therefore understates the difficulty of developing counter-narratives challenging their hegemony. Democratizing marriage is one thing; democratizing the economy is quite another. The problem that needs further consideration by the advocates of counter-narratives and counter-discourses is that originally posed by Friedrich Engels in his 1882 essay, "Socialism: Utopian and Scientific."[41] There, Engels heaps scorn on the idea that a system as centralized as modern industrial capitalism can be overthrown or fundamentally changed by local movements of resistance and social experiments. Rosa Luxemburg posed the same question even more sharply as one of reform or revolution.[42] Let us look more closely at it now.

## System change and conflict resolution practice

What models of change of structured social systems are relevant to conflict resolution practice? What practical methods of conflict resolution are likely to help produce constructive system change? Responding to the first question means confronting the dichotomy of reform or revolution, which has been intensively debated in the century or so since Rosa Luxemburg published her famous essay bearing this title. Responding to the second requires reexamining the methods of third-party practice and possible additions or alternatives to those methods.

We have been inquiring how certain systems, if they generate violent conflict, can be transformed so as to cease producing violence, or, better yet, to establish a sound foundation for positive peace. Transformation, however, is a blurry concept that does not indicate either the quantity or quality of change needed to do the job. What makes the issue particularly tricky is that the system's top dogs have been known to act to preserve their power, property, and privileges by yielding to pressures to change peripheral or nonessential structural features. These pressures may be ecological or political; they may emanate from the natural environment, from within the ranks of highly privileged groups, or from society's lower orders. But ranked systems that survive do so – and continue to generate violence – because their leaders discover how to make moderate, system-maintaining reforms seem progressive, if not revolutionary.

This was precisely the point made by Luxemburg, who insisted that the reform measures advocated by Germany's Social Democrats might give the system a progressive veneer and temporarily reduce political conflict, but without in the least altering capitalism's long-term tendencies to produce economic crises, poverty, imperialism, and war. Genuinely pacificatory change, she thought, would require smashing the bourgeois state and industrial apparatus and replacing them with worker-controlled political and economic institutions. A later critique of the reform/revolution dichotomy reflecting the experience of ineffective reforms *and* Stalinist excesses was offered by the social critic Arthur Koestler in a 1942 essay called "The Yogi and the Commissar." Koestler argued that there are two basic modes of attempted system change, neither of which is fully effective. The reformist 'yogi' seeks to transform society peacefully, one person at a time, by inducing a change of heart in each member. It has the virtue of using pacific means to reach a pacific end, but the defect of taking too long – perhaps forever – to reach the goal of transforming elitist social structures. The revolutionary 'commissar,' on the other hand, seeks to change individuals by changing the system first, if necessary by using violent means. This strategy has the virtue of getting things done organizationally, but the defect – probably fatal – of using violence to achieve peace while leaving individuals spiritually as they were.[43]

In Koestler's view, neither approach really works; what is needed is a synthesis of these perspectives, which, unfortunately, he does not describe. From the perspective of conflict studies, both he and Rosa Luxemburg seem to be right. Reforms that preserve the social system's asymmetrical distribution of power, property, and privilege give the illusion of progress without effectively reducing the system's propensity to generate violence. Reasonable and justified changes like those advocated by the social democrats or the proponents of feminism and LGBT rights, may well be worth fighting for and achieving, but one needs to understand that they provide temporary relief to oppressed groups without guaranteeing further progress toward the goal of pacifying a violent and unjust system. Of course, the violent overthrow of elites does not guarantee such progress either. Revolutions sometimes do redound to the benefit of lower social classes and ethnic out-groups. The Bolshevik revolution in Russia, the Maoist revolution in China, and related movements in Cuba, Vietnam, and elsewhere brought more than a billion people out of desperate poverty, lessened many social inequalities, and helped to modernize formerly underdeveloped nations. Yet the monopolization of decision-making power by a political elite determined to preserve its privileges not only maintained structural violence, but also set the stage for a later restoration of capitalism.

The bad news, as Koestler suggests, is that neither moderate reform nor violent revolution provides the answer sought by people seeking to establish regimes of positive peace. But this dichotomy leaves other possible options out of consideration – for example, the possibility that conflicting parties may agree nonviolently to adopt systemic reforms far-reaching enough to be revolutionary in their effects. How, for example, should we evaluate the social reforms adopted during the 1930s by the American New Deal, the French Popular Front, and similar coalitions? What about the abandonment of South African apartheid and the adoption of a democratic political model engineered by leaders like Nelson Mandela? How is one to analyze the collapse of the Soviet empire in the late 1980s and early 1990s and its replacement by pro-capitalist regimes in more than a dozen nations? The problem is complicated by the fact that we do not yet have theories that clearly and precisely relate degrees and types of system change to reductions in structural, direct, and cultural violence.

Even so, two things seem true of these altered social systems. First, the transformations they accomplished clearly went beyond merely cosmetic reforms. The New Deal created an activist federal government that changed government-citizen and citizen-citizen relations, especially in the field of labor-management relations, in significant ways. The post-apartheid regime in South Africa and post-communist regimes in the former Soviet empire also altered prevailing political patterns and relations in those regions. Second, despite these far-reaching changes, these systems remained highly structured, inegalitarian, and richly productive of social violence. In part, this was the result of trade-offs between political and socioeconomic power. The clearest example of this, perhaps, is South Africa, where black representatives abandoned long-standing demands to expropriate the white minority economically in order to secure agreement to a 'one person, one vote' policy in the political realm. As a result, the South African economy remained largely under the control of local and global capitalist elites, eventually generating intense conflict with workers' organizations. Similarly, while significant socioeconomic changes did take place under the New Deal/Popular Front regimes, the failure of these quasi-revolutions to alter capitalist relations of production set the stage for the creation of a new technological/industrial elite, a surge of global empire-building, further economic crises, and the decline of the trade union movement.

Is a further renegotiation of the social contract in the direction of greater equality and less structural violence possible? For conflict specialists this raises fascinating but difficult issues concerning traditional and novel methods of intervening to help resolve social conflicts. Let me begin, however, by commenting on why many experts in the field of conflict studies have found it difficult to confront the problem of structural conflict directly.

Our earlier discussion of themes in conflict studies praxis suggests part of the answer. Before forms of violent conflict evincing a structural dimension began to appear on a global scale, theorists and practitioners tended to focus either on national and local groups pursuing competitive interests or on ethnic, racial, and national groups defending threatened identities. In the past two decades, however, unexpectedly violent and long-lasting conflicts emerged whose origins and relative intractability pointed beyond group interests and identities to broader structural issues requiring analysis and social action. These phenomena ranged from domestic wars on crime and drugs to regional religious wars, struggles involving transnational terrorism, conflicts over resources driven by climate change and corporate ambitions, and apparently intractable ethnonational conflicts complicated by outside military intervention. What particularly drew analysts' attention to structural issues was the tendency, where 'nested' systems were in play, for conflicts to interact and overlap, so that a religious war might also involve ethnonational ambitions, intense competition for economic resources, and a clash of empires or would-be empires. Indeed, this sort of overlap of interests, identities, and structural drives now seems particularly characteristic of violent struggles in the twenty-first century.

A second reason that the structural turn took so long to develop was both practical and, in a sense still largely unexplored, political. The emerging discipline of conflict studies, involving both theoretical analyses and practical attempts to manage or resolve specific disputes, was in Foucauldian terms a situs and agglomeration of power/knowledge.[44] Its development reflected the interests, ideologies, and worldviews of a number of social groups, not the least of which were Western leaders seeking to make the world safer for democracy and capitalism. Their interests in negotiation, mediation, and other techniques of 'soft power' as lower-cost, more effective alternatives to war emerged more clearly following the U.S. withdrawal from Vietnam, and by the 1990s had produced a strong vein of government support for the field, particularly in the United States.[45] Interest-based negotiation, mediation, and second-track diplomacy were welcomed by many public agencies as potentially useful, nonthreatening forms of conflict management, especially after similar techniques had proved helpful to local authorities and businesses making use of alternative dispute resolution to keep disputes out of the court system. Just as ADR functioned as a supplement rather than an alternative to the system of legal justice, specialists interested in helping to resolve or manage international conflicts were expected to work cooperatively with civil and military officials to advance their government's interests around the world.[46]

A third and final reason had to do with the ethos of the peace studies/conflict resolution field, which was deeply reformist in both admirable and problematic senses. From the earliest formation of the discipline to the present, many scholars and activists came to conflict studies with the intention of helping individuals, groups, and nations to interact less aggressively and more cooperatively. They wanted to improve human relationships, keep people out of court, prevent avoidable injuries, clear up dangerous misunderstandings, substitute dialogue for violence, and save lives. Many of the field's most renowned and memorable figures, such as Elise Boulding, Adam Curle, James H. Laue, Landrum Bolling, and John Paul Lederach, were passionate reformers motivated, at least in part, by religious convictions. Their selflessness, energy, and creativity in dealing with apparently intractable conflicts was reformism's bright side. The more problematic dimension emerged when serious conflicts showed clear signs of structural origin or influence, suggesting that resolution might require a radical alteration of systems.

The perception that a conflict is system-generated presents would-be peacemakers with a difficult choice. Should the conflict specialist use the techniques of mediation and facilitation to obtain the best agreement possible within the constraints of current social and political systems? Or should she become an advocate for system change? If the latter, what are the implications of this mission for conflict resolution practice? Can would-be peacemakers continue to rely on third-party techniques like mediation and facilitation, or are other forms of intervention called for? It may be useful at this point to comment briefly on three broad categories of intervention: new forms of third-party practice; new forms of political practice; and possible combinations of these types.

### Third-party practice

As noted earlier, the practice of mediation, facilitation, or consultation with parties in conflict has taken multiple forms, depending upon the type of dispute to be dealt with and the prevailing assumptions and theories about social conflict. Structural conflicts, however, raise special concerns: how to assist the parties to *recognize* the conflict's systemic dimensions; *identify* the relevant system or systems helping to produce violence; *envision* structural and cultural changes that might eliminate or greatly reduce the violence; *consider* the pros and cons of these changes (including possible unforeseen consequences); and *determine* in detail how to implement them. Each of these steps is essential, and none is easy. Nevertheless, certain fairly well-established forms of practice have undertaken these tasks, although sometimes without focusing specifically on the structural issues at hand.

For example, the problem-solving workshop method pioneered by John Burton and others, Johan Galtung's TRANSCEND approach, the sustained dialogue process advocated by Harold H. Saunders, the interactive conflict resolution techniques used by Ronald Fisher, and the dynamical systems method employed by Peter T. Coleman all invite the parties to discover the hidden roots of their conflict through facilitated joint analysis and to envision methods of altering conflict-generating systems.[47] What these techniques sometimes lack, however, is an express acknowledgment that the parties need to engage in *social-constitutional dialogue and analysis,* which implies a focus on socioeconomic as well as political issues and a determination to deal with the conflict-generating system as a whole. Social-constitutional dialogue is a process that expressly opens up to discussion fundamental social issues that are often considered 'too hot to handle' and are therefore ignored or dealt with only tangentially.

When the United States invaded and occupied Iraq, for example, local parties were *not* invited to explore such crucial issues as the fate of the Baath Party and armed forces, the overall organization of the economy, the distribution of oil company revenues, appropriate relations between the Sunni and Shia communities, or relations with Iran and other neighboring nations.[48] Continuing bloody civil conflict was the price paid for avoiding these discussions. Especially when conflict resolution efforts are sponsored by Great Powers devoted to a particular socioeconomic system or the welfare of particular corporate enterprises, peacemakers are frequently discouraged from facilitating discussions about possible alternative systems and enterprises. By contrast, where interventions are undertaken by relatively independent facilitators, a broader range of socioeconomic issues can be raised, as they have been in Mozambique, Northern Ireland, South Ossetia, and certain other conflict locales.[49]

### Political practice

Every facilitator is called upon to balance the short-term good that can be done by helping parties reach a local settlement against the long-term but often uncertain benefits of encouraging them to attempt a more general and permanent alteration of the conflict's underlying causes. As a result, the desire to achieve some agreement between the parties and stop the carnage often causes facilitators to short-circuit systemic discussions.[50] As reasonable as this choice may be under some circumstances, avoiding the broader discussion often means permitting a more general problem likely to produce new disputes to go unanalyzed and unresolved. Moreover, the method of third-party facilitation itself may incline practitioners to try to obtain the best results possible under an existing system rather than attempt to transform the environment more radically. System transformation often requires activities that are mass-based and political (in a sense that requires careful explication), and which do not fit easily into the third-party model.

Expressly political interventions are not unheard of in the field of conflict resolution, although they are usually avoided. Ordinarily, there are good reasons for the reluctance to 'go political.' Conflict analysis is often deformed when the analyst chooses sides, especially when the choice is made (as it so often is) semiconsciously, under the influence of news media coverage or scholarly interpretations themselves influenced by partisan ideologies.[51] Furthermore, practitioners of conflict resolution are expected to be evenhanded, able to empathize with all the disputants, and dispassionate enough to help them to analyze the root causes of their broken relationship. Additionally, even if it seems clear that a struggle cannot be resolved without transforming a violence-producing system, we know that every system carries with it certain approved methods of politics that are designed, in effect, to preserve the system's essential features. Therefore, 'going political' is often perceived either as playing the system's game or as resorting to illegal and violent methods of system change. Conflict specialists seldom consider seriously the option of practicing other forms of nonviolent politics as part of their professional role, although many are involved in politics as private citizens.

What forms are these? Subsequent chapters of this study will discuss system-changing practices that can be employed in connection with specific forms of structural conflict. Here, on a more abstract level, we can briefly indicate three possible models of political intervention: selective facilitation, selective representation, and selective advocacy.

*Selective facilitation* involves using one's mediatory skills to help conflicting parties or conflicting factions of one party reach agreement on the ambit and nature of the system to be transformed and the most effective and humane manner of transforming it. For example, John Paul Lederach has suggested a tripartite model of intervention in which facilitators can opt to deal with group leaders at the national, mid-range, or grassroots levels as part of a process aimed at empowering them to participate in system transformation.[52]

*Selective representation* takes place when conflict resolution specialists use their skills to promote to a specific vision of system change by representing one party to the conflict in negotiations or problem-solving processes with representatives of other parties. An outstanding example is James H. Laue, a skilled practitioner and associate of Martin Luther King, Jr. who, in effect, represented Dr. King and the Southern Christian Leadership Conference in negotiations with state and local authorities while serving as one of the top mediators of the Community Relations Service of the U.S. Department of Justice.[53]

*Selective advocacy* describes a wide variety of directly political activities in which the intervener helps to organize, train, lead, or participate with groups attempting to achieve specific conflict-resolving system changes. Among conflict specialists, a common mode of advocacy involves the practice of various forms of 'new politics,' including community dialogues and forums, uses of news media and social media, nonviolent demonstrations and occupations, and other forms of direct action, including civil disobedience.

A focus on resolving structural conflicts expands the scope of possible forms of conflict intervention at the same time that it generates new issues – and, perhaps, new problems – for would-be peacemakers. Many of the old reasons for discouraging conflict specialists to engage, as professionals, in overtly political activities remain persuasive. Even so, confining the practitioner to a limited, locally reformist role makes little sense when resolving the conflict clearly calls for a more substantial system change, and, in fact, tends to convert one's practice into a substructure of the system. At best, it means that the specialist is trying to *manage* the conflict within the limits set by existing structures rather than to resolve it. Unfortunately, crucial issues such as the extent to which apparently superficial reforms might actually be transformative, or apparently revolutionary changes actually system-maintaining, are still painfully under-theorized. This does not make it easier for conflict resolvers to make the 'structural turn' in practice that many have made in theory.

Even so, the genie is out of the bottle. We are discovering that ideas and practices that seemed adequate to help parties in dispute manage interest-based and even identity-based conflicts are not adequate to resolve violent system-based conflicts. We turn now to consider these newer forms of struggle.

## Notes

1 An example is Donald L. Horowitz's magisterial *Ethnic Groups in Conflict*, 2nd Edn. (Berkeley, CA: University of California Press, 2000), 95 *et seq.*, which categorizes ethnic groups as "ranked" and "unranked," but goes on to argue (for reasons that I, for one, find unconvincing) that socioeconomic ranking is not as important in understanding ethnic conflicts as political and cultural factors are.

2 Johan Galtung, "International Development in Human Perspective," in John Burton, Ed., *op. cit.*, 309, 321–323, 326–327.

3 "Violence exists when human beings are being influenced so that their actual somatic and mental realizations are below their potential realizations." Johan

Galtung, "Violence, Peace, and Peace Research." *Journal of Peace Research*, 6:3 (1969), 167–191 at 168. In "Cultural Violence." *Journal of Peace Research*, 27:3 (1990), 291–305, at 292, he reframed this definition as "avoidable insults to basic human needs."

4 Johan Galtung, *op. cit.,* 170–171.

5 Ibid., 173.

6 Ibid., 183.

7 Ibid., 171. Galtung does not discuss socialist alternatives to Stalinism, either Trotskyist, Bukharinist, or anarcho-syndicalist, perhaps because of his deep commitment to Gandhian nonviolence and the values of social democracy.

8 Kenneth E. Boulding, "Twelve Friendly Quarrels with Johan Galtung." *Journal of Peace Research*, 14:1 (1977), 75–86; Johan Galtung, "Only One Quarrel with Kenneth Boulding." *Journal of Peace Research*, 24:2 (June 1987), 199–203.

9 Paulo Freire, *Education for Critical Consciousness* (1974) (London and New York: Bloomsbury, 2013). See also Jolle Demmers, *Theories of Violent Conflict* (London and New York: Routledge, 2012), 61–61, 77–87.

10 See Jeffrey Reiman and Paul Leighton, *The Rich Get Richer and the Poor Get Prison: Ideology, Class, and Criminal Justice*, 10th Edn. (London and New York: Routledge, 2016); Gregg Barak, et al., *Class, Race, Gender and Crime: The Social Realities of Justice in America*, 3rd Edn. (Lanham, MD: Rowman and Littlefield, 2010). For a cross-national study of the causes of crime, see Pablo Fajnzylber, Daniel Lederman, and Norman Loayza, "What causes violent crime?" *European Economic Review* 46 (2002), 1323–1357.

11 U.S. Department of Justice, *Special Report: Multistate Criminal History Patterns of Prisoners Released in 30 States* (September 2015). http://www.bjs.gov/content/pub/pdf/mschpprts05.pdf.

12 A somewhat similar concept, "intersocietal systems," is developed by Anthony Giddens in *The Constitution of Society: Outline of the Theory of Structuration* (Berkeley and Los Angeles: University of California Press, 1984), 164, 244. See also Maire Dugan, "A Nested Theory of Conflict." *Leadership Journal: Women in Leadership – Sharing the Vision,* 1:1 (Summer 1996), 14.

13 Galtung, "Cultural Violence," *op. cit.,* at 291. Of course, cultural violence can also be considered structural, since culture is patterned and institutionalized. See, for example, John R. Hall, "Cultural Meanings and Cultural Structures in Historical Explanation." *History and Theory,* 39:3 (October 2000), 331–347.

14 Galtung, "Cultural Violence," *op. cit.,* at 295. "Iron cage" is from Max Weber's *The Protestant Ethic and the Spirit of Capitalism* (New York and London: Routledge, 1992), 123.

15 An example of this disagreement is the difference of opinion between Marxists and Weberians over the role of religion in the development of European capitalism. Max Weber considered the "worldly asceticism" of the early Protestant Reformers, the Calvinists in particular, an essential part of the explanation of why capitalism developed in the West rather than the East. Marxists insist that capitalist relations of production developed in Europe earlier than Weber

thought, and that Protestant ethics were more an effect of this transformation than a cause. See Anthony Giddens, "Introduction" to Weber, *op. cit.,* vii *et seq.*

16 A good illustration is Kwame Ture and Charles V. Hamilton, *Black Power: The Politics of Liberation* (New York: Vintage Books, 1992).

17 See Thomas Janoski, et al., *The Causes of Structural Unemployment: Four Factors that Keep People from the Jobs They Deserve* (Cambridge: Polity Press, 2014); Charles E. Hurst, *Social Inequality: Forms, Causes, and Consequences* (London and New York: Routledge, 2016).

18 Johan Galtung, *Transcend and Transform: An Introduction to Conflict Work* (London: Pluto Press, 2004).

19 Galtung, ibid., 180–181, describes his practice as "liberal in the sense of encouraging small steps; Marxist in the sense of building on transcendence and the dialectics of contradiction; and Buddhist in the sense of having basic needs as the fundamental guide." A full list of his publications and a description of the activities of his TRANSCEND organization is available at http://www.transcend.org.

20 Mark Twain, *The Adventures of Huckleberry Finn* (1884), http://contentserver. adobe.com/store/books/HuckFinn.pdf, 111: "Well," says Buck, "a feud is this way: A man has a quarrel with another man, and kills him; then that other man's brother kills him; then the other brothers, on both sides, goes for one another; then the cousins chip in—and by and by everybody's killed off, and there ain't no more feud. But it's kind of slow, and takes a long time."

21 Marx analyzed the Commune's suppression in *The Civil War in France* (1871), 2nd Edn. (New York: International Publishers, 1989). For a current history of the Commune see John Merriman, *Massacre: The Life and Death of the Paris Commune* (New York: Basic Books, 2014).

22 "Evolutionary socialism" was the brainchild of the German Social Democratic theorist, Eduard Bernstein. See his *Evolutionary Socialism* (1899) (New York: CreateSpace, 2011). For concise histories of the West European left, see David Caute, *The Left in Europe Since 1789*, 2nd Edn. (New York: McGraw-Hill, 1971); Geoff Eley, *Forging Democracy: The History of the Left in Europe, 1850–2000* (Oxford: Oxford University Press, 2002).

23 Rosa Luxemburg, *Reform or Revolution and Other Writings* (New York: Dover Books, 2006).

24 A good overall summary of the Frankfurt School's work is Martin Jay, *The Dialectical Imagination: A History of the Frankfurt School and the Institute of Social Research, 1923–1950* (Berkeley, CA: University of California Press, 1996). Essential works of this school include Herbert Marcuse, *One-Dimensional Man: Studies in the Ideology of Advanced Industrial Society*, 2nd Edn. (Boston: Beacon Press, 1991); Marcuse's *Eros and Civilization: A Philosophical Inquiry into Freud* (Boston: Beacon Press, 1974); and Max Horkheimer and Theodor W. Adorno, *The Dialectic of Enlightenment* (Palo Alto, CA: Stanford University Press, 1991).

25 We discussed this interest-based, utilitarian mindset in connection with Realist thinking; see Chapter 2, *supra,* at 39–44.

26 Marcuse, *Eros and Civilization, op. cit.*

27 Horkheimer and Adorno, *Dialectic of Enlightenment, op. cit.*, and Marcuse, *One-Dimensional Man, op. cit.*

28 On superstructure and base, see Raymond *Williams,* "Base and superstructure in Marxist cultural theory." *New Left Review, 1:82 (November–December 1973).*

29 For Gramsci, see *Hegemony and Revolution: Antonio Gramsci's Political and Cultural Theory* (Brattleboro, VT: Echo Point Books, 2014). For Althusser, see Louis Althusser, *On the Reproduction of Capitalism: Ideology and Ideological State Apparatuses* (London: Verso, 2014).

30 Claude Lévi-Strauss, *The Savage Mind* (Chicago: University of Chicago Press, 1966); Clifford Geertz, *The Interpretation of Cultures* (New York: Basic Books, 1977).

31 Michel Foucault, *Power/Knowledge: Selected Interviews, 1972–1977.* (New York: Vintage Books, 1980), esp. 78 *et seq.*

32 See Harold Berman, *Law and Revolution: The Formation of the Western Legal Tradition* (Cambridge, MA: Harvard University Press, 1963). Foucault analyzed the rise of the medicine, psychiatry, penology, and public administration in similar terms. See, e.g., his *Madness and Civilization: A History of Insanity in the Age of Reason* (New York: Vintage Books, 1988).

33 Michel Foucault, *The Order of Things: An Archaeology of the Human Sciences* (New York: Vintage Books, 1994).

34 Nancy Fraser, *Unruly Practices: Power, Discourse, and Gender in Contemporary Social Theory* (Minneapolis, MN: University of Minnesota Press, 2008), 26. See her enlightening discussion at 22 *et seq.*

35 See the discussion in Chapter 1, *supra*, at 10–11. Giddens and Foucault both insist that power is not merely a negative, coercive force in society but a creative force.

36 Vivienne Jabri, *Discourses on Violence: Conflict Analysis Reconsidered* (Manchester, UK: Manchester University Press, 1996). Using Foucault's concept of "biopolitical" power, Prof. Jabri extended this analysis to include claims to intervene in other nations for humanitarian or "peacebuilding" purposes in *The Postcolonial Subject: Claiming Politics/Governing Others in Late Modernity* (London and New York: Routledge, 2012). To similar effect, see Mark Duffield, *Development, Security, and Unending War: Governing the World of Peoples* (Cambridge: Polity Press, 2007).

37 Sara Cobb, *Speaking of Violence: The Politics and Poetics of Narrative in Conflict Resolution* (Oxford: Oxford University Press, 2013). John Winslade and Gerald D. Monk, *Narrative Mediation: A New Approach to Conflict Resolution* (San Francisco, CA: Jossey-Bass, 2000).

38 Jolle Demmers, *Theories of Violent Conflict: An Introduction* (London and New York: Routledge, 2012), 122.

39 A large and growing literature discusses the contrast between "Marxist" and bourgeois approaches to feminism and GLBT liberation. See, e.g., Herbert Marcuse, "Marxism and Feminism." Lecture delivered at Stanford University

(March 7, 1974). http://platypus1917.org/wp-content/uploads/archive/ rgroups/2006-chicago/marcuse_marxismfeminism.pdf; Shahrzad Mojab, *Marxism and Feminism* (Boston: Zed Press, 2015); Peter Drucker, *Warped: Gay Normality and Queer Anti-Capitalism* (New York: Historical Materialism Books, 2015).

40 Régis Debray, *Revolution in the Revolution? Armed Struggle and Political Struggle in Latin America* (New York: Grove Press, 1967).

41 Friedrich Engels, *Socialism: Utopian and Scientific* (New York: International Publishers, 1972). Also available at https://www.marxists.org/archive/marx/ works/1880/soc-utop/.

42 Rosa Luxemburg, *Reform or Revolution and Other Writings* (New York: Dover Books, 2006).

43 Arthur Koestler, *The Yogi and the Commissar* (1942) (London: Macmillan, 1967), also available on line at http://www.unz.org/Pub/Horizon-1942jun-00381?View=PDF.

44 See Chapter 3, note 33, *supra*.

45 On "soft power," see Joseph S. Nye, Jr., *Soft Power: The Means to Success in World Politics* (New York: PublicAffairs, 2005). An illuminating historical study of these themes in peace studies is Michael English, "The Peace Reform in the Field of Power: The National Peace Academy Campaign and the Establishment of the U.S. Institute of Peace" (Unpublished Ph.D. dissertation, 2015, available at the School for Conflict Analysis and Resolution, George Mason University).

46 The question of relationships between conflict studies specialists and governments is taken up in more detail in the final chapter of this study, *infra*.

47 The relevant works are cited, *supra*, by Burton in Chapter 2, note 28; Galtung in Chapter 1, note 2, and Chapter 3, notes 2, 3, and 18; Saunders and Fisher in Chapter 1, note 4, and Chapter 2, note 31; and Coleman in Chapter 2, note 13.

48 See, e.g., Thomas E. Ricks, *Fiasco: The U.S. Military Adventure in Iraq, 2003 to 2005* (London: Penguin Books, 2007), esp. 156 *et seq*.

49 Andrea Bartoli, "Learning from the Mozambique Peace Process: The Role of the Community of Sant' Egidio," and Susan Allen Nan, "Track One-and-a-Half Diplomacy: Contributions to South Ossetian Peacemaking," in Ronald J. Fisher, Ed., *Paving the Way: Contributions of Interactive Conflict Resolution to Peacemaking* (Oxford: Lexington Books, 2005). See also George Mitchell, *Making Peace* (Berkeley, CA: University of California Press, 2001), 79–104, 161–174.

50 Johan Galtung, for example, expresses a preference for effective limited reforms over "system debate" under certain circumstances in *Transcend and Transform, op. cit.*, 180.

51 See, for example, Richard E. Rubenstein, "On Taking Sides: Lessons of the Persian Gulf War." *Occasional Paper No. 5* (Institute for Conflict Analysis and Resolution, George Mason University (May 13, 1991). http://scar.gmu.edu/ op_5_rubenstein.pdf.

52 John Paul Lederach, *Building Peace: Sustainable Reconciliation in Divided Societies* (Washington, DC: U.S. Institute of Peace, 1997), 38–51.

53 See Joan Orgon Coolidge, "Toward a Just Peace: James H. Laue's Theory of Applied Practice" (2008). Unpublished Ph.D. dissertation, the School for Conflict Analysis and Resolution, George Mason University, www.http://scar.gmu.edu. See also James H. Laue, "Conflict Intervention," in Marvin E. Olsen and Michael Micklin, Eds., *Handbook of Applied Sociology: Frontiers of Contemporary Research* (New York: Praeger, 1981).

## Bibliography

Adamson, Walter L., *Hegemony and Revolution: Antonio Gramsci's Political and Cultural Theory.* (Brattleboro, VT: Echo Point Books, 2014).

Althusser, Louis, *On the Reproduction of Capitalism: Ideology and Ideological State Apparatuses* (London: Verso, 2014).

Barak, Gregg, et al., *Class, Race, Gender and Crime: The Social Realities of Justice in America*, 3rd Edn. (Lanham, MD: Rowman and Littlefield, 2010).

Bartoli, Andrea, "Learning from the Mozambique Peace Process: The Role of the Community of Sant' Egidio," in Ronald J. Fisher, Ed., *Paving the Way: Contributions of Interactive Conflict Resolution to Peacemaking* (Oxford: Lexington Books, 2005).

Berman, Harold, *Law and Revolution: The Formation of the Western Legal Tradition* (Cambridge, MA: Harvard University Press, 1963).

Bernstein, Eduard, *Evolutionary Socialism* (1899) (New York: CreateSpace, 2011).

Boulding, Kenneth E., "Twelve Friendly Quarrels with Johan Galtung." *Journal of Peace Research*, 14:1 (1977), 75–86.

Caute, David, *The Left in Europe Since 1789*, 2nd Edn. (New York: McGraw-Hill, 1971).

Cobb, Sara, *Speaking of Violence: The Politics and Poetics of Narrative in Conflict Resolution* (Oxford: Oxford University Press, 2013).

Coolidge, Joan Orgon, "Toward a Just Peace: James H. Laue's Theory of Applied Practice" (2008). Unpublished Ph.D. dissertation, the School for Conflict Analysis and Resolution, George Mason University, www.http://scar.gmu.edu.

Debray, Régis, *Revolution in the Revolution? Armed Struggle and Political Struggle in Latin America* (New York: Grove Press, 1967).

Demmers, Jolle, *Theories of Violent Conflict: An Introduction* (London and New York: Routledge, 2012).

Drucker, Peter, *Warped: Gay Normality and Queer Anti-Capitalism* (New York: Historical Materialism Books, 2015).

Duffield, Mark, *Development, Security, and Unending War: Governing the World of Peoples* (Cambridge: Polity Press, 2007).

Dugan, Maire, "A Nested Theory of Conflict." *Leadership Journal: Women in Leadership – Sharing the Vision*, 1:1 (Summer 1996), 14.

Eley, Geoff, *Forging Democracy: The History of the Left in Europe, 1850–2000* (Oxford: Oxford University Press, 2002).

Engels, Friedrich, *Socialism: Utopian and Scientific* (New York: International Publishers, 1972). https://www.marxists.org/archive/marx/works/1880/soc-utop/.

English, Michael, "The Peace Reform in the Field of Power: The National Peace Academy Campaign and the Establishment of the U.S. Institute of Peace" (Unpublished Ph.D. dissertation, 2015, available at the School for Conflict Analysis and Resolution, George Mason University).

Fajnzylber, Pablo, Daniel Lederman, and Norman Loayza, "What causes violent crime?" *European Economic Review* 46 (2002), 1323–1357.

Foucault, Michel, *Power/Knowledge: Selected Interviews, 1972–1977.* (New York: Vintage Books, 1980).

———*Madness and Civilization: A History of Insanity in the Age of Reason* (New York: Vintage Books, 1988).

———*The Order of Things: An Archaeology of the Human Sciences* (New York: Vintage Books, 1994).

Fraser, Nancy, *Unruly Practices: Power, Discourse, and Gender in Contemporary Social Theory* (Minneapolis, MN: University of Minnesota Press, 2008), 26.

Freire, Paulo, *Education for Critical Consciousness* (1974) (London and New York: Bloomsbury, 2013).

Galtung, Johan, "Violence, Peace, and Peace Research." *Journal of Peace Research*, 6:3 (1969), 167–191.

———"Only One Quarrel with Kenneth Boulding." *Journal of Peace Research*, 24:2 (June 1987), 199–203.

———"Cultural Violence." *Journal of Peace Research,* 27:3 (1990), 291–305.

———"International Development in Human Perspective," in John Burton, Ed., *Conflict: Human Needs Theory* (London and New York: Palgrave Macmillan, 1990) 309–327.

———*Transcend and Transform: An Introduction to Conflict Work* (London: Pluto Press, 2004).

Geertz, Clifford, *The Interpretation of Cultures* (New York: Basic Books, 1977).

Giddens, Anthony, *The Constitution of Society: Outline of the Theory of Structuration* (Berkeley and Los Angeles: University of California Press, 1984).

Hall, John R., "Cultural Meanings and Cultural Structures in Historical Explanation." *History and Theory*, 39:3 (October 2000), 331–347.

Horkheimer, Max and Theodor W. Adorno, *The Dialectic of Enlightenment* (Palo Alto, CA: Stanford University Press, 1991).

Horowitz, Donald L., *Ethnic Groups in Conflict*, 2nd Edn. (Berkeley, CA: University of California Press, 2000).

Hurst, Charles E., *Social Inequality: Forms, Causes, and Consequences* (London and New York: Routledge, 2016).

Jabri, Vivienne, *Discourses on Violence: Conflict Analysis Reconsidered* (Manchester, UK: Manchester University Press, 1996).

———*The Postcolonial Subject: Claiming Politics/Governing Others in Late Modernity* (London and New York: Routledge, 2012).

Janoski, Thomas, et al., *The Causes of Structural Unemployment: Four Factors that Keep People from the Jobs They Deserve* (Cambridge: Polity Press, 2014).

Jay, Martin, *The Dialectical Imagination: A History of the Frankfurt School and the Institute of Social Research, 1923–1950* (Berkeley, CA: University of California Press, 1996).

Koestler, Arthur, *The Yogi and the Commissar* (1942) (London: Macmillan, 1967), also available online at http://www.unz.org/Pub/Horizon-1942jun-00381?View=PDF.

Laue, James H., "Conflict Intervention," in Marvin E. Olsen and Michael Micklin, Eds., *Handbook of Applied Sociology: Frontiers of Contemporary Research* (New York: Praeger, 1981).

Lederach, John Paul, *Building Peace: Sustainable Reconciliation in Divided Societies* (Washington, DC: U.S. Institute of Peace, 1997).

Lévi-Strauss, Claude, *The Savage Mind* (Chicago: University of Chicago Press, 1966).

Luxemburg, Rosa, *Reform or Revolution and Other Writings* (New York: Dover Books, 2006).

Marcuse, Herbert, "Marxism and Feminism." Lecture delivered at Stanford University, (March 7, 1974). http://platypus1917.org/wp-content/uploads/archive/rgroups/2006-chicago/marcuse_marxismfeminism.pdf.

——*Eros and Civilization: A Philosophical Inquiry into Freud* (Boston: Beacon Press, 1974).

——*One-Dimensional Man: Studies in the Ideology of Advanced Industrial Society*, 2nd Edn. (Boston: Beacon Press, 1991).

Marx, Karl, *The Civil War in France* (1871), 2nd Edn. (New York: International Publishers, 1989).

Merriman, John, *Massacre: The Life and Death of the Paris Commune* (New York: Basic Books, 2014).

Mitchell, George J., *Making Peace* (Berkeley, CA: University of California Press, 2001).

Mojab, Shahrjad, *Marxism and Feminism* (Boston: Zed Press, 2015).

Nan, Susan Allen, "Track One-and-a-Half Diplomacy: Contributions to South Ossetian Peacemaking," in Ronald J. Fisher, Ed., *Paving the Way: Contributions of Interactive Conflict Resolution to Peacemaking* (Oxford: Lexington Books, 2005).

Nye, Joseph S. Jr., *Soft Power: The Means to Success in World Politics* (New York: PublicAffairs, 2005).

Reiman, Jeffrey and Paul Leighton, *The Rich Get Richer and the Poor Get Prison: Ideology, Class, and Criminal Justice*, 10th Edn. (London and New York: Routledge, 2016).

Ricks, Thomas E., *Fiasco: The U.S. Military Adventure in Iraq, 2003 to 2005* (London: Penguin Books, 2007).

Rubenstein, Richard E., "On Taking Sides: Lessons of the Persian Gulf War." *Occasional Paper No. 5* (Institute for Conflict Analysis and Resolution, George Mason University (May 13, 1991). http://scar.gmu.edu/op_5_rubenstein.pdf.

Ture, Kwame, and Charles V. Hamilton, *Black Power: The Politics of Liberation* (New York: Vintage Books, 1992).

Twain, Mark, *The Adventures of Huckleberry Finn* (1884) http://contentserver.adobe.com/store/books/HuckFinn.pdf, 111:John Paul

U.S. Department of Justice, *Special Report: Multistate Criminal History Patterns of Prisoners Released in 30 States* (September 2015). http://www.bjs.gov/content/pub/pdf/mschpprts05.pdf.

Weber, Max, *The Protestant Ethic and the Spirit of Capitalism* (New York and London: Routledge, 1992).

*Williams, Raymond,* "Base and superstructure in Marxist cultural theory." *New Left Review, 1:82 (November–December 1973).*

Winslade, John, and Gerald D. Monk, *Narrative Mediation: A New Approach to Conflict Resolution* (San Francisco, CA: Jossey-Bass, 2000).

# 4

# CLASS CONFLICT AND THE PROBLEM OF CRIME

## Breaking the silence about social class

In the field of conflict studies, as in many other disciplines, class struggle is the conflict 'that dare not speak its name.' Perusing the most comprehensive and popular introductions to the field, one finds repeated discussions of the categories of nationality, ethnicity, race, gender, and religion in conflict, but very little, in most cases, about social class. In part, this reflects a general taboo prevalent in many capitalist societies against 'talking about class' or admitting that social classes – workers and owners in particular – play a significant and contentious role in politics and culture. To cite one well-known example, U.S. newspapers like *The Washington Post* and *The New York Times* seldom print the phrase 'working class,' much preferring to use the broader and vaguer term 'middle class.'[1] Interestingly, the taboo appears to be weakening among Americans at large, even while it remains potent among the news media, politicians, and many academics. In 2015, some 49 percent of Americans identified themselves as working class or 'lower class,' with 51 percent – a considerable drop from previous 60 percent-plus figures – calling themselves middle or 'upper middle' class. (Virtually no one admits to being wealthy.)[2]

In conflict studies, however, there is a more specific reason to avoid focusing on social classes: the assumption that most analysts interested in class conflict are Marxists and are therefore hostile to conflict resolution. Peter Wallensteen's approach to this issue in his *Understanding Conflict Resolution* is fairly typical. In a subchapter on basic needs, he states:

> This thinking is part of a materialist tradition and constitutes a signifi-
> cant element in class analysis. But Marxist theorists seldom have come
> to an understanding of conflict resolution. On the contrary, much
> Marxist thinking is based on the idea of continuous conflict, ending
> only with the defeat of the oppressive system – at this time, capitalism.
> Negotiation and compromise were not part of the political formula,
> or of the academic study. Only in the reformist, social democratic
> version . . . was conflict within capitalism manageable.[3]

As a matter of intellectual history, this statement is accurate enough,
although its assumptions and implications may be questioned. Many leftist
thinkers did oppose conflict resolution, as the authors of another well-
regarded text say, on the grounds that "it attempted to reconcile interests
that should not be reconciled, failed to take sides in unequal and unjust
struggles, and lacked an analysis within a properly global perspective of
the forces of exploitation and repression."[4] Now that the structural turn
in conflict studies has arrived, however, the question is whether class conflict can be dealt with in a way that avoids both radical abstentionism and
pallid reformism. Peter Wallensteen's statement seems to identify conflict
resolution with "negotiation and compromise" – a dated formulation that
does not address the question of whether conflicts generated by the socioeconomic structure play a significant role in producing violence, and, if so,
whether that structure can be transformed sufficiently to resolve them.

That is the subject of our inquiry here. How does the socioeconomic
system generate violence? What can conflict specialists do about this?
Since the conflict scholars' understanding of social class and class conflict was strongly influenced by the three waves of theory and practice
described in Chapter 2, we can begin by looking at the view, still prevalent among most Western academics and politicians, that social classes
are groups sharing common economic interests, particularly interests in
increased incomes, improved working conditions, greater job security and
welfare benefits, and the acquisition of wealth. To use the shorthand term,
those inclined to interpret social conflicts as clashes of competing interests
see working class people, particularly those represented by trade unions,
as an *interest group*.

What does this mean? One implication is that, as large in number as they
may be, workers comprise an interest group like any other. That is, they
strive to become more prosperous, secure, and respected, and are perfectly
able to negotiate with other groups to maximize their benefits under the
overall supervision of the liberal state. A second, more shadowy implication
is that the working class as a whole may not exist in a meaningful sense,

since the immediate economic interests of unionized auto workers, say, are quite different from those of unorganized farm workers, white-collar supervisors, or college professors. On the contrary, under certain circumstances (an intensification of foreign competition, for example), the auto workers' immediate interests seem conjoined with those of investors and executives in the auto industry. Similarly, applying interest group analysis to the business class (in Marx's terms, the bourgeoisie), that class may not exist as a meaningful entity either, since the immediate goals of investors, business owners, managers, professionals, small entrepreneurs, farmers, technical workers and others appear to turn each of these 'classes' into separate interest groups.

From the point of view of conflict studies, this meant incorporating labor-management conflict and other economic disputes into the rubric of alternative dispute resolution rather than conflict resolution. The assumption (characteristic of first wave theory) was that class struggle, redefined as interest group conflict, could be dealt with by a process of continuous bargaining within the existing system, facilitated by lawyers, arbitrators, and mediators.[5] The hallmark of this system was the acceptance by all stakeholders of a set of formal and informal legal, political, and economic rules governing labor-management relations. This reflected a consensus that emerged during the 1930s and 1940s as the result of a historic compromise between business owners and labor unions under the auspices of the New Deal in the United States, the Popular Front in France, and other center-left coalitions in other nations.[6] In an environment of global economic crisis, the labor movement, which was already moving in a reformist direction, abandoned older hopes for an economy and state controlled by workers in order to achieve substantial benefits at the workplace and a place at the political bargaining table.

The medium-range consequences of this compromise were beneficial to many wage earners, especially when, buoyed by military spending, Western economies began to recover from the Great Depression. They were also beneficial to business owners, who had been threatened by a series of massive, violently fought-out strikes that raised fears of a social revolution.[7] Organized workers gained legal recognition of their unions and the right to strike, along with a binding obligation on the part of employers to bargain about wages and working conditions, enforceable wage and hour laws, and laws providing for social security, unemployment compensation, and other welfare benefits.[8] Moreover, an activist state apparently responsive to their needs and desires engaged in innovative economic activities ranging from providing public service jobs for unemployed workers to financing major infrastructure projects such as the Tennessee Valley Authority's dams and irrigation works in the United States. Meanwhile, business owners made important gains, too. They gained recognition of and legal protection for their unqualified rights to own companies, compete in the market, and make 'management decisions' regarding virtually all matters other than wages and working conditions, including what to produce, how to produce and distribute it, what to charge for it, where to locate production facilities, when to shut companies down, and so forth.

In systemic terms, one might say that there had been a *partial* restructuring of the pre-Depression politico-economic system, holding out the prospect of further transformation.[9] But, following the 1945–65 economic boom, old systemic patterns asserted themselves, amplified by trends toward the globalization of capital, rapid technological development, and a determined political effort to limit the expansion of New Deal–type programs. In the United States, as in many other nations, industrial jobs were outsourced or vanished because of international competition, creating a 'Rust Belt' of deindustrialized communities suffering high unemployment and a wide range of social and medical ills.[10] Wages stagnated, forcing more family members to take jobs (if they could find them) in order to maintain family income levels.[11] Trade union membership declined to historic lows – from about 35 percent of the wage and salary workforce in the 1950s to about 11 percent in 2014 (and in the private sector, less than 7 percent).[12] Life expectancies among white working class Americans declined.[13] At the same time, income and wealth disparities not seen since the period before the Great Depression vastly enriched the economic elite while impoverishing millions. While most workers struggled to stay in the same place, those excluded from decently paid employment because of deindustrialization and the explosive growth of low-wage service jobs found themselves and their families falling into deep, persistent, intergenerational poverty.[14]

The result of these developments was a substantial increase in all forms of violence: structural, cultural, and direct. In a moment, we will examine one form of class-based violence in particular – the crime/punishment syndrome. But before doing so, it is worth noting that the interest group framework is hardly the sole or best theoretical lens to employ in interpreting relations between social classes. The concept is neither scientifically 'neutral' nor designed to promote particular class interests; it is rather a recipe for the dissolution of all classes. The basic unit of such a group is the economically self-interested individual, and the interests of the group are the sum total of its members' interests. If people act on this basis, social class solidarity becomes a mere shibboleth, since each person will take the best deal that he or she can get, regardless of its impact on class 'brothers and sisters.' (For this same reason, according to Realist international theory, there can be no permanent alliances between states.) One can make a good case that the near collapse of the labor movement in the United States and its decline in other nations is directly related to the shallowness and transience of interest group consciousness. If union-free Walmart is offering employment when other companies are not, if stagnating wages make it seem disadvantageous to go on paying union dues, or if jobs are shipped abroad, class solidarity comes to an abrupt end.

By contrast, Karl Marx and his early followers thought of a social class not as an agglomeration of individual interests, but as a collectivity with a historic destiny. For Marx, class interests could not be restricted to dollars-and-cents economic goals centered on the workplace. This is because the basic unit of the social class was not the acquisitive individual (an idea that he considered thoroughly bourgeois) but the individual with basic needs, including needs for human development and its *sine qua non*: control over the social system.[15] True, a person's class membership was based on his or her role in the system of production – for most people this means either owning the means of production (capital) or only one's own labor-power (labor). But this social position carried with it shared cultural and ethical values, political ambitions, and personal goals as well as narrow economic interests. As Bertell Ollman puts it:

> It is only . . . because Marx found groups in his society with different relations to the prevailing mode of production, sets of opposing economic interests based on these relations, a corresponding cultural and moral differentiation, a growing consciousness among these groups of their uniqueness and accompanying interest, and—resulting from this consciousness—the development of social and political organizations which promote these interests that he constructed his peculiar concept of "class." Of overriding importance is that "class" in Marxism is not just a label for groups carved out of society on the basis of a discernable set of standards but expresses as well the involved interactions which Marx believed he uncovered between these standards.[16]

On this basis, we can see why Marx and other radicals thought that a class 'struggle' was inevitable – why the conflict between social classes could not be settled via interest group bargaining and negotiation, but would have to involve a contest for state power and social hegemony. Marx did *not* think of the capitalist economy as a zero-sum game in which one class's gain was the other's loss; in fact, he described capitalism as the first economic system capable of revolutionizing its own methods of production, and denied that class struggle was primarily about wages and working conditions.[17] It was about satisfying the basic needs of the whole person. Two great systemic obstacles stood in the way of this satisfaction, one requiring immediate change and the other to be transformed over a somewhat longer term: the *capitalist* system and the *class* system.

The capitalist system, in Marx's eyes, was basically self-destructive and out of control – in our terms, like a driverless car accelerating toward a cliff. As social historians have often pointed out, the stability and longevity of any ranked social system depends upon the elite's ability to take care of the lower classes – to fulfill the implicit social contract that calls for labor, services, respect, and obedience to be exchanged for security, identity, prosperity, or whatever other values are recognized as essential in that society.[18] Capitalism could provide these satisfactions sporadically, in the short run, but never in the long run. This was a result of the basic system dynamics outlined in Marx's *Capital* and since elaborated and extended by other analyses: for example, the inexorable drive to replace human labor-power with technology, reducing workers' ability to buy products and services in the market, and leading to crises of overproduction; the tendency of concentrated capital to put real economic and political power in the hands of a few tycoons while decimating small and medium-sized entrepreneurs; the growing predominance of finance capital, with its ungovernable credit bubbles and speculation-driven market crises; the intensification of military competition and wars between nations and would-be empires defending their companies, and more.[19] At bottom, the capitalist class could not stop pursuing profits as their number one priority, while the rest of society could not stop trying to satisfy their own basic needs.

Workers would suffer because of the system's addiction to the profit motive and its tendency to produce global crises, but negative motivations were not the only incitements to rebellion. The Marxists believed that modern workers constituted the first genuinely *social* – or perhaps I should say sociable – class, since they were not forced, as capitalists were, to compete to the point that others would be destroyed. Rather, the experience of working together to produce and distribute products inclined them toward cooperation. The system's greatest contradiction was the clash between the business owners' private appropriation of the economic surplus and the cooperative, public methods used by workers of all sorts to produce it.[20] After all, the whole society collaborates to produce goods and services by collectively supplying everything needed for production except private capital. This public investment, whose size dwarfs private investment, provides the education, medical care, and social security needed by workers and business managers; the public roads, rails, and airways used to transport personnel, products, and equipment; the airways and cyberspace used for communications and advertising; the scientific research used in the development of new products and services; the legal system and public order needed to secure people and property; a stable currency and credit system, backed if necessary by 'bailouts' of crisis-ridden industries; and even the military establishment used to guarantee business's access to international markets, freedom of the seas, and more.

Marxists thought that the basic unfairness of this situation would become evident to workers and provoke them to question the class structure that underpins it. The vast bulk of resources essential to business – even the expenses of commuting to factories and offices – are supplied by working people at their own expense, without any acknowledged right to a share of the proceeds beyond their wages and whatever welfare benefits companies or governments may provide. The owners of capital continue to pocket the entire net profit of business enterprises, allegedly because they have raised the funds needed to finance these businesses, and because they make the managerial decisions on which profits partly depend. But even if these are valuable services (at least when sound decisions are made), they hardly constitute a basis for presuming to rule the world! Crucially, the capitalist elite's economic power converts easily into political and cultural power, which puts them in a position to make decisions for world society based on their own value system – a code, seldom exposed plainly, that ranks profit-making the highest of human activities, justifies the privatization and commercialization of virtually every good and service; defends concentrated wealth and power on social-Darwinist grounds; preaches the virtues of competition and 'necessary' military force; and is prepared to sacrifice natural resources endlessly in order to preserve the existing mode of production.[21]

Compared with the savagery of the bourgeoisie in thought and action, to many radicals the workers seemed by far the more 'civilized' class. This was a key reason, above and beyond their vulnerability to exploitation and economic crises, that they were thought to be the appropriate successor to the business class as rulers of state and society. But we must not forget the second obstacle to the satisfaction of long-unsatisfied needs for human development: not just the domination of the business class, but the very existence of a class-based society. Any hierarchical socioeconomic structure, even one dominated by the worker majority acting as an international class, would generate structural violence insofar as it failed to satisfy people's basic material, psychic, and cultural needs. Therefore, the fundamental purpose of taking control of the economy and the state was to produce the abundance of goods, services, and opportunities that, combined with an egalitarian ethic and practice, would make possible the 'withering away' of the state. A workers' government would open the door to replacement of the coercive, top-down state – in Engels's words, "the government of people" – by a democratic, consensus-based organization: "the administration of things."[22]

From the perspective of conflict studies, this formulation, so often derided as dreamy utopianism, should be considered neither impossible nor unimportant. We can hypothesize that the violence generated by social and political structures founded on an unequal, elitist distribution of power can be radically decreased by transforming the system so as to empower the lower classes to satisfy their basic needs. A principal source of social violence – the modern state – can become a vastly less coercive, repressive, and warlike organization if two changes are made. First, overcome the inhibitions inherent in a profit-driven system against producing the goods, services, and cultural products that people want and need in ways consistent with the survival of the planet. Second, make this new abundance available to people on the basis of their basic needs rather than their rank in some economic or social hierarchy. *Shared abundance*, says the hypothesis, will reduce the need for coercion by private and public authorities. Less coercion will reduce the incitement to rebel, which will obviate the need for violent repression and war. Structural violence will decline, and with it, direct and cultural violence.

How do we research such hypotheses? We will have more to say about this shortly, but one place to start may be in societies that have achieved a high level of abundance combined with an ethic of democratic decision-making and egalitarian sharing. The Global Peace Index produced by the Institute for Economics and Peace, which also publishes reports discussing the relevant issues, ranks nations each year on a sophisticated scale of peacefulness.[23] In addition, conflict scholars could expand their field of attention to include regions of peace, including affluent communities in their own nations, many of which have experienced both substantial decreases in crime and domestic violence and dramatic improvements in local policing, public administration, and community problem-solving. Some critics may consider it 'utopian' to think that people living in impoverished urban or rural communities could one day enjoy the abundance now showered upon a few wealthy neighborhoods, but the first question to investigate is whether there are demonstrable causal links between shared abundance, social peace, and the withering away of coercive state institutions. If these links exist, the idea that structural violence can be radically reduced is not utopian. It is just unfeasible under current political conditions.

### Crime, punishment, race, and class

The connection between class and crime is not one of life's mysteries. I have given many lectures on crime and punishment in which I have

told students, the members of religious congregations, or people attend-
ing community forums that criminal, police, and prison violence in the
United States – the enormously wealthy nation that currently leads the
world in the number of people it arrests, tries, and incarcerates – is a
product of our socioeconomic system. Most audiences are not shocked by
this idea, although they are sometimes a bit startled to hear it stated publicly. That poverty and economic inequality are major causes of crime can
hardly be doubted in light of more than fifty years of research on the topic
by scholars in the United States and abroad concluding that crime rates
(rates of violent crime in particular) rise predictably with higher unemployment, lower income levels, the economic decline of neighborhoods,
and growing income and wealth inequality.[24]

The authors of the pioneering U.S. crime commission report, "The
Challenge of Crime in a Free Society" (1965), put the matter simply:
"Warring on poverty, inadequate housing and unemployment, is warring
on crime."[25] A more recent transnational study extends the same analysis
globally, but puts special emphasis on the correlation of overall economic
growth, income inequality, and violent crime:

> Both economic growth and income inequality are robust determi-
> nants of violent crime rates. Furthermore, even after controlling for
> country-specific effects (including systematic measurement error),
> there is clear evidence that violent crime is self-perpetuating. These
> variables (economic growth, inequality, and past crime rates) worked
> well for homicides and remarkably well for robbery rates. Their sign
> and statistical significance survived the addition of other explanatory
> variables, including measures of crime deterrence, illicit drug activi-
> ties, demographic characteristics, and cultural traits.[26]

In fact, it is not only violent crime that increases with the growth of social
inequality, but also a wide variety of violent conflicts, including ethnonational, racial, and religious clashes. As a recent study by Ravi Kanbur for
the International Peace Academy puts it: "Theory and evidence support
the view that it is the between-group dimension of inequality that is
crucial. Given structural cleavages such as caste, religion, ethnicity, race
and region, if income disparities align with these splits they exacerbate
tension and conflict."[27] This finding has important implications for the
connection of crime with race and ethnicity, as we will see in a moment.

If there are clear connections, then, between people's socioeconomic
position and the likelihood that they or their neighbors will be involved
either as perpetrators or as victims in violent crime, one would expect
conflict specialists to seek to resolve the conflict between lawbreakers and

authorities by helping the parties discover how to combat poverty, inequality, and 'precarity' — that problematic, increasingly common situation in which workers, particularly those employed irregularly or in low-wage jobs, teeter on the edge of poverty.[28] To be sure, this is not the only task that conflict resolvers might undertake, but it seems essential, as does the further investigation of the systemic sources of poverty and inequality. *Are* poverty, inequality, and precarity (or PIP, as some have begun to call these conditions) the inevitable products of capitalism at its current stage of development — problems whose elimination will require some sort of large-scale system transformation? Or, are they remediable glitches that can be eliminated or mitigated by enacting sensible within-system reforms? In either case, what practical measures to combat them make sense?

These are important questions, one would think, but few conflict studies scholars and practitioners of the 'second wave' considered them of primary importance. To the extent that the specialists recognized crime as involving intergroup conflict rather than individual deviance, like many other scholars concerned with crime/punishment issues, they conceived of clashes between criminals and authorities as racially, ethnically, or culturally grounded. Conflicts between the police and the community were thus typed as *identity group* struggles rather than products of the class structure, a classification that led naturally to academic studies, intergroup dialogues, and government-funded projects designed to improve police-community relations by altering police attitudes and behaviors, or the behaviors of potential criminals. These efforts produced a number of reform programs, many of them related to the movement for 'community policing' — an attempt to develop police practices more attuned to the problems, needs, and concerns of people in impoverished minority communities.[29] Many of these programs seem quite sensible, and some have apparently had a favorable impact on police-community relations. Nevertheless, it seems clear that the continuing state of war between authorities and lawbreakers in many communities will continue until the conflict's systemic causes have been identified and removed.

As Elliott Currie puts it in the updated 2013 edition of *Crime and Punishment in America*:

> Today, as in the 1990s, the United States is distinguished by its unusually high levels of poverty, its wide spread of income inequality, and its relatively weak and hesitant provision of social benefits to the vulnerable. The key difference is that these problems have worsened since the first edition [of this book], and that has a great deal to do with why America's cities remain the most violent in the advanced industrial world.[30]

We need to focus on these words: "America's cities remain the most violent in the advanced industrial world." What people lacking a systemic framework for interpreting this situation are unable to understand is that the fundamental problem in these cities is neither bad criminals nor bad cops. It is a system that has turned large urban areas into war zones. In a war zone, one is not surprised to learn of soldiers who abuse their power and brutalize civilians, or armed civilians who consider soldiers their enemy and fair game for retaliation. In almost all discussions of the crime/punishment syndrome, even colloquies among well-meaning reformers, the extent to which all the actors in the drama play roles scripted by the socioeconomic structure itself tends to be downplayed or even ignored. Partisan moralism rears its head even among the experts, who look for some rogue police or citizens to blame. But it is the situation that creates them, not the other way round.

How to characterize that situation is a critically important question. *Is* the clash between police and communities, which in the United States has produced intense movements of resistance such as Black Lives Matter, also a racial or ethnic identity group struggle? Certainly! Reliable statistics in the United States and other nations show that a disproportionately high number of people of color are arrested, convicted, and imprisoned for crime and suffer its effects as victims.[31] To some extent, this is the result of discrimination against minority communities in law enforcement; there is no doubt that police and prosecutors focus intense attention on ethnic and racial ghettos, that racial profiling by police takes place as a matter of course, and that many criminal laws are designed to treat people of color more harshly than whites.[32] But Elliott Currie is surely right to insist that the underlying reality is an overlap between economic deprivation and race: "Being poor in America *means* being at the bottom of an exceptionally harsh system of inequality; being black greatly increases the chances of being impoverished and, therefore, trapped at the lower end of the social ladder." Empirical studies show a particularly sharp correlation between *extreme* poverty and crime, with the result that extremely poor white neighborhoods "suffered more violence than somewhat less poor, but still deprived black communities. And they suffered almost twice the violent crime rates of black neighborhoods characterized by 'low' poverty."[33]

Class inequality and racial injustice are interlinked sources of crime and incarceration, but race and ethnicity rather than class remains the center of public attention. One reason for this, surely, is that, as the old saying has it, 'the squeaky wheel gets the grease.' On the one hand, many fearful or angry people who do not wish to link the crime problem to the way the socioeconomic system operates link it instead to culture, in particular, to race or nationality. Crime in America is said by some to be "a black (or Hispanic) problem" and in France "an Arab problem." On the other hand, for at least half a century, African-Americans have demonstrated their anger at what they consider brutal and unfair treatment by the police and court systems, as have people of South Asian or Caribbean descent in the United Kingdom, people of Arab or Muslim descent in France, and ethnic or religious minorities elsewhere. In fact, protests against mistreatment by cultural minorities are more common, intense, and sometimes violent than protests by workers in general.

Pierre Bourdieu and Johan Galtung explain this discrepancy by noting that in many societies direct violence, such as police brutality against minorities, is visible and outrageous, while structural violence seems so natural as to be virtually invisible.[34] But this seems a bit facile. As Galtung's theory suggests, structural, cultural, and direct violence produce each other. It also seems clear that the *perception that direct violence is a product of an unjust structure* is a prime mover of rebellion by the system's bottom dogs.[35] Why, then, are the victims of racial or ethnic oppression sometimes more inclined to rebel than the system's class victims?

I say sometimes, because ethnic oppression is clearly no guarantee of rebellion. During the Prohibition years in the United States, for example, intense police violence was directed against the Italian-American and Irish-American communities, already the subjects of discrimination and obloquy by the native majority, without generating a violent response. Moreover, African-Americans were arrested at will, manhandled, and gunned down by white police for decades before the Los Angeles ghetto exploded in 1965. What are the conditions under which 'an exceptionally harsh system of inequality' based on class privilege and discrimination tends to vanish from people's agendas, to be replaced by a consciousness of inequality based on nationality, race, ethnicity, gender, or other forms of cultural identity?

A useful explanation seems particularly urgent at present, when many workers in Europe and North America have focused resentments arguably generated by the operations of the class system against the members of ethnic, racial, and religious out-groups, particularly those migrating from poorer to wealthier regions in search of safety, freedom, and better jobs. At the same time, of course, in nations like Greece and Spain, working people and students more inclined to act on the basis of class-based ideas and goals have organized substantial new political parties, as well as movements within established parties like the Bernie Sanders 'insurgency' in the United States. This poses a related question: under what conditions will class-conscious political mobilizations take place?

First, as to the frequent 'invisibility' of class: explanations based on cultural diversity in certain societies, or on how well the capitalist and liberal democratic systems have worked to satisfy most people's needs abound, but are growing visibly tattered.[36] A more telling response, in my view, is suggested by the message on a political button that recently caught my eye: *They only call it class warfare when we fight back.* Class struggle is unceasing, but if the power disparity between classes is great enough, there may seem to be no struggle at all. If business owners, for example, have virtually absolute power, recognized both in law and in custom, to close an enterprise down or move it to another location, the workers' failure to greet plant or office relocations with militant protests makes their class membership seem nonexistent as a relevant factor in political and social life. If they don't protest collectively, this is because they believe that it will be a waste of time and energy to do so, *and* because they lack an ideological, moral, and narrative framework for acting as the members of a mistreated class. Defeated as an interest group, there is no basis for their continuing to fight unless they have a concept of themselves as a component of a faulty and transient system − that is, as a collectivity with a destiny. On the other hand, in some locales or industries in which interest group consciousness has not entirely ousted class consciousness, workers have begun to question alleged 'management rights' like the right to close down or relocate businesses at will.

Certainly, class structure is not invisible because structural violence is less obvious than direct violence. When people lose their jobs or their homes because of business failures or relocations, when some turn to drugs, alcohol, or criminal activities as a result, or when whole neighborhoods or regions are depressed by economic reversals, these effects are quite visible. What disappears from view is the *connection* between these effects and their systemic causes. The sufferers have learned *not* to view the business closure or the depressed neighborhood as an avoidable insult to their basic needs produced by a profit-driven system. The messages delivered constantly and in multifarious ways by cultural agencies from the school and church to the television drama are that business trends (and catastrophes) are as mysterious and uncontrollable as the weather; that the free market system is basically beneficent and healthy, although it needs tweaking now and then; that, in any case, there is no conceivably better alternative system; and that individuals are ultimately morally responsible for their own economic fates.[37]

Note that this is not a result of ideological brainwashing, as some social critics seem to think. During periods of strong capitalist growth and expansion, these credos and mea culpas seem to be borne out by events in the real world. Thus, Max Weber, a pioneering sociologist writing during an era of rapid industrial growth, pointed out that modern social classes did not

define themselves only by their role in economic production, but also –
perhaps primarily – by their patterns of consumption, which is to say that
they tended to think of themselves as *status* groups.[38] The Critical Theorist
Herbert Marcuse, writing during an even more spectacular boom period
(1945–70), opined that consumer consciousness had become almost a "second nature" to workers in advanced industrial societies.[39] To the extent that
this is true, social classes as self-conscious communities tend to dissolve, and
we get an almost infinite number of status-based groupings defining themselves as blue-collar, white-collar, or unemployed; highly educated or less
so; sophisticated urban or down-home rural; high-tech or low-tech; white
or nonwhite, and so forth. When the boom period ends, however, and most
workers find their status as well as their wages under attack, class consciousness may reassert itself and working people begin to challenge the principles
accepted as common sense in easier, more optimistic days. Of course, these
periods of stagnation or crisis are precisely the times at which the old system's defenders try to convince workers to think of themselves as members
of national or cultural identity groups rather than as a social class.

Our analysis suggests two conclusions relevant not only to crime/pun-
ishment and class struggles, but also to structural conflicts in general. First,
most serious structural conflicts are *simultaneously* class-based, cultural, and
political. These overlaps, in fact, are what often make them seem forbid-
dingly complex and intractable.[40] Hegel's insight that social systems tend
toward total integration remains true, as does his idea that they are eventually disrupted by contradictions.[41] This means that social conflicts need to
be defined by reference to the *whole* system rather than by reference to their
immediate parties. What some call the conflict between lawbreakers and
authorities ('cops vs. robbers' in popular parlance) is also a conflict between
majority and minority racial and ethnic groups, but one that is inseparable
from a struggle between socioeconomic classes. Furthermore, these manifestations of systemic conflict are not as neatly nested as Johan Galtung's
famous Chinese box metaphor may suggest. For example, conflicts about
crime and punishment often pit racial and ethnic minority communities
against majorities, but since minorities are also disproportionately the victims of crime, some may ally themselves (quietly or not) with the majority.
Structural conflicts overlap, but they do so sloppily.

To consider cops vs. robbers or 'the police vs. the community' a coherent
conflict in itself effectively redefines conflict resolution – the elimination of
a conflict's causes – as within-system conflict management, or ADR. One
can do this consciously, of course, by reasoning that because the whole system is unreachable, too hard to transform, or too beneficial to change, some
temporary amelioration of the situation is the best that one can accomplish.

One's inability to transform the system as a whole is certainly no reason to avoid doing what one can – especially if there is reason to believe that a specific reform is a step toward system transformation rather than away from it. Many conflict specialists, however, tend either to ignore the overarching system or to insist as a matter of faith that immediately feasible reforms can transform it from within.[42] The question that clearly requires further discussion is how to determine whether a proposed reform is system-transforming or not.

A second conclusion is that making the structural turn in conflict studies may be particularly difficult to accomplish when the context of the conflict is not the apparent anarchy of international relations or a 'failed state,' but a functioning nation-state. Conflict specialists working in relatively anarchic milieus understand either that an existing system established to manage conflict has failed, or that no such system has ever existed. For this reason, they sometimes feel free to convene workshops or dialogues in which conflicting parties are invited to imagine and to plan a system that promises to satisfy their basic needs. (Even here, it is easier to facilitate discussions of a new political constitution than of a new socioeconomic system.) In the context of a functioning state, however, assisting parties to consider the whole system and to imagine the changes needed to eliminate structural violence seems a direct challenge to state power, provoking fears of revolution and repression. Oddly enough, therefore, it may be less difficult to convene a discussion of a new constitution in Northern Ireland or Liberia than to talk about the system changes that could eliminate crime in Mexico or the United States.

## Socioeconomic change and the peacemaker's role

The problem, in a nutshell, is how to accomplish a socioeconomic transformation that is both radical and nonviolent. Inegalitarian class structures which fail to satisfy basic human needs generate violent conflict in two ways: directly, as when social classes struggle for economic and political supremacy, and indirectly, as when frustrated people conditioned to think of themselves in national, racial, ethnic, or religious terms hold other identity groups responsible for their problems and target them for punishment. Conflict resolution requires that ranked socioeconomic structures be altered in order to satisfy the basic needs and vital interests of lower-class groups. But how can this be accomplished without provoking violence by the old regime and its challengers? And, if a nonviolent social transformation *is* feasible, what roles can specialists in conflict resolution play in the process?

The first question demands attention because of the historic association of radical social revolutions with intense mass violence. In some situations where the goal was to replace or alter legal and political institutions *without* overturning the old socioeconomic order, fundamental change took place without large-scale bloodshed. The nonviolent movement led by Mahatma Gandhi and the Congress Party ousted the British from India, and the campaign led by Nelson Mandela and the African National Congress overthrew the apartheid system in South Africa, without a revolutionary civil war, but also without reordering those nations' economic structures and priorities.[43] Other upheavals that aimed at transforming the system of class and property relations as well as the system of governance proved more destructive. In certain instances (the Russian and Chinese revolutions come to mind), significant system changes were, indeed, accomplished, but state and revolutionary violence exacted a very high price both in terms of human lives and subsequent political deformation. Of course, this does not mean that leaving an old social regime in place produces peace! The slow collapse of a defunct system (for example, the centuries-long decay of feudalism in Europe) can be even more costly, generating religious upheavals, communal wars, and struggles between secular rulers, as well as horrendous structural violence.

This history must give one pause. On the other hand, we know that in some cases, significant socioeconomic changes were made relatively rapidly *without* serious violence. Two instances already noted were the mass mobilizations led by New Dealers and social democrats that legitimized the labor movement and created the welfare/interest group state. During the 1930s, a series of hard-fought strikes and demonstrations led by far-left organizations posed the threat of a violent mass uprising and enabled those advocating structural reforms to portray themselves as relative moderates. Revolutionary violence was avoided, although many of the tactics employed by the labor movement were either quasi-legal or illegal, and were branded violent by the old regime. Such innovations in the United States as 'sit-down strikes' (i.e., factory occupations) and 'one-cent sales' (mass demonstrations to prevent property foreclosures) were borderline tactics that the state decided not to challenge in order to avoid a dangerous conflict escalation. One also recalls that American courts declared much of the original New Deal legislative program unconstitutional before the U.S. Supreme Court finally decided to validate it. Interestingly, the size and militancy of the mass movement seems to correlate positively with the avoidance of civil violence. When people are politically aroused to demand significant structural change, but also have the organizational means to express themselves collectively, nonviolent transformations can occur.

That being said, the extent to which these reform movements actually succeeded in altering the old social system remains a matter of debate. Franklin D. Roosevelt's enemies branded him a revolutionary tyrant, and the new principles and institutions brought to life by the New Deal were more than cosmetic, but in hindsight, the claim that his administration rescued American capitalism by reforming labor-management relations, creating the welfare state, and regulating the banking and securities industries seems not at all far-fetched.[44] While the changes implemented by the New Deal and social democratic movements were in some ways quite substantial, they did *not* eliminate old classes or create new ones, permanently reverse relations of class domination/subordination, or transform the system of property relations that reflects and embodies the power of these groupings. In fact, many of the activists who advocated more radical change saw the New Deal reforms, combined with mass organizing by groups like the Congress of Industrial Organizations (CIO), as steps on the road to a thoroughgoing social transformation. This seems to have been an error – but it leaves a key question for us, which current social science has done little to answer. How can we evaluate the transformative potential of a specific reform program? To do this requires a better understanding of the processes of system change than the field of conflict studies now possesses.

A second example of substantial nonviolent socioeconomic change is the rapid and unexpected movement of former communist systems in the direction of capitalism that has taken place over the past two or three decades in Russia, the former Soviet Republics, Eastern Europe, China, and Vietnam. In the former Union of Soviet Socialist Republics and its dependencies, as well as in Yugoslavia, the old system virtually collapsed and was replaced by a version of Western-style oligopoly capitalism, while in China and Vietnam, capitalist institutions and markets were permitted to develop under Communist Party control. Major questions concerning these developments remain unanswered. Was violence largely avoided because bureaucratic elites were able to maintain political power or to transform themselves into business elites under the new system? Can the parties now in control of formerly communist regimes prevent the return of the gross inequalities and related social ills associated with capitalism? Do their activities in the world represent a new model of international behavior, or are they repeating the process of empire-building that has so often led to global warfare?

Even with these major issues awaiting exploration, the historical materials suggest that rapid and far-reaching socioeconomic changes *can* be made without unleashing state and revolutionary violence, at least under certain conditions, and that conflict specialists can play a role in facilitating processes of transformation. Taking Crane Brinton's classic study of violent revolutions, *The Anatomy of Revolution*, as a rough template, one can imagine an 'Anatomy of Nonviolent Transformation' that would involve the following four stages of development.

*Stage 1 – The old social system's functions and basic unfairness become evident, provoking multifarious and contradictory demands for change.*

Historians such as Brinton discuss the decline of the *ancien régime* at length, emphasizing the role played by the "transfer of allegiance of the intellectuals" in delegitimizing old authority systems.[45] Conflict specialists can play a role in this process by focusing attention on the systemic causes of social problems, the forms of structural violence, and the possibilities of helping to create less violent systems. Like the French encyclopedists, scholars in conflict studies and related fields can produce *publications, new course offerings, conferences,* and *practice projects* applying the 'structural turn' to specific issues of class analysis and class conflict. The audiences for such presentations can be students, community residents, journalists, or policymakers. In January 2016, for example, several scholar/activists at George Mason University's School for Conflict Analysis and Resolution organized a two-day conference at the United Nations headquarters in New York to discuss "Poverty, Inequality, and Global Conflict," and to consider what types of national and international policies might help to solve the problems of system-generated violence. A report of the conference was distributed to a group of opinion-makers who could help spread the word that poverty and inequality were systemic causes of violence that needed to be combated by new national and international policies, as well as new community-based programs.[46]

*Stage 2 – In a growing atmosphere of crisis, mass movements organize and demand that substantial changes, not yet carefully specified, be made in the old system. They support their demands by resorting to unusual political tactics.*

A further sign that the situation may be ripe for systemic change is the emergence of political movements both to the left and to the right of established elite-dominated parties. This indicates that people are moving toward accepting the need for some sort of social and political reconstruction, although they have not yet agreed on its content. As feelings of disenchantment with the existing socioeconomic order spread, people feel the need for public and private discussions of what has gone wrong with the system and what the possibilities are of changing it. Under these circumstances, conflict resolvers are well positioned to facilitate various forms of *public dialogue* that may be convened by community groups to help people air their discontents, identify key social structures requiring alteration, and envisage possible methods of altering them.[47] They can offer to inform political groups formally or informally of the results of relevant academic research, as well as undertaking *new research* needed to throw further light on systemic problems and possible solutions. Skilled facilitators can also offer to assist such groups to work through their internal differences and/or their differences with competing organizations by using the *problem-solving workshop* methods developed by practitioners like John Burton, Herbert Kelman, and Christopher Mitchell, the *sustained dialogue* approach pioneered by Harold Saunders, Johan Galtung's *Transcend and Transform* methods, and other relevant techniques for intergroup analysis and communication.[48]

*Stage 3 – As ferment spreads, social-constitutional discussions erupt on street corners, in churches, and in workplaces, while economic and social experiments take place in numerous communities.*

People mobilizing for change select new leaders at the local as well as national and international levels. Rather than await the outcome of some final struggle, however, they begin to imagine and implement local solutions to the problems that most concern them. Conflict specialists can play various useful roles in this process, including *advising the members of new organizations how to use tactics that are militant and nonviolent,* and how to employ conflict resolution techniques in dealing with their political adversaries. Moreover, they are well positioned to investigate, evaluate, and publicize the *community-based programs and experimental projects* that have already begun to appear in response to perceptions that the current socio-economic system is in crisis.

In contemplating further system change, people want to know 'what works.' What existing programs already help to get young people in poor neighborhoods off the streets, provide them with useful, well-paid work, and keep them out of the hands of violent gangs?[49] How have older people and others declared 'superfluous' by the market economy managed to provide services for each other in exchange for 'time-dollars': a program now operating in more than thirty U.S. cities?[50] What alternative forms of cooperative business and public service enterprise already permit workers and local residents in scores of communities to own their own companies and plan their own economic futures?[51] Some activists believe that the spread of these local initiatives and cooperative enterprises is the key to a nonviolent socioeconomic transformation.[52] Others fear that local movements will be co-opted or repressed as the struggle intensifies. Conflict specialists can make a valuable contribution to the discussion by studying and evaluating the evidence for these claims and working to develop programs that they believe are transformative.

*Stage 4 – Political conflict intensifies at local and national levels, with old elites dividing and political coalitions reorganizing to support competing visions of system change. Specific programs for structural transformation are presented to the public in elections, referenda, and other forms of public decision-making.*

As political conflict escalates and moves toward a possible resolution, conflict specialists could play very important, although virtually unprecedented, roles in facilitating agreement on a new social constitution. All the third-party techniques mentioned earlier can be employed to assist the parties to reach specific agreements on needed changes. Moreover, conflict resolvers skilled in improvising new public decision-making processes could help design political forums to permit open and thoughtful discussion of proposed structural changes.[53] They could also advise conflicting parties how to deal with two factors that often obstruct nonviolent agreement on new socioeconomic relations: elite groups' fear of total loss, and all parties' reluctance to consent to irrevocable changes. Conflict resolvers will understand the need to assure privileged groups that changes agreed upon will not render them non-people, expose them to vengeance, or ignore their basic human needs. They will also work to ensure that any new structural arrangement embodies the 'principle of reversibility.' In the same way that citizens can now work to amend a political constitution, the parties to class conflicts need to be assured that restructured socioeconomic systems can also be re-altered to reflect changes in the popular will.

Surely, one has to recognize that participatory processes aimed at altering existing social structures substantially, deliberately, and peacefully break new ground. There are not many ready-made, easily comprehended examples of how to accomplish this. But (as the remaining chapters of this study make clear) socioeconomic transformation is essential to the resolution of structural conflicts in general, including those featuring cultural and political clashes. The paucity of relevant contemporary cases also suggests the need for conflict specialists to pay more attention to a number of academic fields that received short shrift in the days of first wave (interest-based) and second wave (identity-based) conflict studies. Each wave drew on fields relevant to its main interests. Analysts and resolvers interested primarily in clashing interests drew on law, political science, game theory, international relations, and neoliberal economics, while those focusing on identities relied strongly on social psychology, cultural anthropology, psychoanalytic theory, and ethnosociology. Those making the structural turn in conflict studies will continue to consult and utilize these valuable sources, but they may well spend more time studying social history, narrative theory, radical economics, philosophy, ethics, and world literature than their predecessors did. Their need is not only to understand the social, psychological and epistemological roots of structural change but to imagine how new systems might be created and how they would operate – a task that novelists may be more apt to accomplish than social scientists.

What has given the field of conflict studies flexibility and relevance thus far has been its willingness to redefine its basic interests and tasks, consult newly relevant intellectual sources, and attract theorists and practitioners reflecting these new perspectives. One hopes that these values will help the field to remain vital and useful to many people in a period of increasing political danger.

## Notes

1 See, e.g., Derek Willis, "The Rise of 'Middle Class' as an Ordinary American Term." *New York Times* (May 14, 2015). http://www.nytimes.com/2015/05/15/upshot/the-rise-of-middle-class-as-a-mainstream-description.html?_r=0.

2 Frank Newport, "Fewer Americans Identify as Middle Class in Recent Years." *Gallup Poll* (April 28, 2015). http://www.gallup.com/poll/182918/fewer-americans-identify-middle-class-recent-years.aspx.

3 Peter Wallensteen, *Understanding Conflict Resolution*, 4th Edn. (Los Angeles and London: Sage Publications, 2015), 23.

4 Oliver Ramsbotham, et al., *Contemporary Conflict Resolution*, 4th Edn. (Cambridge, UK and Malden, MA: Polity Press, 2016), 3.

5 The training of labor lawyers, arbitrators, and mediators in the United States has become the province of the law schools and schools of public administration. See, e.g., Michael R. Carrell and Christina Heavrin, *Labor Relations and Collective Bargaining: Private and Public Sectors*, 10th Edn. (London and New York: Pearson, 2012).

6 I have described this bargain in "Analyzing and Resolving Class Conflict," in Dennis J.D. Sandole and Hugo van der Merwe, Eds. *Conflict Resolution Theory and Practice* (Manchester, UK: Manchester University Press, 1993), 146–157. See also William E. Leuchtenburg, *Franklin D. Roosevelt and the New Deal, 1932–1940* (New York: Harper Perennial, 2009).

7 See, e.g., Farrell Dobbs, *Teamster Rebellion*, 2nd Edn. (New York: Pathfinder, 2004); Philip A. Korth and Margaret Beegle, *I Remember Like Today: The [Toledo] Auto-Lite Strike of 1934* (Lansing, MI: Michigan State University Press, 1988); William F. Dunne, *The Great San Francisco General Strike: The Story of the West Coast Strike* (New York: Workers Library, 1934).

8 Unorganized and local workers – the majority of the work force – were not so lucky. The longest section of the U.S. National Labor Relations Act of 1935 was the exempted employee section.

9 See Jefferson Cowie, *The Great Exception: The New Deal and the Limits of American Politics* (Princeton, NJ: Princeton University Press, 2016).

10 See Jefferson Cowie and Joseph Heathcott, Eds., *Beyond the Ruins: The Meanings of Deindustrialization* (Ithaca, NY: ILR Press, 2003).

11 "For most workers," as a Pew Research Poll puts it, "wages have barely budged for decades." Drew Desilver, Pew Research Center (October 9, 2014), http://www.

pewresearch.org/fact-tank/2014/10/09/for-most-workers-real-wages-have-barely-budged-f. The same Foundation reported in 2015 that the share of two-parent households in which both parents worked full-time had risen to 46 percent, up from 31 percent in 1970. http://www.pewsocialtrends.org/2015/11/04/raising-kids-and-running-a-household-how-working-parent. See also Lawrence Mishel, "Causes of Wage Stagnation." Economic Policy Institute (January 17, 2015). http://www.epi.org/publication/causes-of-wage-stagnation/.

12 Drew Desilver, "American union membership declines as public support fluctuates." Pew Research Center (February 20, 2014). http://www.pewresearch.org/fact-tank/2014/02/20/for-american-unions-membership-trails-far-behind-public-support/.

13 It is widely thought that recent statistics showing an unprecedented decline in the life expectancy of less educated white American males related to high levels of alcoholism, drug abuse, and suicide is related to the despair generated by deindustrialization and economic decline. See, e.g., Olga Khazan, "Middle-Aged White Americans are Dying of Despair." *The Atlantic* (November 24, 2015). http://www.theatlantic.com/health/archive/2015/11/boomers-deaths-pnas/413971/.

14 On rising inequality, see Thomas Piketty and Arthur Goldhammer, *Capital in the Twenty-First Century* (Cambridge, MA: Belknap Press, 2014) and *The Economics of Inequality* (Cambridge, MA: Belknap Press, 2015). See also Chad Stone, et al., "A Guide to Statistics on Historical Trends in Income Inequality." Center for Budget and Policy Priorities (October 26, 2015). http://www.cbpp.org/research/poverty-and-inequality/a-guide-to-statistics-on-historical-trends-in-income-inequality. On poverty in the United States, see Peter Edelman, *So Rich, So Poor: Why It's So Hard to End Poverty in America* (New York: New Press, 2013); Sasha Abramsky, *The American Way of Poverty: How the Other Half Still Lives* (New York: Nation Books, 2014).

15 Marx's more than economistic approach to class becomes clear if one reads the selections from his work edited by Neil Smelser, in *Karl Marx on Society and Social Change: With Selections by Friedrich Engels* (Chicago: University of Chicago Press, 1975); Marx and Engels's *Economic and Philosophical Manuscripts of 1844 and the Communist Manifesto* (Amherst, NY: Prometheus Books, 1988); and Marx's *Grundrisse: Foundations of the Critique of Political Economy* (London and New York: Penguin, 1993).

16 Bertell Ollman, "Marx's Use of Class." *Dialectical Marxism: The Writings of Bertell Ollman* (2016), available at https://www.nyu.edu/projects/ollman/docs/class_content.php.

17 Karl Marx and Friedrich Engels, *The Communist Manifesto, op. cit.*; Karl Marx, *Wages, Price and Profit* (New York: CreateSpace, 2014).

18 A particularly compelling presentation of this theme is Barrington Moore's *magnum opus, Social Origins of Dictatorship and Democracy: Lord and Peasant in the Making of the Modern World* (Boston: Beacon Press, 1967).

19 See Karl Marx, *Capital, Volume 1: A Critique of Political Economy* (New York: Dover Press, 2011). For a clear oral exposition and commentary, see "Reading

Marx's Capital with David Harvey" (2010), http://davidharvey.org/reading-capital/, published as *A Companion to Reading Capital* (London, Verso, 2010).

20  This contradiction is discussed at length by Engels in his *Socialism: Utopian and Scientific, III, Historical Materialism*, available online at https://www.marxists.org/archive/marx/works/1880/soc-utop/ch03.htm.

21  Capitalism's implicit ethic of predatory exploitation has proved a matter of major concern for Pope Francis and the Roman Catholic Church. See John Cassidy, "Pope Francis's Challenge to Global Capitalism." *The New Yorker* (December 3, 2013). http://www.newyorker.com/news/john-cassidy/pope-franciss-challenge-to-global-capitalism.

22  Frederick Engels, *Anti-Dühring: Herr Eugen Dühring's Revolution in Science* (New York: CreateSpace, 2015), 407 *et seq.*

23  See http://www.visionofhumanity.org/#/page/indexes/global-peace-index.

24  See the comprehensive and judicious summary of research in "The Causes of Crime," David F. Greenberg's Introduction to *Crime and Capitalism: Readings in Marxist Criminology* (Philadelphia, PA: Temple University Press, 1993), 58–99. For updated research, see Elliott Currie, *Crime and Punishment in America*, Rev. Edn. (London and New York: Picador, 2013), 106–142.

25  "The Challenge of Crime in a Free Society," Report of the President's Commission on Law Enforcement and the Administration of Justice (Washington, DC: U.S. Government Printing Office, 1967), 6. https://www.ncjrs.gov/pdffiles1/nij/42.pdf. The same conclusion is reached with more elaboration by James S. Campbell, et al., of the Task Force on Law and Law Enforcement of the National Commission on the Causes and Prevention of Violence in their report entitled, "Law and Order Reconsidered" (1970), 44 *et seq.* https://archive.org/stream/laworderreconsid00camprich/laworderreconsid00camprich_djvu.txt. See also Ramsey Clark, *Crime in America*.

26  Pablo Fajnzylber, et al., "What causes violent crime?" *European Economic Review* 46 (2002), 1323–1357 at 1349. Cf. Elliott Currie, *op. cit.*, at 120: "Countries where there is a wide gap between rich and poor routinely show higher levels of violent crime . . . Societies with weak 'safety nets' for the poor and economically insecure are more likely than others at a comparable level of development to be wracked by violence."

27  Ravi Kanbur, "Poverty and Conflict: The Inequality Link." *Coping With Crisis Working Paper Series* (New York: International Peace Academy, 2007), 3. See also Henk-Jan Brinkman, et al., "Addressing Horizontal Inequalities as Drivers of Conflict in the Post-2015 Development Agenda" (New York: UN Peacebuilding Support Office, February 2013).

28  See, e.g., Sanford F. Schram, *The Return of Ordinary Capitalism: Neoliberalism, Precarity, Occupy* (Oxford: Oxford University Press, 2015).

29  David L. Carter, *The Police and the Community*, 7th Edn. (London and New York: Pearson, 2001); Vinita Pandey, "Community Policing for Conflict Resolution and Community Resilience." *International Journal of Social Work and Human Services Practice*, 2:6 (December 2014), 228–233, http://www.hrpub.org/down-

load/20141201/IJRH4-19290153.pdf; Megan Clare Price, "The Processes and Partnerships Behind Insight Policing." *Criminal Justice Policy Review* (2015), 1–15.

30 Elliott Currie, *op. cit.*, 223.

31 See, e.g., Michelle Alexander, *The New Jim Crow: Mass Incarceration in the Age of Colorblindness, op. cit.*; Shaun L. Gabbidon and Helen Taylor Greene, *Race and Crime*, 4th Edn. (New York: Sage, 2015); UK Ministry of Justice, *Statistics on Race and the Criminal Justice System, 2014* (26 November 2015), https://www. gov.uk/government/uploads/system/uploads/attachment_data/file/480250/ bulletin.pdf.

32 A commonly cited example is the law punishing the sale and possession of crack cocaine more severely than the sale and possession of powdered cocaine. But there is also a vast differential in the enforcement of laws against street crime and "white-collar" crime. See D.O. Friedrichs, *Trusted Criminals: White-Collar Crime in Contemporary Society*, 4th Edn. (Boston: Wadsworth, 2009). See also the well-researched senior honors thesis by Joseph P. Martinez, "Unpunished Criminals: The Social Acceptability of White Collar Crimes in America" (Ypsilanti, MI: Eastern Michigan University, 2014), http://commons.emich.edu/cgi/view-content.cgi?article=1381&context=honors.

33 Elliott Currie, *op. cit.*, 122, 126.

34 See Chapter 2, *supra*, at 36.

35 This connection seems to be implicit in analyses of the 1960s' racial uprisings, such as Robert E. Conot, *Rivers of Blood, Years of Darkness* (New York: Bantam Books, 1967); Stokeley Carmichael and Charles V. Hamilton, *Black Power: The Politics of Liberation* (New York: Vintage Books, 1967); and *Report of the National Advisory Committee on Civil Disorders* (Kerner Report) (New York: Bantam Books, 1968). See also Richard E. Rubenstein, *Rebels in Eden: Mass Political Violence in the United States* (Boston: Little Brown, 1970).

36 Probably the most thoughtful of these explanations, at least for the United States, is Seymour Martin Lipset and Gary Marks, *It Didn't Happen Here: Why Socialism Failed in the United States* (New York: W.W. Norton, 2000). But see also, Gar Alperovitz, "Inequality's Dead End – And the Possibility of a New Long-Term Direction." *Nonprofit Quarterly* (March 10, 2015). https://nonprofitquar-terly.org/2015/03/10/inequality-s-dead-end-and-the-possibility-of-a-new-long-term-direction/; Shannon Jones, "It didn't happen here: Why socialism failed in the United States – The failure of reformism, not socialism." *World Socialist Website* (6 March 2002). https://www.wsws.org/en/articles/2002/03/ book-m06.html.

37 The classic study of the impact of these messages on industrial workers in the United States is Richard Sennett and Jonathan Cobb, *The Hidden Injuries of Class* (New York: W.W. Norton, 1993). See also Nancy Isenberg, *White Trash: The 400-Year Untold History of Class in America* (New York: Viking, 2016).

38 H.H. Gerth and C. Wright Mills, Eds., *From Max Weber: Essays in Sociology* (Oxford: Oxford University Press, 1958), 180–195. The essay "Class, Status

and Party" is also available online at http://sites.middlebury.edu/individual-andthesociety/files/2010/09/Weber-Class-Status-Party.pdf. See also Erik Olin Wright, "The Shadow of Exploitation in Weber's Class Analysis" (2002), http://www.ssc.wisc.edu/~wright/Weber-revised.pdf.

39 Herbert Marcuse, *One-Dimensional Man, op. cit.* at 120: "The so-called consumer society and the politics of corporate capitalism have created a second nature of man which ties him libidinally and aggressively to the commodity form."

40 This seems to me an underlying implication of Dennis J.D. Sandole's fine study of violent postwar ethnic conflict, *Capturing the Complexity of Conflict* (London and New York: Routledge, 1999).

41 See Slavoj Zizek, *Less Than Nothing: Hegel and the Shadow of Dialectical Materialism* (London: Verso, 2013).

42 See my discussion of the "reforming from within" issue in "State Security, Human Security, and the Problem of Complementarity," in Edwin Daniel Jacob, Ed., *Rethinking Security in the Twenty-First Century* (Palgrave Macmillan, 2016).

43 Barrington Moore discussed "the price of peaceful change" in India in *Social Origins of Dictatorship and Democracy: Lord and Peasant in the Modern World, op. cit.* See also Alex Callinicos, "South Africa after Apartheid." *Socialist Review* 2:70 (March 1996). http://pubs.socialistreviewindex.org.uk/isj70/safrica.htm. Of course, the forty-year struggle against apartheid involved periods of armed struggle, state repression, extra-judicial killings, and mass uprisings in the townships. See Sheridan Johns and R. Hunt Davis, Eds., *Mandela, Tambo, and the African National Congress: The Struggle Against Apartheid, 1948–1990* (Oxford: Oxford University Press, 1991).

44 See, e.g., Barton J. Bernstein, *Towards a New Past: Dissenting Essays in American History* (New York: Pantheon, 1968).

45 Crane Brinton, *The Anatomy of Revolution* (New York: Random House, 1965), 39 *et seq.*

46 The Conference on Poverty, Inequality, and Global Conflict (January 11–12, 2016) was cosponsored by George Mason University, the UN Academic Impact, and the Chicago-based People Program International. The Conference Report is available from the School for Conflict Analysis and Resolution at scar.gmu.edu.

47 See, for example, the descriptions of "public dialogue," "policy dialogue," and "public conversations" at *Beyond Intractability* (Peter S. Adler and Kristi Parker Celico, "Policy Dialogue," December 2003). http://www.beyondintractability.org/essay/policy-dialogue. See also Public Conversations Project website, http://www.publicconversations.org/.

48 See Chapter 2, *supra*, at 46–47.

49 Unfortunately, most programs designed to combat or prevent gang violence define the gang problem in noneconomic terms and do not contain plans for economic reconstruction of poor communities. Some, however, have produced good results, however temporary, in lowering rates of violence. See James C. Howell, "Gang Prevention: An Overview of Research and Programs." *OJJDP*

*Juvenile Justice Bulletin* (Washington, D.C.: U.S. Department of Justice, Office of Juvenile Justice and Delinquency Prevention, December 2010). https://www. ncjrs.gov/pdffiles1/ojjdp/231116.pdf.

50 Edgar S. Cahn, *No More Throw-Away People: The Co-Production Imperative*, 2nd Edn. (London: Essential Books, Ltd., 2004).

51 Gar Alperovitz, *What Then Must We Do? Straight Talk About the Next American Revolution* (White River Junction, VT: Chelsea Green Publishers, 2013).

52 The project is described at http://democracycollaborative.org/content/next-system-project and thenextsystem.org.

53 Lawrence E. Susskind and Sarah McKearnan, 'The Evolution of Public Policy Dispute Resolution." *Journal of Architectural and Planning Research*, 16:2 (Summer 1999), 96–115. Peter Wallensteen, *Understanding Conflict Resolution*, 4th Edn. (Los Angeles and London: Sage Publications, 2015), 23. Oliver Ramsbotham, et al., *Contemporary Conflict Resolution*, 4th Edn. (Cambridge, UK and Malden, MA: Polity Press, 2016), 3.

## Bibliography

Abramsky, Sasha, *The American Way of Poverty: How the Other Half Still Lives* (New York: Nation Books, 2014).

Adler, Peter S. and Kristi Parker Celico, "Policy Dialogue." *Beyond Intractability* (December 2003). http://www.beyondintractability.org/essay/policy-dialogue.

Alexander, Michelle, *The New Jim Crow: Mass Incarceration in the Age of Colorblindness* (New York: The New Press, 2012).

Alperovitz, Gar, *What Then Must We Do? Straight Talk About the Next American Revolution* (White River Junction, VT: Chelsea Green Publishers, 2013).

——"Inequality's Dead End – And the Possibility of a New Long-Term Direction." *Nonprofit Quarterly* (March 10, 2015). https://nonprofitquarterly. org/2015/03/10/inequality-s-dead-end-and-the-possibility-of-a-new-long-term-direction/.

Bernstein, Barton J., *Towards a New Past: Dissenting Essays in American History* (New York: Pantheon, 1968).

Brinkman, Henk-Jan, et al., "Addressing Horizontal Inequalities as Drivers of Conflict in the Post-2015 Development Agenda" (New York: UN Peacebuilding Support Office, February 2013).

Brinton, Crane, *The Anatomy of Revolution* (New York: Random House, 1965).

Cahn, Edgar S., *No More Throw-Away People: The Co-Production Imperative*, 2nd Edn. (London: Essential Books, Ltd., 2004).

Callinicos, Alex, "South Africa After Apartheid." *Socialist Review*, 2:70 (March 1996). http://pubs.socialistreviewindex.org.uk/isj70/safrica.htm.

Campbell, James S., et al., "Law and Order Reconsidered" (Washington, DC: Task Force on Law and Law Enforcement of the National Commission on the Causes and Prevention of Violence, 1970). https://archive.org/stream/laworderreconsid00camprich/laworderreconsid00camprich_djvu.txt.

Carmichael, Stokeley and Charles V. Hamilton, *Black Power: The Politics of Liberation* (New York: Vintage Books, 1967).

Carrell, Michael R. and Christina Heavrin, *Labor Relations and Collective Bargaining: Private and Public Sectors*, 10th Edn. (London and New York: Pearson, 2012).

Carter, David L., *The Police and the Community*, 7th Edn. (London and New York: Pearson, 2001).

Cassidy, John, "Pope Francis's Challenge to Global Capitalism." *The New Yorker* (December 3, 2013). http://www.newyorker.com/news/john-cassidy/pope-franciss-challenge-to-global-capitalism.

Clark, Ramsey, *Crime in America: Observations on Its Nature, Causes, Prevention and Control* (New York: Simon & Schuster, 1970).

Conot, Robert E., *Rivers of Blood, Years of Darkness* (New York: Bantam Books, 1967).

Cowie, Jefferson, *The Great Exception: The New Deal and the Limits of American Politics* (Princeton, NJ: Princeton University Press, 2016).

——and Joseph Heathcott, Eds., *Beyond the Ruins: The Meanings of Deindustrialization* (Ithaca, NY: ILR Press, 2003).

Currie, Elliott, *Crime and Punishment in America*, Rev. Edn. (London and New York: Picador, 2013).

Desilver, Drew, "American union membership declines as public support fluctuates." Pew Research Center (February 20, 2014). http://www.pewresearch.org/fact-tank/2014/02/20/for-american-unions-membership-trails-far-behind-public-support/.

Dobbs, Farrell, *Teamster Rebellion*, 2nd Edn. (New York: Pathfinder, 2004).

Dukes, E. Franklin, *Resolving Public Conflict: Transforming Community and Governance* (New York: St. Martin's Press, 1996)

Dunne, William F., *The Great San Francisco General Strike: The Story of the West Coast Strike* (New York: Workers Library, 1934).

Edelman, Peter, *So Rich, So Poor: Why It's So Hard to End Poverty in America* (New York: New Press, 2013).

Engels, Friedrich, *Socialism: Utopian and Scientific, III, Historical Materialism*, https://www.marxists.org/archive/marx/works/1880/soc-utop/ch03.htm.

——*Anti-Dühring: Herr Eugen Dühring's Revolution in Science* (New York: CreateSpace, 2015), 407 *et seq.*

Fajnzylber, Pablo et al., "What causes violent crime?" *European Economic Review* 46 (2002), 1323–1357.

Friedrichs, D.O., *Trusted Criminals: White-Collar Crime in Contemporary Society*, 4th Edn. (Boston: Wadsworth, 2009).

Gabbidon, Shaun L. and Helen Taylor Greene, *Race and Crime*, 4th Edn. (New York: Sage, 2015).

Gerth, H.H. and C. Wright Mills, Eds., *From Max Weber: Essays in Sociology* (Oxford: Oxford University Press, 1958).

Greenberg, David F., *Crime and Capitalism: Readings in Marxist Criminology* (Philadelphia, PA: Temple University Press, 1993).

Harvey, David, "Reading Marx's Capital with David Harvey" (2010). http://davidharvey.org/reading-capital/, published as *A Companion to Reading Capital* (London: Verso, 2010).

Howell, James C., "Gang Prevention: An Overview of Research and Programs." *OJJDP Juvenile Justice Bulletin* (Washington, D.C.: U.S. Department of Justice, Office of Juvenile Justice and Delinquency Prevention, December 2010). https://www.ncjrs.gov/pdffiles1/ojjdp/231116.pdf.

Isenberg, Nancy, *White Trash: The 400-Year Untold History of Class in America* (New York: Viking, 2016).

Johns, Sheridan and R. Hunt Davis, Eds., *Mandela, Tambo, and the African National Congress: The Struggle Against Apartheid, 1948–1990* (Oxford: Oxford University Press, 1991).

Jones, Shannon, "It didn't happen here: Why socialism failed in the United States – The failure of reformism, not socialism." *World Socialist Website* (6 March 2002). https://www.wsws.org/en/articles/2002/03/book-m06.html.

Kanbur, Ravi, "Poverty and Conflict: The Inequality Link." *Coping With Crisis Working Paper Series* (New York: International Peace Academy, 2007).

Khazan, Olga, "Middle-Aged White Americans are Dying of Despair." *The Atlantic* (November 24, 2015). http://www.theatlantic.com/health/archive/2015/11/boomers-deaths-pnas/413971/.

Korth, Philip A. and Margaret Beegle, *I Remember Like Today: The [Toledo] Auto-Lite Strike of 1934* (Lansing, MI: Michigan State University Press, 1988).

Leuchtenburg, William E., *Franklin D. Roosevelt and the New Deal, 1932–1940* (New York: Harper Perennial, 2009).

Lipset, Seymour Martin and Gary Marks, *It Didn't Happen Here: Why Socialism Failed in the United States* (New York: W.W. Norton, 2000).

Martinez, Joseph P., "Unpunished Criminals: The Social Acceptability of White Collar Crimes in America" (Ypsilanti, MI: Eastern Michigan University, 2014). http://commons.emich.edu/cgi/viewcontent.cgi?article=1381&context=honors.

Marx, Karl, *Grundrisse: Foundations of the Critique of Political Economy* (London and New York: Penguin, 1993).

——*Capital, Volume 1: A Critique of Political Economy* (New York: Dover Press, 2011).

——*Wages, Price and Profit* (New York: CreateSpace, 2014).

Marx, Karl and Friedrich Engels, *Economic and Philosophical Manuscripts of 1844 and the Communist Manifesto* (Amherst, NY: Prometheus Books, 1988).

Mishel, Lawrence, "Causes of Wage Stagnation." Economic Policy Institute (January 17, 2015). http://www.epi.org/publication/causes-of-wage-stagnation/.

Moore, Barrington, *Social Origins of Dictatorship and Democracy: Lord and Peasant in the Making of the Modern World* (Boston: Beacon Press, 1967).

Newport, Frank, "Fewer Americans Identify as Middle Class in Recent Years." *Gallup Poll* (April 28, 2015). http://www.gallup.com/poll/182918/fewer-americans-identify-middle-class-recent-years.aspx.

Ollman, Bertell, "Marx's Use of Class." *Dialectical Marxism: The Writings of Bertell Ollman* (2016). https://www.nyu.edu/projects/ollman/docs/class_content.php.

Pandey, Vinita, "Community Policing for Conflict Resolution and Community Resilience." *International Journal of Social Work and Human Services Practice*, 2:6 (December 2014) 228–233). http://www.hrpub.org/download/20141201/IJRH4-19290153.pdf.

Piketty, Thomas and Arthur Goldhammer, *Capital in the Twenty-First Century* (Cambridge, MA: Belknap Press, 2014).

——*The Economics of Inequality* (Cambridge, MA: Belknap Press, 2015).

President's Commission on Law Enforcement and the Administration of Justice, "The Challenge of Crime in a Free Society," Report of the President's Commission on Law Enforcement and the Administration of Justice (Washington, DC: U.S. Government Printing Office, 1967), 6. https://www.ncjrs.gov/pdffiles1/nij/42.pdf.

Price, Megan Clare, "The Processes and Partnerships Behind Insight Policing." *Criminal Justice Policy Review* (2015), 1–15.

Ramsbotham, Oliver, et al., *Contemporary Conflict Resolution*, 4th Edn. (Cambridge, UK and Malden, MA: Polity Press, 2016).

*Report of the National Advisory Committee on Civil Disorders* (Kerner Report) (New York: Bantam Books, 1968).

Rubenstein, Richard E., *Rebels in Eden: Mass Political Violence in the United States* (Boston: Little Brown, 1970).

——"Analyzing and Resolving Class Conflict," in Dennis J.D. Sandole and Hugo van der Merwe, Eds. *Conflict Resolution Theory and Practice* (Manchester, UK: Manchester University Press, 1993), 146–157.

——"State Security, Human Security, and the Problem of Complementarity," in Edwin Daniel Jacob, Ed., *Rethinking Security in the Twenty-First Century* (Palgrave Macmillan, 2016).

Sandole, Dennis J.D., *Capturing the Complexity of Conflict* (London and New York: Routledge, 1999).

Schram, Sanford F., *The Return of Ordinary Capitalism: Neoliberalism, Precarity, Occupy* (Oxford: Oxford University Press, 2015).

Sennett, Richard and Jonathan Cobb, *The Hidden Injuries of Class* (New York: W.W. Norton, 1993).

Smelser, Neil J., Ed., *Karl Marx on Society and Social Change: With Selections by Friedrich Engels* (Chicago: University of Chicago Press, 1975).

Stone, Chad, et al., "A Guide to Statistics on Historical Trends in Income Inequality." Center for Budget and Policy Priorities (October 26, 2015). http://www.cbpp.org/research/poverty-and-inequality/a-guide-to-statistics-on-historical-trends-in-income-inequality.

Susskind, Lawrence E. and Sarah McKearnan, 'The Evolution of Public Policy Dispute Resolution." *Journal of Architectural and Planning Research*, 16:2 (Summer, 1999), 96–115.

Ture, Kwame and Charles V. Hamilton, *Black Power: The Politics of Liberation* (New York: Vintage Books, 1967)

U.K. Ministry of Justice, *Statistics on Race and the Criminal Justice System, 2014* (26 November 2015). https://www.gov.uk/government/uploads/system/uploads/attachment_data/file/480250/bulletin.pdf.

Wallensteen, Peter, *Understanding Conflict Resolution*, 4th Edn. (Los Angeles and London: Sage Publications, 2015).

Willis, Derek, "The Rise of 'Middle Class' as an Ordinary American Term." *New York Times* (May 14, 2015). http://www.nytimes.com/2015/05/15/upshot/the-rise-of-middle-class-as-a-mainstream-description.html?_r=0.

Wright, Erik Olin, "The Shadow of Exploitation in Weber's Class Analysis" (2002). http://www.ssc.wisc.edu/~wright/Weber-revised.pdf.

Zizek, Slavoj, *Less Than Nothing: Hegel and the Shadow of Dialectical Materialism* (London: Verso, 2013).

# 5

# CULTURAL CONFLICT AND THE PROBLEM OF RELIGIOUS VIOLENCE

## The mysterious renaissance of religious violence

One of the most shocking and disconcerting features of many recent social conflicts is the extent to which they involve clashes of passionately held religious beliefs and cultural values. Frequently, one hears even knowledgeable observers declare that, while many sorts of violent struggles are difficult to resolve, religious or cultural conflicts are virtually impossible to settle peacefully. Why? Because of the parties' fanaticism, their dogmatic conviction that only they possess the Truth, their 'all or nothing' absolutism, and their conviction that theirs is a holy cause, or, as the analyst Mark Juergensmeyer puts it, that they are fighting a "cosmic war" under God's command.[1] One can answer, quite correctly, that secularist movements have been far more violent than any religiously motivated campaign, but there is clearly something especially terrifying – especially to the inhabitants of wealthy nations who are used to employing impersonal, hi-tech weapons of war – about facing a God-intoxicated warrior seeking martyrdom. Moreover, it is not just their violence that makes religious or cultural-nationalist movements seem resistant to conflict resolution, but their apparent unwillingness to engage in reasonable discussion and to make compromises. *"Gott mit uns!"* (God is on our side) is not an invitation to bargain.

Adding to the difficulty of understanding the new forms of struggle which have now produced an apparently endless war on terror by nations feeling themselves under attack is what one might call historical shock. Of course, beliefs were known to be important factors in violent conflict. Two world wars and the Cold War had underlined the importance of ideological motivations for fighting, and several decades of ethnic conflict had demonstrated that people would risk and take lives to defend cultural identities they believed to be threatened. Even so, what James Davison Hunter called the "culture wars" and what Samuel P. Huntington termed the "clash of civilizations" represented something new – or, perhaps, the revival of something unaccountably old – in world political culture.[2] Neither academic analysts nor policymakers predicted that, in the late 1970s, Iran would experience the first religiously motivated revolution since the English Revolution of the seventeenth century. Nor did they foresee a great outburst of sectarian strife in the Islamic world, the rise of Hindu nationalism in India, the emergence of militant religious movements among Palestinians and Israelis, the spread of violent jihadism from the Middle East to Africa and Asia, or the emergence of evangelical Christianity as a significant factor in political conflicts in the Americas.

An important feature of many of these events still not well explained is the transformation of some secular social struggles into religious conflicts – what one might call the *sacralization* of conflict.[3] In a number of conflict zones, ranging from Algeria and Syria to Sri Lanka and Kashmir, where ethnic or national conflicts were initially organized and fought out by secular leaders wielding secular ideologies, a rapid shift occurred at a certain point toward religious leadership, ideology, and mobilization. Four situations seem to generate this sort of development. First, the conflict becomes protracted, so that no quick victory or defeat is possible. Second, the secular leadership is discredited by lack of military success, political corruption, and inability to maintain morale. Third, military or political reverses compel the group losing ground to choose between surrender, a disadvantageous or shameful compromise, and 'keeping the faith.' Finally, religious allies elsewhere produce much-needed financial, logistical, and moral support for the struggle. The apparent salience of these conditions directs one's attention to locales like France and England, where youths of immigrant background have rioted with little reference to religious leaders or doctrines. There is a danger in such cases that *if* the issues generating discontent are not identified and dealt with, the conflict can become protracted – a prelude to asymmetrical struggle and possible sacralization.

This brings us to the crucial question of how to understand these new (or old/new) forms of cultural conflict. What drives them? What are their structural aspects? How can they be resolved? Recall, to begin with, that structural conflicts are not *either* socioeconomic *or* cultural *or* political but involve all these dimensions (and perhaps one or two more, as we shall see) simultaneously. Recall, too, that interests do not cease to exist because identity needs are involved nor identity issues vanish because the conflict is structural. Interests and needs are defined and their relationships are organized by sociocultural systems. The key to resolving complex violent conflicts, I have been arguing, is to understand how these systems can be identified, how they work, and how they might be changed. Nonetheless, confronted by current cultural conflicts like the struggle between the Islamic State, say, and its Muslim and non-Muslim enemies, many analysts are tempted to ignore structural issues and to treat the struggle either as a disguised clash of interests or an identity-based conflict writ large: a "clash of civilizations." Neither of these approaches, I am sorry to say, does much to advance our understanding of the problem or to suggest a feasible solution.

One reason that the reappearance of religiously motivated conflict on the world stage came as such a surprise to most academic analysts was the prior commitment of many of them to modernization theory – an updated version of Max Weber's social theory that included secularization as part of the inexorable movement of societies from a traditional to a modern state.[4] As capitalist development, scientific thinking, bureaucratization, and other aspects of modernization proceeded, the world was expected to follow the lead of the West, which had responded to its own era of religious wars (roughly 1520–1690 CE) by depoliticizing religion, secularizing the state, developing a culture of religious tolerance and pluralism, and lowering the general level of religious zeal to the point religiously motivated violence became a rarity. The causal nexus between almost two centuries of savage Catholic-Protestant warfare and the subsequent era of de-Christianization and 'state-building' in Europe seems quite clear, although many Westerners repressed the memory of their own communal bloodletting while continuing to marginalize the members of non-Christian faiths.[5] The result of this selective memory is to make the regime of relative tolerance seem a timeless, essential feature of the Western character, as opposed to the alleged fanaticism and intolerance of Muslim, Hindu, Eastern Orthodox, and Chinese civilizations.

What remains of the assumption that all systems will tend, over time, to converge on some variant of Western-style social order? One optimistic view sees religious zealotry and violence as an atavistic protest against modernization that is bound to disappear as capitalist enterprise, scientific inquiry, and modern methods of governance become instilled worldwide. Analysts like Francis Fukuyama remain wedded to the notion that human history is, at bottom, the history of Reason, which flowered definitively in the European Enlightenment but continues to put out shoots everywhere. In this view, it is only a matter of time until religious fundamentalists of various stripes recognize that you can't turn back the clock, and that, in any case, the recognition they desire can be obtained under a modern liberal capitalist system.[6] A more sober variation on the same theme (recalling the first wave of conflict studies praxis) sees religious rebellions as disguised and distorted expressions of immediate economic and political interests. The implication is that if these interests are recognized and dealt with, religious and cultural commitments will lose their power to incite violence, as they did in the West.

The British-Tunisian analyst Soumaya Ghannoushi summarizes this viewpoint nicely:

> Rather than scripture and theology, it is in politics and economics, in power balances, foreign interventions, and the scramble for influence and resources that the causes of its ills reside. Religious faith, sect and ethnic affiliations are spontaneously recalled, or willfully exploited within the conflicts raging around the Muslim world, but are in reality neither their primary cause nor the sole key to their resolution.[7]

One wants to agree with this, because it brings conflict resolution into sight, and because it is clear that religiously motivated conflicts are not only about religion – that, in fact, their virulence arises from the use of religious identity as a kind of magnifying glass that focuses and multiplies energies generated by other conflicts. The leaders of the Islamic State movement, for example, clearly have interests in administering a state, controlling oil and gas supplies, supplying their followers with jobs, and playing a powerful role in regional and global politics. But does this mean that ISIS's religious commitments and cultural values are a mere mask for economic and geopolitical interests? Can conflicts to which they are a party be settled by interest-based bargaining? Answering this question requires some thought; we will return to it after briefly examining the more pessimistic position embraced by analysts like Samuel P. Huntington.

To Huntington and his followers, religiously motivated conflicts are neither transient expressions of antimodernist nostalgia nor ideological disguises for other interests, but symptoms of an intractable and frequently violent clash of large, culturally defined identity groups or civilizations.[8] Advocates of this view see Enlightenment values as inextricably linked to Western culture and predict a long period of violent conflict between the West and other civilizations defining themselves in terms of idiosyncratic religious and cultural commitments. The civilization, says Huntington, has replaced the interest group and the social class as the primary unit of global conflict. It has also replaced the ethnic group, although it is, in effect, an ethnic group writ large reminiscent of the 'pan' movements (pan-Germanism, pan-Slavism, pan-Arabism, etc.) of the late nineteenth and early twentieth centuries.[9] Like Thomas Hobbes's *homo lupus*, each civilization is an enemy to every other civilization, with the master conflict being that which pits "the West against the Rest." Huntingtonians expect such culture clashes to continue even after each civilization modernizes (witness the Chinese road to modernity).[10] The lesson that they do not hesitate to draw: negotiate alliances where you can, but keep your powder dry!

This theory has two major virtues. It correctly predicts the rising importance of religious beliefs and cultural value commitments in world politics, and it does not dismiss these commitments as mere window-dressing or epiphenomena.[11] It makes some sense to consider groups like the Islamic State, for whom the 'near enemy' has always been more important than the 'far enemy,' contenders for the title of chief civilizational representative. Where Huntington's approach goes wrong, in my view, is in creating a mirror image of the modernization school's error by converting other identities and interests, such as those associated with interest groups, local ethnic groups, and social classes, into epiphenomena. It does this, I believe, because of failure to adopt a systemic perspective that would show how culture and class, religious values and other group interests are interrelated in the context of overarching internal (epistemic) and external (power-based) structures. The same sort of one-dimensionality deprives the modernization viewpoint of critical depth and practical usefulness. To attempt to negotiate with leaders of the Islamic State, say, about territory, oil, or employment opportunities without taking into account the structural aspects of their struggle and the role of religious culture in that structure would be an exercise in futility.

Please understand that I am *not* assuming, as Huntington seems to do, that conflicts involving religious beliefs and cultural values are irresolvable except through the use of force or threats of military action. As a matter of fact, the advocates of interest-based bargaining also rely in the last analysis on threats of force ('bargaining from strength') as an indispensable component of conflict resolution. What both schools fail to grasp is that violent conflicts can be sustainably resolved only when the disputants' basic needs are satisfied – a result seldom achieved through power-based bargaining. Why seldom? Because power/knowledge, to use Foucault's terminology, is part of the problem. Power is not prediscursive but is defined by and exercised through a structured system – the same system that denies the bottom dogs fulfillment of their basic needs and vital interests. Without identifying that system and considering how it might be altered, neither a modernizing, interest-based perspective nor a "clash of civilizations," culture-based approach can explain the resurgence of religious violence or guide the construction of new conflict-resolving processes.

Four decades of social strife involving religious organizations and beliefs constitute neither a hiccup in the modernization process nor an expression of some insoluble civilizational clash. As Kevin Avruch has pointed out, what generates violence in such situations is not each side's preexisting cultural repertoire alone, but an *interaction* between culture and context, systems of belief and systems of power and status.[12] To account for the style and content of such imagining therefore requires more than a catalogue of popular narratives, beliefs, images, and other cultural praxes. In my view, it requires an understanding of the interaction between a people's deep culture and the social transformations generated by an aggressively globalizing world system. Because such conflicts are rooted in this interaction, not just in inherited cultural norms, there is cause to hope, *pace* Huntington and other cultural determinists, that they may one day be resolved. But the assumption that modernization under Western auspices is the cure seems to me equally untenable. It is only by restructuring systemic relationships between "the West and the Rest" that the current plague of religious violence can be brought under control.

## Neo-imperialism and its discontents

The theory that religiously motivated violence is a response to modernization does contain a nugget of truth. The systemic transformation that some Western scholars call modernization goes by other names as well – for example, globalization, development, and nation-building – but is widely known by those subject to its power and temptations as neo-colonialism or neo-imperialism. It may be helpful to distinguish between neo-imperialism and globalization. Globalization is a multifaceted, self-engendering process involving the rapid multiplication and proliferation of transnational contacts and relationships of all sorts. Globalization is taking place when we study each other's languages and learn each other's songs. Neo-imperialism is globalization promoted, shaped, and ultimately limited by elites exporting and expanding their own business infrastructure and commercial values, methods of research and communication, and basic principles of government, education, family life, and consumer culture. What is sent abroad, of course, is an 'export version' of the imperialists' home system – a technique first developed by the Romans in order to diffuse the fundamentals of Roman law throughout their empire.[13] Even so, it is a *total* system that is exported, including socioeconomic, political, and cultural structures.

This neo-imperial system, I contend, provides the structural context needed to help us to understand the plague of religious violence and related warfare that has beset the world since the 1980s. The nature of this system, of course, is a contested issue. It is — and should be — a hot topic among conflict specialists in particular. After a long period of relative silence, the study of empire, fueled by the perception that the United States has succeeded to the role once played by the old imperial powers, is again acceptable in some academic and journalistic circles. An early study of the conflict between Muslim jihadists and pro-Western forces called the neo-imperial system "McWorld": Benjamin Barber's way of describing the rapid and pervasive spread of American economic, military, political, and cultural influence around the globe after 1945, culminating in America's emergence as the world's sole military superpower following the Cold War.[14] This vast expansion of influence has been perceived by many groups abroad, particularly in volatile, resource-rich regions subject to foreign economic and military intervention, as an 'invasion' that undermines local and regional autonomy, divides and conquers subject peoples, generates massive political corruption, disrupts long-established patterns of social interaction, and exposes local communities to a barrage of imports that challenge traditional religious values and threaten people's core identities.

Invasion, of course, is far more than a metaphor. The modern era of religious politicization and extremism may have begun with the Iranian Revolution and accelerated with U.S. aid to jihadi forces rebelling against the Soviet occupation of Afghanistan, but it did not involve attacks against the West until the first President Bush sent an army to Saudi Arabia and invaded Kuwait in 1991. The stated purpose of the invasion was to expel Iraqi president Saddam Hussein's troops from Kuwait, but Bush's war was also intended to inaugurate a new era of U.S. neo-imperial activism by overcoming the so-called 'Vietnam syndrome' and eliminating Saddam's Iraq as a major player in Middle Eastern affairs.[15] The first communiqué issued by al-Qaeda leader Osama bin Laden called for the United States to remove its troops from Saudi Arabia's sacred soil, terminate military operations and deadly civil sanctions against Iraq, and end its one-sided support to Israel.[16] Little more than a decade later, lured by the promise of oil wealth, regional 'democratization,' and the establishment of U.S. control over the region, the second President Bush invaded Iraq proper. Saddam Hussein was deposed and killed, and the region was plunged into sectarian chaos. From the recipients' perspective, it seemed clear that, stylistic differences aside, the Americans' neo-imperial 'mission' differed hardly at all from that of the Western imperialists who had carved up the Middle East following World War I, and who had dominated most of the non-Western world ever since the eighteenth century.

Military imposition, however, is not an adequate explanation for the success (at least temporarily) of the neo-imperial project or for the current wave of rebellions against it. Although force was clearly used to expand and maintain the system, it is also true that certain groups in the receiving nations welcomed the spread of Western economic and cultural influence in their lands, at least up to a point. Younger, more urbanized people in particular have displayed great interest in Western consumer goods, technologies, and fashions; in greater freedom of expression, travel, and opportunities to study in Europe or America; in gender rights, internet access, and parliamentary democracy; online investment opportunities, pop music, and religious pluralism; TV satellite dishes, mobile phones, and a whole panoply of American and European lifestyles and politico-cultural values.[17] Yet the desire for these goods and services can be intensely ambivalent and guilt-producing, since they threaten traditional identities, patterns of social order, and belief systems, and often extract a heavy price in the loss of personal dignity and national independence. For decades, to cite just one example, this price has included the wholesale bribery of public officials and business executives in nations incorporated into the neo-imperial system.[18] Intense ambivalence about Western mores may help to explain why the al-Qaeda operatives living in Florida prior to the September 11, 2001 attacks on U.S. targets imbibed alcohol and visited strip bars before going into battle – it was one way to 'sharpen the contradictions.'[19]

The two faces of neo-imperialism are therefore intimidation and temptation, a combination that has been a potent stimulus to religious terrorism throughout history. One recalls the popular resistance to the French in the Maghreb, to the British in old China, India, and East Africa, to the Russians in Central Asia, and to the United States in Iraq. Everywhere that secular leadership was unwilling or unable to push back against foreign political and economic domination, religious leaders mobilized mass insurgencies by fusing traditional values and behaviors with modern ideas and organizing techniques. Religious movements not only offered followers the opportunity to purify themselves and defend their traditions, they often provided the only opposition capable of organizing across the lines of class, region, and ethnicity. Moreover, they linked the promise of personal transformation – repentance and spiritual rebirth – to the achievement of social reform. Frequently, they practiced what they preached by organizing social welfare and relief programs that corrupt or callous governments seemed incapable of providing, as well as organizing resistance to imperial claims and impositions. These examples of sacrificial action linked to promises of personal and social transformation appealed to many believers at a time when secular movements that promised radical change had been discredited, and when Western thought no longer inspired movements of cultural revival and national liberation. Given the choice between a pallid, collaborationist secularism and a fiery religious fundamentalism, it is not surprising that many people yearning for change prefer the latter.

Ironically, the religious turn in movements of resistance to empire was often the unintended result of the empire-builders' own policies and activities. By outlawing India's secular nationalists, Great Britain laid the groundwork for Mahatma Gandhi's *satyagraha* movement. By its activities in the Cold War, the United States deprived the Third World of militant secular leaders and – in Afghanistan, in particular – actively promoted the rise of an extremist religious alternative. By defeating Saddam Hussein in Iraq, the United States brought to power the world's second Shia government, the first having been the revolutionary government of Iran, whose religious origins many trace to America's overthrow of the secular nationalist Mohammad Mosaddegh in the 1950s. Some analysts have called this sort of eventuality 'blowback' – the unanticipated violent consequences of covert warfare. But it is much more than that. I would argue that it is the inevitable result of the imperialist project, which cannot help denying subject peoples their autonomy, dignity, and identity. As we noted earlier, conflicts are mostly likely to be sacralized when they become protracted and when combatants are unable either to win or to give up the fight. Because people will not give up the fight for autonomy, dignity, and identity, the imperial system invariably becomes a system permanently at war.

One example that seems particularly apposite in view of recent events is the Jewish rebellion against the Seleucid Greeks in the second century BCE – the Maccabean-led uprising that eventually expelled the forces of Antiochus II from Judea and created the Hasmonean Kingdom. The context for this struggle was an imperialist campaign that involved the increasing penetration of the Palestinian Jewish community by the culturally sophisticated, politically advanced, and economically expansionist Greek Empire. The heirs of Alexander the Great controlled an invincible military machine. At the same time, their worldly, tolerant, permissive culture was admired and welcomed by key elements of the Jewish ruling class, who went so far as to educate their children in the Greek style and to adopt themselves to Greek customs and lifestyles. This behavior was seen as a political and a cultural betrayal by more 'fundamentalist' elements of the community that were committed to the twin goals of communal political autonomy and religious purity. The revolt began with what is perhaps the first recorded instance of political terrorism: the stabbing of a Greek official and Jewish collaborator by a fundamentalist militant in the hill town of Modin.[20] After six years of guerrilla warfare, the Greeks were finally driven from the land, which enjoyed a brief (roughly one-century) period of independence before the Roman legions arrived to resume imperial rule.

Three features of this episode are particularly significant in light of modern events. First, the exercise of imperial power was perceived by those subject to its demands not just as an imposition but a *desecration*. (Antiochus's attempt to introduce a statue of Olympian Zeus into the Jerusalem Temple was the final straw.) This tells us something about one of the social situations most likely to generate religious violence. Not imperial power alone, but power associated with impurity drives subject populations to engage in religiously motivated rebellions. Second, the imperialists used their assumed military and cultural superiority not just to threaten and control local people who might otherwise have resisted, but to impress them with their inferiority – that is, to *humiliate* them.[21] Third, the rebellion was aimed both at the foreign imperialists and their Jewish collaborators, a large and influential Hellenizing Party strongly attracted to Greek culture as well as the advantages of Greek trade.[22] In *Violent Politics*, William R. Polk points out that, in most protracted insurgencies, the insurgents' primary initial targets are domestic forces that collaborate with foreign occupiers.[23]

This returns us to the theme of violence as a product of social structure, for rebel attacks on both a near enemy and a far enemy signify that a transnational system, foreign-directed but involving local representatives, is implicated in the conflict. At the same time, this structural issue suggests the need for further development of the theory of cultural violence. Recall that, in explicating the role of cultural systems in generating violence, Johan Galtung focused on what might be called the cognitive elements in culture: religion, ideology, language, science, and cosmology.[24] The problem of religious revolt suggests the need to add another cultural dimension: the depth-psychological and spiritual. Both in the case of the Maccabean Revolt and in later cases of insurgency, what fuels the uprising is not only rage against local collaborators but also the self-loathing produced by the insurgents' own prior inclination to collaborate. The temptations presented by a powerful empire representing a sophisticated, worldly culture and offering access to forbidden pleasures are undeniably powerful. One can easily imagine the psychic and ethical conflicts that yielding to them must generate, especially in the minds of educated, relatively prosperous natives caught between the stern demands of their own tradition and foreign blandishments. Under these circumstances, religious nationalists can offer these sufferers one of religion's traditional gifts: the opportunity to purify oneself and one's people by engaging in sacred violence on behalf of the faith.[25]

Current rebellions against neo-imperial controls provide a particularly dramatic example of the sacralization of conflict. Ancient empires sometimes threatened the cultural and religious identities of subject peoples, but, since they ordinarily permitted vassal states to enjoy a high degree of local autonomy, the Maccabean situation was the exception rather than the rule.[26] The old empires did not usually transform traditional livelihoods, undermine local political institutions, or alter the customs of family life. Modern empires and neo-empires are far more threatening to traditionalists, since they tend to produce radical socioeconomic and cultural transformations in societies subject to their power. As Michel Foucault teaches, no traditional society ever attempted to exercise the degree of control over whole populations exercised by modern social systems.[27] An interesting but difficult problem produced by this fact is that the residents of 'exporting' nations – those sending their systems of production and values abroad – have little consciousness of the revolutionary impact of incorporating 'importing' societies into the system. Movements of resistance therefore come to them as a great surprise, and they are tempted to attribute them to religious fanaticism, power-lust, or some other evil or deviant personal motivation, rather than seeing them as directly related to a system that, as Johan Galtung says, has come to seem entirely "natural" to them.

Neo-imperialism, then, is an enormously ambitious project that aims at incorporation of virtually the entire world population in its systemic operations.[28] Since exercising direct coercive control over those incorporated is unfeasible, the corollary is to involve large numbers of subjects voluntarily in the system. Modern capitalist hegemony sustains itself by involving subject populations in a variety of complicities.[29] For example, local peoples may participate actively in the armed forces, government, business community, or other sectors of society effectively dominated by outsiders, virtually 'Westernizing' themselves for the sake of power, income, social status, or enjoyment. They may participate less actively but still significantly in the economy and culture, for example, by consuming imported physical and cultural goods, providing low-wage labor, hustling on the margins of the economy, or relying on foreign or government assistance in the absence of remunerative and dignified jobs. Or, they may become socially inactive, unable or unwilling to participate in the imperialist project, but deterred from resisting openly by intimidation, disorientation, and self-doubt. It seems clear, in any case, that the attempt to globalize the Western social system creates the raw material for religious rebellions, which in turn generate the long, costly, and equally cruel campaign of state violence known as the war on terror. The question before us now is whether understanding the systemic dimensions of this conflict can suggest a more peaceful and effective strategy for resolving it.

## Getting beyond neo-imperialism

As always, when one comes to the point of asking what can be done to resolve a structural conflict, the questions that come immediately to mind are these: Is it possible to change the violence-producing system nonviolently? What structural reforms are most likely to have transformative effects? How can these measures be agreed upon and implemented? How, after a time, can they be evaluated and, if necessary, altered? Dealing with these practical and political issues, however, requires that a prior step be taken. Those involved, as parties or potential peacemakers, must agree – or at least suspect! – that the conflict implicates a structured system that requires definition, analysis, and serious change. The structural turn, in other words, needs to be taken not only by conflict specialists but also by the disputants and other interested parties. The last chapter of this study will suggest some general rules for making this transition to structural thought. Our immediate task is to focus on the problem of recognizing and analyzing neo-imperialism's role in generating religious violence and the so-called war on terror.

Although it may seem odd to say so, the first practical step to be taken in dealing with the problem of neo-imperialism is theoretical. Even a brief perusal of the literature reveals strong disagreement among the academic experts on a number of basic issues, including the nature of the international system, whether neo-imperialism is a useful way to describe it, what role the United States and other Great Powers play in it, and what alternative forms of world order are currently evolving or might be created. A lively discussion of these issues, under the heading of "the globalization debate," has begun among scholars in international studies, economics, and the social sciences.[30] A related discussion in the field of conflict studies has focused on 'peacebuilding' – a generic name for varied efforts to create social and political conditions (particularly in post-conflict environments) conducive to the reconciliation of formerly warring or alienated groups and the prevention of new civil conflicts.[31] Many discussions of peacebuilding, however, have tended to sidestep the problem of neo-imperialist structures and their effects.[32] The time seems ripe – indeed, it may be overripe – to put these issues at the center of discussions in the field of conflict studies, and to do so in a way that does not prejudice the outcome.

Now that a structural turn is taking place in the field, five areas of inquiry seem particularly germane. We cannot discuss them in detail here, but we can put them on our intellectual agenda.[33]

First, how shall we understand the current structure and dynamics of global power in their relationship to prior world systems? Do we inhabit an imperial or neo-imperial system, and is the United States (alone or in alliance with the European Union and NATO) "the new Rome"?[34] If this is not an accurate description of the current world system, what is a better one?

Second, to what extent and in what ways do empires old and new generate violent conflict, including structural and cultural violence? Are anti-imperial rebellions and ensuing wars to suppress them, or inter-imperial struggles and wars to prosecute them, inevitable under neo-imperial rule? Are racism, cultural chauvinism, and the obsolescence of democratic values natural byproducts of neo-imperialism?

Third, to what extent and in what ways do empires function as preventers, managers, or resolvers of conflict? We have heard much about the Pax Romana, the Pax Britannica, and other claimed benefits of imperial rule. Do these systems effectively deter internal conflicts by force or threats of force? Do they effectively mediate between themselves and subject states, between competitive subject states, and between themselves and Great Power competitors?

Fourth, what forms of global organization might serve as practical alternatives to the imperial/neo-imperial model? What became of the United Nations' promise to become such an alternative? Does a reformed United Nations hold promise of fulfilling this promise? If not, are other 'world society' models feasible?

Finally, what are the implications of these answers for the theory of conflict and the practice of conflict resolution? Should conflict analysts and resolvers attempt to work within the present system to reform or humanize it? Should they seek to play the role of a pressure group on government or attempt to remain independent of all global power centers? In any case, what practical methods seem most likely to result in a nonviolent transformation of the current world system?

This last question requires at least a partial answer at this stage of our inquiry. Discussing the present global system in academic institutions or think tanks, while clearly important, will not impact ongoing conflicts unless the discussions are extended to include the parties directly in conflict, including representatives of the neo-imperial system and those in rebellion against them. In practical terms, this seems to me to require the convening of public conferences and confidential workshops in which group leaders, or influential people close to them, are invited to analyze the systemic sources of a specific conflict in depth, to see if they can agree on an identification of some of its key sources, and, if so, to discuss concrete proposals for system change.

To illustrate, imagine a process designed to generate nonviolent alternatives to the costly, inconclusive 'war on terror' that the United States and certain allies have conducted for the past fifteen years against a battery of violent Islamist groupings, most prominently, al-Qaeda and the Islamic State. The project could be called "Toward a Just Peace: Nonviolent Alternatives to Jihad and the War on Terror." Respected conflict specialists working independently of any government would convene a series of conferences and workshops giving knowledgeable parties, influential at various levels of the struggle, the opportunity to discuss matters of common concern in great depth. The public conferences would be attended by academic figures; business, labor, and community leaders, including religious leaders; former government officials; journalists, and other professionals with knowledge of how the world system works, or with experience in the regions affected by the war on terror, or both. The confidential workshops would be attended by persons influential in the lives of groups directly implicated in Islamist and counter-Islamist violence, ranging from high-level political and clerical advisors to civil society leaders, journalists, students, and grassroots organizers. Some conferences or workshops would be organized to deal with more specialized topics: for example, creative responses to the escalated struggle between Sunni and Shia Muslims, or the possible role of religious leaders in peacemaking. All meetings would take place over the course of an eighteen-month period, at the end of which the parties would agree either to move the discussions to the level of official diplomacy, renew them for another year, or abandon them altogether.

When such proposals are made, people's responses often betray confusion. Initially, practical, technical, or apparently common sense objections predominate. For example, 'Religious fanatics will not participate in this sort of discussion. It is unlikely that the impartial facilitators will be acceptable to all the parties. Western officials are too busy and politically vulnerable to attend such meetings. The conflict is too bloody to permit rational discussion. You can't negotiate with terrorists,' and so forth. But the practical-technical objections can be answered with relative ease. The more serious obstacles to proceeding are political and psychological.

### Practical objections

Many of the interactive, dialogic processes in common use by conflict specialists (e.g., problem-solving workshops, sustained dialogues, public conversations, and multilevel peacebuilding forums) seem well suited to conduct the proposed conferences and workshops.[35] Capable, experienced facilitators and mediators already understand how to select participants at various levels (national, mid-range, grassroots) who will be influential enough to help shape outcomes and open-minded enough to participate actively. Certain religious figures or government officials may well be too fanatical or committed to a previously fixed position to join in the dialogue, but others close to them who can represent their views and feelings often prove quite able to participate meaningfully. The best conflict specialists are strikingly skilled at helping people deeply committed to their own causes and previously disinclined to parley to become deeply involved in analytical, imaginative (and, yes, risky) discussions. Expert facilitators understand how to help participants move from an alienated discourse based on fears, threats, and dogma to a self-reflexive, interactive dialogue about the possibilities of solving common problems – and to do this without substituting their judgment for that of the parties. When should discussions be recessed to permit participants to consult with their colleagues at home? How can discussants move from agreeing on abstract principles to making concrete proposals and costing them out? Answering such questions successfully is the conflict resolver's stock in trade.

### Political objections

The more salient objection, then, is the political response, which is one all too familiar to conflict resolvers: 'You can't talk with those people.' Hiding behind the alleged practical obstacles is an unwillingness to engage with the enemy (or with those close enough to the enemy to stand in his shoes) in any mode other than that of warfare. This attitude is understandable, although no less one-sided and oversimplified for that. It takes us back to the description of partisan moralism that opened this study. 'These cruel fanatics are killing innocents and would like to kill us. We need to destroy them, not dialogue with them. They will view any offer to talk as weakness.' Yes, but every participant in a war says the same thing about his or her enemy (they certainly say the same thing about us). Although there is often truth in such accusations, the situation is almost always more complex than partisan moralists think. For example, some elements of the enemy are less cruel and fanatical than others; the conflict has causes other than the enemy's malice; and, in most cases, we will end up talking with them anyhow, sooner or later. Charges made against the Afghani Taliban organization at the time of the U.S. invasion of that country in 2001 were virtually identical to those made later against al-Qaeda and the Islamic State, yet peace talks between the Taliban and a quartet of states (the United States, China, Pakistan, and Afghanistan) have been held with some regularity since 2012 and may be continued in 2016 despite an escalation in the fighting.[36]

This suggests, first of all, that conferences and workshops aimed at illuminating the systemic causes of conflict and possibly generating agreements to alter those systems need not be considered impractical or immoral because fighting is still going on. Although negotiating cease-fires may at some point become a topic for negotiation, participating in social-constitutional dialogue does not require a prior cease-fire. Moreover, the dialogue processes advocated here are *not* negotiations of the sort that could expose participants to the charge of 'selling out' to the enemy. Not only are they confidential, they are analytical processes designed to discover if, by changing the systemic context of the conflict, it is possible to make peace *without* engaging in the sort of compromise that so often produces these accusations. Conflict resolution is not power-based negotiation. Its aim is not compromise but social and political change. Thanks to work done by conflict specialists at the U.S. Institute of Peace and elsewhere, this is not a distinction entirely unfamiliar to officials of major governments. Therefore, if parties to the conflict such as the United States fail to move in the direction of conflict resolution, this must be because they think either (a) that they can win a war on terror by military means, (b) that dialogues would subject them to intolerable political reprisals at home, or (c) that, even though the war is unwinnable, conducting it provides more advantages than disadvantages to their constituents (for example, military industrial companies).

The question thus raised for conflict specialists is how best to pursue the goal of resolving structural conflicts through systemic change when states (including one's own state) are parties to the conflict and do not seem to want it to be resolved nonviolently. Even though the structural turn in conflict studies is of fairly recent vintage, this issue is already causing dissension in the field, since many specialists (especially in the United States) have become dependent upon government grants, contracts, and employment opportunities; others, while not immediately dependent, wish to remain 'policy-relevant' and to influence government from a position of close proximity; and still others, while seeking to maintain their independence of thought and action, are strongly averse to activities that seem political in a partisan sense. The final chapter of this study is devoted to a reflection on the relationship of states to conflict studies and the future of structural conflict resolution.

## Notes

1 Mark Juergensmeyer, *Terror in the Mind of God: The Global Rise of Religious Violence*, 3rd. Edn. (Berkeley, CA: University of California Press, 2003).
2 James Davison Hunter, *Culture Wars: The Struggle to Define America* (New York: Basic Books, 1991); Samuel P. Huntington, *The Clash of Civilizations: And the Remaking of World Order* (New York: Simon & Schuster, 2002). Both books are discussed in more detail in *infra* at 114–116, 140.

3 The discussion of sacralization is based on my article, "Religious Conflict, Empire-Building, and the Imagined Other," in Mahmoud Eid and Karim H. Karim, Eds., *Re-imagining the Other: Culture, Media, and Western-Muslim Intersections* (Palgrave Macmillan, 2014).

4 Max Weber, *Economy and Society: An Outline of Interpretive Sociology*, 2 Vols. (Berkeley, CA: University of California Press, 1978). See also Michael E. Latham, *Modernization as Ideology: American Social Science and "Nation Building" in the Kennedy Era* (Chapel Hill, NC: University of North Carolina Press, 2000).

5 Richard S. Dunn, *The Age of Religious Wars, 1559–1715* (New York: W.W. Norton, 1979); Mack P. Holt, *The French Wars of Religion, 1562–1629* (Cambridge: Cambridge University Press, 2005); Michel Vovelle, *Ideologies and Mentalities* (Chicago: University of Chicago Press, 1990).

6 Francis Fukuyama, *The End of History and the Last Man* (New York: Harper, 1993). James Davison Hunter, although somewhat less optimistic in tone, reaches a similar conclusion in his study of the United States' "culture wars."

7 Soumaya Ghannoushi, "Terrorism and the Crisis of Sunni Islam." *Huffington WorldPost* (October 19, 2015). http://www.huffingtonpost.com/soumaya-ghannoushi/terrorism-and-the-crisis-of-sunni-islam_b_.

8 Samuel P. Huntington, *op. cit.* See also Richard E. Rubenstein and Jarle P. Crocker, "Challenging Huntington," *Foreign Policy* 96 (Autumn 1994), 113–128.

9 For a critical treatment of the "pan" movements portraying them as precursors of fascism, see Hannah Arendt, *Imperialism: Part Two of The Origins of Totalitarianism* (New York: Mariner Books, 1968), 102–146.

10 See, e.g., Randall Peerenboom, *China Modernizes: Threat to the West or Model for the Rest?* (Oxford: Oxford University Press, 2008).

11 But see Kevin Avruch's entry, "The Clash of Civilizations (Huntington)," in *The Wiley Blackwell Encyclopedia of Race, Ethnicity and Nationalism*, referring to critics who consider Huntington's theory a "'folk theory' for influential political actors": "Rather than predicting the state of the world and global conflict . . . the 'Clash of Civilizations' helped to bring it about." http://onlinelibrary.wiley.com/doi/10.1002/9781118663202.wberen012/pdf.

12 Kevin Avruch, *Context and Pretext in Conflict Resolution: Culture, Identity, Power, and Practice.* (Boulder, CO: Paradigm Press, 2012). See also Jolle Demmers, *op. cit.*, at 116–138.

13 See, e.g., George Mousourakis, *Roman Law and the Origins of the Civil Law Tradition* (New York: Springer, 2015), esp. 84 *et seq.*

14 Benjamin R. Barber, *Jihad vs. McWorld* (New York: Ballantine Books, 1995).

15 On March 1, 1991, in the midst of Operation Desert Storm (Iraq), President Bush gave a speech at the Executive Office Building in Washington, D.C. in which he stated, "It's a proud day for America. And we've kicked the Vietnam syndrome once and for all." http://www.presidency.ucsb.edu/ws/?pid=19351. On U.S. war aims, see my essay, "On Taking Sides: Lessons of the Persian Gulf War" (Lynch Lecture), *Occasional Paper No. 2* (George Mason University Institute for Conflict Analysis and Resolution, 1991), available online at scar.gmu.edu.

16 See Sharon Otterman, "Saudi Arabia: Withdrawal of U.S. Forces." *Council on Foreign Relations Backgrounder* (May 2, 2003). http://www.cfr.org/saudi-arabia/saudi-arabia-withdrawl-us-forces/p7739.

17 Barber, *op. cit.,* 17–20, *passim.* See also Thomas L. Friedman, *The Lexus and the Olive Tree: Understanding Globalization* (New York: Picador, 2012), which portrays the process as essentially consumer-driven.

18 See, e.g., Janine Wedel, *The Shadow Elite: How the World's New Power Brokers Undermine Democracy, Government, and the Free Market* (New York: Basic Books, 2009).

19 Cf. Juan Cole, "Sharpening Contradictions: Why al-Qaeda attacked Satirists in Paris." *Informed Comment* (January 7, 2015). http://www.juancole.com/2015/01/sharpening-contradictions-satirists.html.

20 See Jonathan Goldstein, *I Maccabees (Anchor Bible)* (New Haven, CT: Yale University Press, 1976).

21 The great study of humiliation of the colonized by the colonizer, and the reaction that it produces, is Frantz Fanon, *Black Skin, White Masks– New Edition* (New York: Grove Press, 2008).

22 Paul Johnson, *A History of the Jews* (New York: Harper & Row, 1987), 98–106.

23 William R. Polk, *Violent Politics: A History of Insurgency, Terrorism & Guerrilla War, from the American Revolution to Iraq* (New York: HarperCollins, 2007).

24 Johan Galtung, "Cultural Violence," *op. cit.,* at 296–302. See also Chapter 3, *supra,* at 64.

25 I have elaborated this argument in "The Psycho-Political Causes of Terrorism," in Charles W. Kegley, Jr., *The New Global Terrorism: Characteristics, Causes, Controls* (Upper Saddle River, NJ: Prentice Hall, 2002).

26 King Cyrus's Persian Empire is generally credited with initiating the system of imperial control over locally autonomous units. See T. Cuyler Young, "The Early History of the Medes and the Persians and the Achaemenid Empire to the Death of Cambyses," in John Boardman, et al., Eds., *The Cambridge Ancient History,* 2nd Edn., Vol. IV (Cambridge: Cambridge University Press, 1988), 61 *et seq.*

27 This theme is found throughout Foucault's work, but it may be best exemplified by his *Discipline and Punish: The Birth of the Prison* (New York: Vintage, 1995).

28 This theme is explored at length by Michael Hardt and Antonio Negri in their trilogy: *Empire* (Cambridge, MA: Harvard University Press, 2001), *Multitude* (London and New York: Penguin, 2005), and *Commonwealth* (Cambridge, MA: Belknap, 2011).

29 These issues are thoughtfully discussed in Albert Memmi, *The Colonizer and the Colonized* (Boston: Beacon, 1991) and Frantz Fanon and Jean-Paul Sartre, *Black Skin, White Masks* (New York: Grove Press, 1991).

30 See, e.g., William I. Robinson, *A Theory of Global Capitalism: Production, Class, and State in a Transnational World* (Baltimore, MD: Johns Hopkins University Press, 2004); Joseph E. Stiglitz, *Globalization and Its Discontents* (New York: W.W. Norton, 2003) and *Making Globalization Work* (New York: W.W. Norton, 2007); David Held and Anthony McGrew, *Globalization/Anti-Globalization: Beyond the*

*Great Divide*, 2nd Edn. (London: Polity Press, 2007), and their edited book, *Globalization Theory* (London: Polity Press, 2007).

31 See, e.g., Dennis J.D. Sandole, *Peacebuilding* (London: Polity Press, 2011); Craig Zelizer, Ed., *Integrated Peacebuilding: Innovative Approaches to Transforming Conflict* (Boulder, CO: Westview Press, 2013); *Alliance for Peacebuilding* website, www.allianceforpeacebuilding.org.

32 For a critical view of these discussions, see Vivienne Jabri, "Peacebuilding, the Local and the International: A Colonial or Post-Colonial Rationality?" *Peacebuilding*, 1:1 (2013). https://www.academia.edu/9277599/Vivienne_Jabri_2013_._Peacebuilding_the_Local_and_the_International_A_Colonial_or_a_Postcolonial_Rationality_Peacebuilding_.

33 These questions are based on my essay, "Conflict Resolution in an Age of Empire: New Challenges to an Emerging Field," in Dennis J.D. Sandole, Sean Byrne, et al., Eds., *A Handbook of Conflict Analysis and Resolution* (London and New York: Routledge, 2008).

34 Cullen Murphy, *Are We Rome? The Fall of an Empire and the Fate of America* (New York: Houghton Mifflin, 2007). For affirmative critical answers, see Michael W. Doyle, *Empires* (Ithaca, NY: Cornell University Press, 1986); Richard Falk, *Predatory Globalization: A Critique* (Cambridge: Polity Press, 1999); David Harvey, *The New Imperialism* (Oxford: Oxford University Press, 2003); Immanuel M. Wallerstein, *The Modern World-System, Vol. 1* (New York and London: Academic Press, 1996); and William Appleman Williams, *Empire As a Way of Life: An Essay on the Causes and Character of America's Present Predicament Along With a Few Thoughts About an Alternative* (New York: Ig Publishers, 2006). For less critical views, see Robert Kagan, *Of Paradise and Power: America and Europe in the New World Order* (New York: Knopf, 2003); Niall Ferguson, *Empire: How Britain Made the Modern World* (London: Penguin Books, 2004), and *Colossus: The Price of America's Empire* (London: Penguin Books, 2006).

35 See the discussion in Chapter 2, *supra*, at 45–47. See also John W. Burton and Frank Dukes, *Conflict: Practices in Management, Settlement, and Resolution* (London and New York: Palgrave Macmillan, 1990); John Paul Lederach, *Building Peace: Sustainable Reconciliation in Divided Societies* (Washington, DC: U.S. Institute of Peace, 1998); Bruce W. Dayton and Louis Kriesberg, Eds., *Conflict Transformation and Peacebuilding: Moving from Violence to Sustainable Peace* (London and New York: Routledge, 2009).

36 See, e.g., Hashmat Moslih, "The Taliban and Obstacles to Afghanistan Peace Talks," *Al Jazeera English* (February 27, 2016). http://www.aljazeera.com/indepth/features/2016/02/taliban-obstacles-afghanistan-peace-talks-160225095920107.html.

## Bibliography

Arendt, Hannah, *Imperialism: Part Two of The Origins of Totalitarianism* (New York: Mariner Books, 1968).

Avruch, Kevin, "The Clash of Civilizations (Huntington)," in *The Wiley Blackwell Encyclopedia of Race, Ethnicity and Nationalism*. http://onlinelibrary.wiley.com/doi/10.1002/9781118663202.wberen012/pdf.

——*Context and Pretext in Conflict Resolution: Culture, Identity, Power, and Practice*. (Boulder, CO: Paradigm Press, 2012).

Barber, Benjamin R., *Jihad vs. McWorld* (New York: Ballantine Books, 1995).

Burton, John W. and Frank Dukes, *Conflict: Practices in Management, Settlement, and Resolution* (London and New York: Palgrave Macmillan, 1990).

Bush, George H.W., Speech (March 1, 1991). http://www.presidency.ucsb.edu/ws/?pid=19351.

Cole, Juan, "Sharpening Contradictions: Why al-Qaeda attacked Satirists in Paris." *Informed Comment* (January 7, 2015). http://www.juancole.com/2015/01/sharpening-contradictions-satirists.html.

Dayton, Bruce W. and Louis Kriesberg, Eds., *Conflict Transformation and Peacebuilding: Moving from Violence to Sustainable Peace* (London and New York: Routledge, 2009).

Demmers, Jolle, *Theories of Violent Conflict: An Introduction* (London and New York: Routledge, 2012).

Doyle, Michael W., *Empires* (Ithaca, NY: Cornell University Press, 1986).

Dunn, Richard S., *The Age of Religious Wars, 1559–1715* (New York: W.W. Norton, 1979).

Falk, Richard, *Predatory Globalization: A Critique* (Cambridge: Polity Press, 1999).

Fanon, Frantz, *Black Skin, White Masks – New Edition* (New York: Grove Press, 2008).

——and Jean-Paul Sartre, *Black Skin, White Masks* (New York: Grove Press, 1991).

Ferguson, Niall, *Empire: How Britain Made the Modern World* (London: Penguin Books, 2004).

——*Colossus: The Price of America's Empire* (London: Penguin Books, 2006).

Friedman, Thomas L., *The Lexus and the Olive Tree: Understanding Globalization* (New York: Picador, 2012).

Foucault, Michel, *Discipline and Punish: The Birth of the Prison* (New York: Vintage, 1995).

Fukuyama, Francis, *The End of History and the Last Man* (New York: Harper, 1993).

Ghannoushi, Soumaya, "Terrorism and the Crisis of Sunni Islam." *Huffington WorldPost* (October 19, 2015). http://www.huffingtonpost.com/soumaya-ghannoushi/terrorism-and-the-crisis-of-sunni-islam_b_.

Goldstein, Jonathan, *I Maccabees (Anchor Bible)* (New Haven, CT: Yale University Press, 1976).

Hardt, Michael and Antonio Negri, *Empire* (Cambridge, MA: Harvard University Press, 2001).

——*Multitude* (London and New York: Penguin, 2005).

——*Commonwealth* (Cambridge, MA: Belknap, 2011).

Harvey, David, *The New Imperialism* (Oxford: Oxford University Press, 2003).

Held, David and Anthony McGrew, *Globalization/Anti-Globalization: Beyond the Great Divide*, 2nd Edn. (London: Polity Press, 2007).

——*Globalization Theory* (London: Polity Press, 2007).

Holt, Mack P., *The French Wars of Religion, 1562–1629* (Cambridge: Cambridge University Press, 2005).

Hunter, James Davison, *Culture Wars: The Struggle to Define America* (New York: Basic Books, 1991).

Huntington, Samuel P., *The Clash of Civilizations: And the Remaking of World Order* (New York: Simon & Schuster, 2002).

Jabri, Vivienne, "Peacebuilding, the Local and the International: A Colonial or Post-Colonial Rationality?" *Peacebuilding*, 1:1 (2013). https://www.academia.edu/9277599/Vivienne_Jabri_2013_._Peacebuilding_the_Local_and_the_International_A_Colonial_or_a_Postcolonial_Rationality_Peacebuilding_.

Johnson, Paul, *A History of the Jews* (New York: Harper & Row, 1987).

Juergensmeyer, Mark, *Terror in the Mind of God: The Global Rise of Religious Violence*, 3rd. Edn. (Berkeley, CA: University of California Press, 2003).

Kagan, Robert, *Of Paradise and Power: America and Europe in the New World Order* (New York: Knopf, 2003).

Latham, Michael E., *Modernization as Ideology: American Social Science and "Nation Building" in the Kennedy Era* (Chapel Hill, NC: University of North Carolina Press, 2000).

Lederach, John Paul, *Building Peace: Sustainable Reconciliation in Divided Societies* (Washington, DC: U.S. Institute of Peace, 1998).

Memmi, Albert, *The Colonizer and the Colonized* (Boston: Beacon, 1991).

Moslih, Hashmat, "The Taliban and Obstacles to Afghanistan Peace Talks," *Al Jazeera English* (February 27, 2016). http://www.aljazeera.com/indepth/features/2016/02/taliban-obstacles-afghanistan-peace-talks-160225095920107.html.

Mousourakis, George, *Roman Law and the Origins of the Civil Law Tradition* (New York: Springer, 2015).

Murphy, Cullen, *Are We Rome? The Fall of an Empire and the Fate of America* (New York: Houghton Mifflin, 2007).

Otterman, Sharon, "Saudi Arabia: Withdrawal of U.S. Forces." *Council on Foreign Relations Backgrounder*, (May 2, 2003). http://www.cfr.org/saudi-arabia/saudi-arabia-withdrawl-us-forces/p7739.

Peerenboom, Randall, *China Modernizes: Threat to the West or Model for the Rest?* (Oxford: Oxford University Press, 2008).

Polk, William R., *Violent Politics: A History of Insurgency, Terrorism & Guerrilla War, from the American Revolution to Iraq* (New York: HarperCollins, 2007).

Robinson, William I., *A Theory of Global Capitalism: Production, Class, and State in a Transnational World* (Baltimore, MD: Johns Hopkins University Press, 2004).

Rubenstein, Richard E., "On Taking Sides: Lessons of the Persian Gulf War" (Lynch Lecture), *Occasional Paper No. 2* (George Mason University Institute for Conflict Analysis and Resolution, 1991), available online at scar.gmu.edu.

——"The Psycho-Political Causes of Terrorism," in Charles W. Kegley, Jr., *The New Global Terrorism: Characteristics, Causes, Controls* (Upper Saddle River, NJ: Prentice Hall, 2002).

——"Conflict Resolution in an Age of Empire: New Challenges to an Emerging Field," in Dennis J.D. Sandole, Sean Byrne, et al., Eds., *A Handbook of Conflict Analysis and Resolution* (London and New York: Routledge, 2008).

——"Religious Conflict, Empire-Building, and the Imagined Other," in Mahmoud Eid and Karim H. Karim, Eds., *Re-imagining the Other: Culture, Media, and Western-Muslim Intersections* (Palgrave Macmillan, 2014).

——and Jarle P. Crocker, "Challenging Huntington," *Foreign Policy* 96 (Autumn 1994), 113–128.

Sandole, Dennis J.D., *Peacebuilding* (London: Polity Press, 2011).

Stiglitz, Joseph E., *Globalization and Its Discontents* (New York: W.W. Norton, 2003).

——*Making Globalization Work* (New York: W.W. Norton, 2007).

Vovelle, Michel, *Ideologies and Mentalities* (Chicago: University of Chicago Press, 1990).

Wallerstein, Immanuel M., *The Modern World-System, Vol. 1* (New York and London: Academic Press, 1996).

Weber, Max, *Economy and Society: An Outline of Interpretive Sociology*, 2 Vols. (Berkeley, CA: University of California Press, 1978).

Wedel, Janine, *The Shadow Elite: How the World's New Power Brokers Undermine Democracy, Government, and the Free Market* (New York: Basic Books, 2009).

Williams, William Appleman, *Empire As a Way of Life: An Essay on the Causes and Character of America's Present Predicament Along With a Few Thoughts About and Alternative* (New York: Ig Publishers, 2006).

Young, T. Cuyler, "The Early History of the Medes and the Persians and the Achaemenid Empire to the Death of Cambyses," in John Boardman, et al., Eds., *The Cambridge Ancient History*, 2nd Edn., Vol. IV (Cambridge: Cambridge University Press, 1988), 61 *et seq.*

Zelizer, Craig, Ed., *Integrated Peacebuilding: Innovative Approaches to Transforming Conflict* (Boulder, CO: Westview Press, 2013).

# 6

# STRUCTURAL CONFLICT RESOLUTION

## Toward a new politics

### Resolving structural conflicts in the shadow of the state

The general movement of this study has been toward crisis – a large crisis in world society and a small crisis in the field of conflict studies. We began by showing that many violent conflicts are not just the results of misunderstanding or malice but are generated by oppressive and exploitative social structures. We then explored the socioeconomic and cultural dimensions of certain local conflicts (crime and punishment in particular) and discussed their relationship to a 'total system' of globalizing capitalism. Finally, discussing religiously motivated conflict, we linked this system to neo-imperialism and raised the question of the state's role in maintaining the current world order. The large crisis, it seems to me, is the result of an attempt to keep this global system afloat notwithstanding its instability and vast, regular production of violence. Military confrontations and build-ups involving other Great Powers (or would-be empires) are now taking place all along the borders of regions dominated by the United States and its allies, from Eastern Europe and Ukraine to the South China Sea. The current moment, with its spread of global insurgencies and its endless war on terror, may actually be seen as a kind of hiatus in violence compared with the inter-imperialist wars that took more than 100 million lives in the twentieth century; a level of violence that may well resume unless the present order is restructured.

The far more parochial crisis in conflict studies is directly related to this same dynamic. Once we have begun to discover the connections between the total system and local violence, the question is what to do, practically speaking, with this knowledge. Discussions of structural conflicts and their resolution seem to follow a pattern in which structuralist insights are respectfully noted, but immediately qualified by a warning: just because some great transformation has not yet produced 'positive peace,' conflict specialists should not cease working for immediately feasible settlements or reforms that might produce 'negative peace.' In a knowledgeable essay that asks, "Does Our Field Have a Centre?" Kevin Avruch describes a tension between "American Pragmatists" and "European Structuralists" and concludes, in effect, that our field does *not* have a 'centre,' although it does have some shared understandings about conflict.[1] With greatest respect for these colleagues, it seems to me that most commentaries to date fail to respond to substantive challenges raised by a structuralist perspective in three interrelated problem areas: the state as a party to conflict; system-maintaining vs. system-transforming reforms; and the need for a new politics.

### The state as a party to conflict

If it is true that American conflict specialists tend to be more pragmatic than European structuralists, this is very likely related to the fact that since 1945, the United States has been the dominant global power, with the world's strongest economy and more than 800 military bases in approximately eighty nations around the globe.[2] The United States remains dominant, yet confronted by political challenges to mere military prowess that have inclined virtually all national administrations since that of Richard Nixon to seek 'soft power' supplements to the 'hard power' policies that proved ineffective to prevent the communist unification of Vietnam.[3] In order to maintain global supremacy without exhausting itself in costly neo-imperial wars, the U.S. government has developed a strong interest in the vocabulary, concepts, and practices of conflict resolution. From the 1980s onward, in addition to creating and funding the U.S. Institute of Peace, the American political establishment created an Office of Conflict Management and Mitigation within the U.S. Agency for International Development, a Bureau of Conflict and Stabilization Operations in the U.S. Department of State, and a number of offices in the Department of Defense and courses at the National Defense University, all aimed at applying conflict management skills to the problems of global governance. American pragmatism may have roots in U.S. colonial history, as theorists like Louis Hartz used to argue,[4] but its current status in conflict studies seems clearly related to the reluctance of many scholars and practitioners to challenge the U.S.-dominated system at its source. 'Pragmatic,' in this context, does not have its normal meaning as a synonym for nondogmatic, experimental, or improvisatory; here it means willing to adapt one's praxis to the reality of U.S. neo-imperialism.

What should conflict resolvers do when the state is not only a party to a conflict but the primary manager of a structured system that generates multiple conflicts as part of its normal operations? To warn conflict specialists not to fixate on the total system or denigrate the worthiness of moderate reforms does not respond to this challenge. Even where no violence-generating system exists, an elementary principle of conflict resolution practice requires facilitators to be nonpartisan between the conflicting parties. But when such a system does exist, I would contend, the specialist is obliged to recognize that fact and to practice her trade in a way that reflects this recognition. If, ignoring the systemic context, she attempts to practice conflict resolution under the aegis (or in the shadow) of the neo-imperial state, she effectively becomes an agent of that system.

An example drawn from personal experience may clarify this point. In 2004, following the U.S. invasion and occupation of Iraq, I was informed that the U.S. Institute of Peace had established an office in the Green Zone of Baghdad.[5] Conflict specialists were being encouraged to assist the agency's efforts to resolve interreligious and intertribal disputes in Iraq as part of the overall U.S. strategy in that nation. (Later, they would be invited to assist the Provincial Reconstruction Teams formed by the U.S. Army to 'stabilize' pacified areas in Iraq and Afghanistan.) I responded that I did not wish to play a role in the American conquest of Iraq even under the label of 'conflict specialist' and questioned both the efficacy and morality of attempting to practice "conflict resolution under the gun." My interlocutor answered that this would be an opportunity to learn about the conflict in detail, to help to make the U.S. role more rational and humane, and, perhaps, even to save lives. "The U.S. is in Iraq and is going to stay there," he said. "Using this as an opportunity to help resolve violent, long-standing conflicts is better than doing nothing." The exchange taught me that one can always find a way of rationalizing one's participation in an imperial system, especially when the opportunity is held out of helping to build a *Pax Americana*.

Ten years later, a similar issue (or so I thought) was raised when I learned that the U.S. Institute of Peace was conducting conflict resolution workshops with certain groups forming part of the Syrian opposition to President Bashar al-Assad. At a public forum, I asked why the organization did not attempt to resolve the main conflict between Assad and the Opposition. The question was somewhat rhetorical, since it seemed clear that U.S. foreign policy, which a government-funded agency dare not challenge, was to support certain (non-Islamist) elements of the Opposition in order to overthrow the Iranian- and Russian-backed Assad regime. The answer, however, took me aback. "We are working with the Opposition because its members are too divided to participate in peace negotiations. We need to assist them to prepare for real conflict resolution." This presented a more persuasive rationale for participating as an insider in the neo-imperial system. Rather than seeing the system as a coherent, relatively unified operation aimed at maintaining U.S. supremacy by any means necessary, it implied (or hypothesized) a more complex, divided, and changeable reality – a discourse, if you like – in which many differing voices competed, and in which one might participate meaningfully by adding one's own voice.

### System maintenance versus system reform

This colloquy pointed to a second problem area: the question of the effect of reform on a violence-producing system. Warning conflict specialists not to despise feasible conflict settlements or reforms misses the point that the reform/revolution dichotomy is not particularly useful in discussions of system transformation. We need to be able to distinguish between those reforms that make peripheral changes while leaving the system's violence-generating capacity intact (or even strengthening it) and those that have the potential to 'pacify' a system by transforming it structurally. The discussion about Syria, evoking an image of an incoherent and changeable Establishment, suggested that I might have been too quick to condemn the Peace Institute's attempts to mediate among Opposition groups, since the situation in that stricken nation (stricken, in large part, by the U.S. decision to allow its Saudi and Gulf States allies to arm the Opposition) was shifting, opening up the possibility of a joint effort by the Americans, Soviets, and regional powers to settle the conflict. A Syrian peace settlement, although still a distant possibility, would not only end the unutterable agony of the Syrian people and permit the return of millions of refugees, it would arguably continue the slow decline of the neo-imperial system. Indeed, the only likely gainer, if successful peace negotiations were to take place, would be the Russians, who had been successful to that point in defending the Assad regime, and who were calling for direct peace talks.

My argument here, then, is not that conflict resolvers must under any and all circumstances refrain from working with agencies of the neo-imperial state. Neither should they assume that well-intended reform efforts will usually be rewarded by transformative results. Our theory and practice should be guided by a structuralist understanding of the obstacles to and possibilities of serious systemic change. One must admit, of course, that a great deal of work needs to be done to develop usable, historically based concepts of system analysis and transformation. We do *not* yet have a solid theoretical basis for distinguishing between system-maintaining and system-transforming reform measures. It seems clear, for example, that the neo-imperial state is neither a coherent monolith driven purely by *raison d'état* nor an incoherent, malleable "X" awaiting transformation by peace-oriented activists. We need to know to what extent and under what conditions such a system can be transformed and what early moves are likely (or not) to produce transformative effects. With regard to practice, there has been virtually no evaluation of the systemic effects of practical interventions like those I have just described. What are the medium-term and long-term effects of the Peace Institute's efforts in Baghdad's Green Zone or their attempts to reconcile Syrian oppositionists? Structurally based evaluations are needed to help us to transcend the old reform/revolution dichotomy and to redesign our practice.

### The need for new politics

The third challenge still not sufficiently understood by many conflict specialists is political. Earlier in this study, I referred to the technocratic assumptions of much conventional third-party practice and suggested that a focus on transforming systems would require conflict resolvers to integrate politics more overtly into their praxis. I also noted that, since all social systems include political institutions, and the values and practices designed to resolve disputes without altering the system's basic structure, a structuralist perspective would very likely require a new politics – perhaps several varieties of new politics. When I began research for this study, I did not foresee that historical events would outrun my speculations – that major political formations to the right and the left of traditional center-left and center-right political parties would appear throughout the West, and that we would be plunged into an era of great political ferment and uncertainty. It seems to me that these events both validate a structural perspective and make its further development even more necessary and urgent.

In the United States and in Europe, a growing sentiment expressed across broad divisions of the population converges, despite disagreements, on certain structural fundamentals: that there is a social system which is malfunctioning or in crisis, that long-established political institutions and parties are part of the problem, and that serious reconstruction is necessary. In some respects, of course, this consensus is purely formal. Attempts to define the nature of the failing structures, the extent of the crisis, and the kind of reconstruction required reveal very sharp divisions, with traditional political parties splitting into factions and new political organizations extending the political spectrum in all directions. In general, the divisions reflect how various groups define the system requiring change, and, by implication, what needs to be done to restructure it. Thus, to traditional conservatives, the problem is unresponsive, self-interested bureaucracy; to traditional liberals, it is insufficiently regulated big business. Leftists from Jeremy Corbyn to Bernie Sanders define the system as corporate capitalism or as neo-imperialism, while rightists from Donald Trump to Marine Le Pen define it as pro-immigrant cosmopolitanism or as secularism. Interestingly, the new politicization also discloses unexpected conjunctions – for example, an agreement by the far left and libertarian right that the neo-imperial system lacks legitimacy, costs too much, and should be reconstituted on a much more limited basis.

The fact that systemic perspectives are emerging among people not accustomed to thinking in structural terms provides major new challenges for conflict specialists. These seismic shifts in public opinion raise the question whether we can play a constructive role in facilitating discussions between political groupings increasingly divided by differing conceptions of the system, anxiety syndromes, and political values. In the United States, where extreme partisanship and gridlock has brought conventional politics into general disrepute, a long and inconclusive discussion of the nation's 'culture wars' has given way to more complex analyses of working class resentment, nationalist resurgence, and the decay of the two-party system.[6] From a conflict studies perspective, it seems clear that efforts to make peace between political partisans by attempting to convince them to be more civil and cooperative are almost certain to fail, precisely because they do not expose the systemic sources of the partisanship. Conflict specialists can, however, invite the members of conflicting groups to participate in social-constitutional dialogues that would explore what has gone wrong with the old system and what new alternatives might be constructed to restore the health of the body politic. As a start, such dialogues could take place on the local level or in connection with more narrowly defined conflicts in order to demonstrate their general usefulness and scalability. But the time to begin them is now.

The current situation also raises the question of what other activities conflict specialists could undertake to help bring about the construction of a more egalitarian, less violent social system. If we conceive of our function as purely facilitative, a potential contradiction emerges between the goal of helping to create a more just and peaceful system, as most of us would define these terms, and the vision of a new society that might conceivably emerge as the result of a facilitated process. Imagine that a wave of fear, racism, and xenophobia responding to some new terrorist attack or similar disaster were to generate widespread agreement that the political system needs to be restructured along authoritarian, militaristic lines in order to institutionalize an aggressive nationalist ideology and interests. It would then be clear, if it is not clear already, that, for us, system transformation is not a formal, quantitative category; it has a concrete political meaning which qualifies our neutrality as 'third parties.' Our view (if I may presume to speak for my colleagues) is that inegalitarian, inequitable, and exploitative systems produce poverty, misery, and violence, and that these ills can be remedied by constructing a more just and humane system. Politics, as Hannah Arendt taught, is ultimately an ethical discipline, which means that, for those interested in resolving structural conflicts, political activity is unavoidable.[7]

## Conflict resolution and government: supplement or replacement?

A determination to help resolve structural conflicts, as we have seen, immediately puts in issue the relationship of conflict specialists to the state. Clearly, to define conflict resolution professionals as servants of the state disables them from challenging the social systems that brought the state into being and that government is designed to protect. But this leaves open the question of how they should relate to government institutions that, as time goes on, play an increasingly active role in adopting their language, funding their research, employing their students, and seeking consultative relationships. Common responses describe the conflict studies field and governmental institutions as engaged in 'complementary,' 'supplementary,' or 'overlapping' activities. One hears this particularly when discussing the congeries of activities now called peacebuilding and an alleged convergence of perspectives between nongovernmental conflict specialists and state agencies interested in 'sustainable development,' 'civil society–building,' and 'democratization.' But these phrases beg the question originally posed by founders of the field like John Burton and Johan Galtung, and perhaps more important now than when it was first formulated: *Is the field of conflict resolution destined to be a supplement to the system of elite-dominated power or a means of replacing that system?* And is this a question permitting diverse answers within a roughly unified discipline, or is it a 'wedge issue' likely to divide conflict specialists along political as well as professional lines?

John Burton's opening salvo on this topic was a 1988 essay called "Conflict Resolution as a Political System." "The appearance of conflict resolution," he argued, "signals the decadence of formalistic and coercive

rule by elites. It is in the context of this continuing trend that conflict resolution merges into political philosophy." Burton was not inclined to discuss
the social basis for the existing elite's authority, the ways by which social
structures could be transformed, or what a more egalitarian and humane
system might look like. In fact, he expressly disclaimed an interest in these
topics in order to focus exclusively on the consensual, analytical processes
that he considered the essence of conflict resolution.[8] Our job, he declared,
was not to define a "perfect system" but to describe and practice a superior
method of solving social problems. In Burton's view:

> Conflict resolution processes have the potential to take the place of
> courts and power-based negotiation. Conceivably they could deal
> with many problems of distribution of roles and resources as well.
> Insofar as conflict results in such alterations in institutions and norms
> as problem solving may require, insofar as it is a major influence for
> change, and also for adjustments to changing conditions, it becomes a
> system of decision making.[9]

As he saw it, the problem was adversarial, power-based decision-making,
and the solution was analytical, problem-solving processes focused on
human needs.

The idea that conflict resolution processes could substitute generally
for existing legal and political modes of decision-making may seem far-
fetched, but the underlying thrust of Burton's argument is powerful. It
rests on an either/or proposition. Either conflict resolution will present
an alternative to the existing elite-dominated political system or it will
become another of the elite's governance tools. "There is always the
danger," he warned presciently, "that the [conflict resolution] process can
be captured and used to advantage by elites that already control existing
decision making processes. Already there is evidence that this is happen-
ing."[10] In fact, the process of elite co-optation of the field has proceeded
more quickly than even Burton expected. The repeated mantra of government agencies interested in conflict resolution or peacebuilding, by
which they mean the peaceful, efficient management of disputes *within*
the bounds of existing elite-dominated political and socioeconomic systems, is that it provides a useful supplement to politics-as-usual, or that it
complements existing state practices. In this formulation, the field poses
no threat to the established order. On the contrary, it becomes a device
that gives the established order a human face as well as providing methods of settling disputes that are lower in cost, more effective, and more
sustainable than the crude manifestations of brute power.

Conflict resolution, in this formulation, is again equated in political significance to alternative dispute resolution – a set of concepts and practices developed primarily by lawyers and community-based mediators to keep disputes out of the courts and to produce results more satisfactory to the parties and more stabilizing to existing legal and political systems. To take a typical example, many jurisdictions in the United States now require the parties to child custody disputes to attempt mediation before engaging in more formal legal processes. Since the issues involved in such cases are more 'equitable' than 'legal,' the results of mediation are more likely to be in the child's best interests than the results of adversary legal procedures. But, of course, such processes *supplement and effectuate* the authority of the overarching legal system rather than undermining or replacing it. The parties to ADR processes ordinarily retain their access to the judicial system (for example, the right to go to court or to file appeals if mediation efforts fail), and violent or potentially violent disputes are almost always handled by the regular courts on the grounds that vulnerable parties require the formality and protection of the state's (coercive) judicial system. Almost by definition, a supplementary system does not handle the most serious conflicts. Thus, Victim-Offender Reconciliation Programs and other forms of restorative justice have been quite successful at providing alternative methods of processing minor criminal cases, but almost all felony cases are directly managed by the state.

A supplementary system like restorative justice has beneficial effects, of course; I am personally familiar with people whom it has rescued from being processed through an unfeeling, often destructive criminal justice system. But there is little doubt that its function overall is to strengthen that system as a whole. Similarly, the notion of complementarity is often used to stabilize and expand the reach of violently coercive systems by incorporating less coercive elements within them. One might call this the institutionalized exception that stabilizes the rule. An interesting example is provided by the United Nations Development Programme's attempt to define the relationship between the new doctrine of 'human security' (whose goals strongly resemble that of conflict resolution) and the much older concept of state security.

How do these doctrines differ? According to the UN Commission on Human Security:

> Whereas state security concentrates on threats directed against the state, mainly in the form of military attacks, human security draws attention to a wide scope of threats faced by individuals and communities. It focuses on root causes of insecurities and advances

people-centered solutions that are locally driven, comprehensive and sustainable. As such, it involves a broader range of actors: e.g. local communities, international organizations, civil society as well as the state itself.[11]

In other words, while state security involves short-term military responses to real or fancied military threats, human security deals with a wide range of long-run insecurities (or denials of human needs) and possible solutions. There is clear evidence, which I outline in a recent article, that the UN officials and advisors who created the human security doctrine felt that it would gradually *replace* the doctrine of state security or, through a process of transition, become the dominant thread in the tapestry of overall security discourse.[12] But one decade later, the Commission on Human Security, reacting to pressure from Great Powers jealously guarding their prerogatives, states that "Human security . . . is not intended to displace state security." Rather, their relationship is "complementary." "Without human security, state security cannot be obtained, and vice versa."[13]

Of course, this caveat took the wind out of the new doctrine's sails. Human security was never intended to deny the right of ordinary nations to defend their territory against military attack; it was, however, an implicitly critical doctrine aimed at neo-imperialist powers that provoked violence by expanding their own spheres of influence and creating obstacles to the human development of other peoples. Complementarity, after all, means that two ideas or entities are compatible and that they complete each other to make a coherent whole. For Peru or Tajikistan, state security and human security may, indeed, be complementary. But are superpowers armed to the teeth compatible with a world system that promotes human development and inspires peaceful relations between peoples? To ask the question, it seems to me, is to answer it.

'Hard' and 'soft' power may well be compatible if a nation is practicing what some call 'defensive defense': a military and intelligence posture limited to responding to imminent threats of an armed attack on one's own country and not capable of launching aggressive warfare against others. The idea that these concepts are not only generally compatible but mutually necessary, however, rests on a serious fallacy: the notion that all states are essentially the same in essence, enjoying similar rights and possessing similar interests. On the contrary, an empire or neo-empire is not a state. In many respects, in fact, it is an antistate. In a superpower's hands, concepts like 'security,' 'sovereignty,' 'national interest' and 'self-defense' utterly change shape, to the point that they end up meaning the opposite of what normal states mean when they use these terms. Residents of the United States, for example, begin by asserting that they, as a nation, need and deserve national security. Recognizing that their nation is also the world's leading economic and military power, many go on to argue that *that* transnational entity – the neo-imperial order – is what needs and deserves security. The fact that imperial security is incompatible with human security – that securing imperial power 'un-secures' everyone else – is swept aside or repressed, at least until the Americans themselves begin to realize (as many now seem to be doing) that it also un-secures *them*.

What sort of new politics does this sort of analysis imply? If conflict resolution is meant to be more than a supplement or complement to existing systems of power and privilege, how can it assist more effectively in creating a practical and just alternative? The tension that continues to exist in conflict studies and related fields, it seems to me, is not so much a conflict between pragmatists and structuralists, but more a clash between facilitators and advocates. The strong bias of the profession is toward facilitation. Even radical innovators and practitioners like Johan Galtung, Adam Curle, John Paul Lederach, and the late John Burton hesitated to describe the system that they thought would finally eliminate structural violence and pave the way toward positive peace, preferring to focus on processes intended, in Galtung's words, to "transcend and transform" the conflict situation.[14]

This was in part a result of their trust in facilitated processes designed to decentralize decision-making to the level of the conflicting parties. It was also, I think, a reflection of their disenchantment with Stalinized communism and other failed large-scale social experiments, and their desire to create a discipline that would not be stereotyped as conventionally leftist. In the current era, which Alain Badiou and others have described as post-anti-communist, conflict specialists may feel more comfortable discussing the large issues of politics among themselves and involving others in the dialogue.[15] There are indications that this has already begun to happen, among them, peace journalism efforts like Johan Galtung's TRANSCEND Media Service, the development of other online networks and tools for public discussion, and growing interest among conflict scholars in normative issues and the ethics of conflict resolution.[16] Once these discussions have reached the point of outlining possible alternatives to current violence-producing systems, two further questions will be posed: how to harmonize this understanding with facilitative practice, and how to advocate most effectively for preferred alternatives. The challenge of advocacy revives an old debate in the field about the proper relationship between conflict resolution praxis and the practice of Gandhian or Kingian nonviolent resistance and what one analyst calls "positive peacebuilding."[17] We are at the beginning of a very interesting stage in the development of this field.

## Reprise: from partisan moralism to structural praxis

This brings our discussion full circle. The work of peaceful system transformation must involve public education on a large scale. Strenuous new
efforts are required to help our fellow citizens and fellow humans worldwide, at a time of increasing insecurity and frustration, to move beyond
partisan moralism to a new appreciation of their own responsibility and
the system's responsibility for avoidable violence. The bad news is that,
where violent conflict is concerned, no party to the conflict and few
bystanders are guiltless. The good news is that no party is solely responsible
for violence sponsored or provoked by an oppressive social structure. And
the best news is that, once people decide to transform such a structure,
they can help each other to do so. Each of these steps – acknowledging
responsibility for violence, perceiving that a system is also responsible for
it, and deciding to change that system through collective effort – challenges peacemakers to overcome serious (but not insuperable) political and
psychological obstacles to public understanding of such issues.

A first step in overcoming these obstacles, in my view, is an all-out
attack on the thinking that divides the world into 'perpetrators' and 'victims' of violence.[18] Dramatic literature and media products can help people
understand that each party to a violent conflict, the weaker as well as the
more powerful, is both a perpetrator *and* a victim. In *The Confessions of Nat
Turner*, William Styron's Pulitzer Prize-winning novel about a slave revolt
in Virginia, the author stirred up fierce controversy by portraying some
slaveholders as benevolent figures and some rebellious slaves as psychopaths
and brutes.[19] At the same time, he presented the system of chattel slavery
as the overarching 'script' that degraded everyone who played a role in it,
and that thus required total transformation. Recall our earlier discussion of
the prison system. The fact that some prison authorities are kindly altruists
and some prisoners violent sadists does not alter the fact that the system as
a whole tends to brutalize *all* who participate in it. The system as a whole
has to be overthrown to eliminate the victim/perpetrator and the perpetra-
tor/victim.

What other measures might help people implicated in conflict to accept
an appropriate share of responsibility for violence rather than blaming it
entirely on some enemy? Our response to partisan moralism is unlikely to
be effective unless it takes into account the psychological vulnerabilities
and strong emotions that move conflicting parties to exculpate themselves
by inculpating others. This sort of accounting is particularly important
at a time like the present, when people in many lands seem passionately
driven to defend the goodness and purity of their national 'family' and to

brand those who criticize the nation as haters of the family and lovers of its enemies. Thanks to psychoanalytic peace theorists like Wilhelm Reich and Vamik Volkan, we know something about the fears, anxieties, and repressed desires that inspire an aggressive, authoritarian nationalism.[20] It is not yet clear, however, how conflict specialists can help fellow citizens to do the sort of self-reflective work required to deal more dispassionately with these emotional issues. Wilhelm Reich's attempt to establish neighborhood psychotherapy centers for Germans in the pre-Hitler period was unrealistic and, perhaps, foolish, but at least it recognized a real need.[21] We may be able to facilitate community workshops or forums that at least permit such issues be discussed openly rather than allowing them to fester in secret.

How one moves from partisan moralism toward an appreciation that a system is also responsible for generating violence can be illustrated by one fairly hopeful example. During the 1960s, numerous large cities in the United States were struck by serious riots in which African-Americans alienated by perceived mistreatment and infuriated by acts of police violence burned down substantial areas of the inner cities, looted stores, and attacked or were attacked by the police. In general, people outside the areas hit by civil disorders reacted to the violence with a mixture of horror and moral disapproval, mitigated only slightly by sympathy for the plight of the poor and excluded. When the Watts ghetto of Los Angeles exploded in 1965, President Lyndon B. Johnson equated the rioters with the violent racists of the Ku Klux Klan, declaring that "A rioter with a Molotov cocktail in his hands is not fighting for civil rights any more than a Klansman with a sheet on his back and a mask on his face."[22] Johnson would later attribute the urban uprisings to the activities of "a few mean and willful men" – a view widely shared at first by experts as well as the public.[23]

Following the Watts riot, a California investigatory commission headed by former CIA director John McCone emphasized the rioters' rootlessness and lack of community ties, while also attributing their anger to poor living conditions in the inner city (the so-called 'riff-raff' theory of rioting).[24] In a fairly short time, however, this understanding began to deepen and to become more complex. A two-year study by scholars at the UCLA Institute of Government and Public Affairs concluded that most rioters had *not* been 'riff-raff' but typical members of the community motivated by deep-rooted feelings of deprivation and alienation.[25] Then, after major riots occurred in Newark, Detroit, and other cities, the National Advisory Commission on Civil Disorders (Kerner Commission) issued its famous report concluding that the causes of the uprisings were historical and systemic. The United States was "moving toward two societies, one black, one white – separate and unequal," said the Commission in 1967, with the black society subjected to systematic discrimination and deprivation.[26]

One year later, large-scale riots shook the black communities of Chicago, Baltimore, Washington, New York, and scores of other towns in the wake of Martin Luther King's assassination, while largely white protestors confronted the police at the Democratic National Convention and other sites of antiwar activity. In response, a National Commission on the Causes and Prevention of Violence (Eisenhower Commission) was created. Its reports, published over the next two years, presented in-depth social and historical analyses of a wide range of related forms of violence and disorder, from assassinations and other crimes of violence to 'police riots,' prison uprisings, and confrontational political protests.[27] The focus of these reports was on dysfunctional political and legal systems rather than mad or bad individuals or organizations. The question of how to restructure such systems in order to produce a substantially lower level of violence was also discussed, but the Commission's recommendations were confined to specific limited reforms. Except for noting the impact of racial discrimination in employment, public contracts, and housing, the socioeconomic order was left virtually unanalyzed.

What we learn from this history, it seems to me, is that public attitudes can change in a relatively short period of time, even when the initial response to a violent crisis is fearful, angry, and defensive. In the case of the riot commissions, it was a liberal establishment fearful of escalating civil violence and recognizing the need for some social and political reforms that took the lead in public education. The challenge for current students of conflict may be to take the lead themselves, with whatever political allies and funding sources can be discovered, in organizing and staffing truth and reconciliation commissions and councils to investigate the systemic sources of specific forms of direct, structural, and cultural violence. One can imagine community-based task forces commissioned to study, take testimony, and make recommendations with regard to poverty, inequality, and deindustrialization; crime, police violence, and the prison system; militarism and the 'war on terror'; religious differences and the search for an ethical consensus; political partisanship, gridlock, and the decay of the two-party system; and neo-imperialism and the threat of a new world war.

On the basis of such activities, national and international conversations could begin aimed at imagining and implementing systems designed to produce positive peace. What might such systems look like? This is not a question that most conflict specialists ask, perhaps because, historically speaking, their field has been so sensitive to the charge of being 'utopian.'

Following the disaster of World War I, socialists and pacifists in Europe and North America bitterly criticized militaristic 'jingoism' and minimized the threat of a new war. In 1933, the Oxford Union famously passed a resolution that read: "Resolved: We will not fight for King or country." As a result, when World War II began, the peace advocates were accused by Realists of practicing a blind and destructive utopianism. This legacy affected conflict studies at its inception and had much to do with decisions to label the field of practice 'conflict resolution' or 'conflict transformation' rather than peace advocacy.

Although this aversion to the peace label has now largely dissipated, many scholars and practitioners continue to cultivate a hard-edged, realistic style and remain wary of behavior that might seem dreamy or impractical. Nevertheless, the times demand an imaginative response to the urgent need for new socioeconomic, political, and cultural systems. If I may say so, dreaming is now the new practicality. We have seen that crises in the fields of crime and punishment, poverty and inequality, religious mobilizations and terrorism, neo-imperial conflicts, and political polarization all call for new ideas about alternative systems. In addition to facing these forms of system-generated violence, the inhabitants of our planet are now threatened by unprecedented dangers due to climate change and other ecological crises. Without realizable dreams of a social system that prioritizes planning to satisfy human needs over profit and privilege, our species could sacrifice centuries' worth of hard-won gains in physical security and cultural development. In developing these ideas, conflict specialists may find science fiction or cybernetics more helpful than political science. We should resolve to seize inspiration wherever we can find it.

To imagine workable new systems, finally, is to respond to an understandable public skepticism about the possibilities of transformations that would not only be radical, but also radically beneficial. People may profess a belief in social equality, for example, but they also want to know what equality means in practice. *Can* our social system become more egalitarian without eliminating incentives to do superior work? If income or wealth differentials should be narrowed, how narrow should they be? Can poverty be eliminated by guaranteeing all citizens decently paid jobs and a minimum income, or through other means? Can cultural equality be encouraged by promoting genuinely integrated schools, workplaces, and housing – and, if so, can we do this by relying on persuasive processes of conflict resolution? All these questions deserve answers, as do queries about feasible alternatives to a failed system of mass incarceration, the possibilities of democratic economic planning in the computer age, and how to transform a neo-imperial system into a partnership of nations.

People will join in the quest for more just and peaceful social systems only when they have reason to believe that there *are* alternatives that make sense and that will solve problems rather than exacerbate them. They must have hope as well as desperation. By reaching out to specialists in other fields, those interested in resolving structural conflicts may soon find themselves participating in a new venture of major practical and intellectual importance.

## Notes

1 Kevin Avruch, "Does Our Field Have a Centre? Thoughts from the Academy." *International Journal of Conflict Engagement and Resolution*, 1:1 (January 2013). See also Oliver Ramsbotham, et al., *Contemporary Conflict Resolution*, 4th Edn. (Cambridge, UK and Malden, MA: Polity Press, 2016), 47–48.

2 David Vine, "The U.S. Probably Has More Foreign Military Bases than Any Other People, Nation, or Empire in History." *The Nation* (September 14, 2015). https://www.thenation.com/article/the-united-states-probably-has-more-for-eign-military-bases-than-any-other-people-nation-or-empire-in-history/.

3 Joseph S. Nye, Jr.'s seminal book, *Bound to Lead: The Changing Nature of American Power*, Rev. Edn. (New York: Basic Books, 1991) made the connection between "soft power" and maintaining America's global hegemony post-Vietnam explicit.

4 See Louis Hartz, *The Liberal Tradition in America* (New York: Harvest Books, 1991).

5 See, e.g., https://www.usip.org/publications/iraq-back-the-green-zone (July 2, 2007).

6 See James Davison Hunter, *Culture Wars: The Struggle to Define America, op. cit.*; Andrew Hartman, *A War for the Soul of America: A History of the Culture Wars* (Chicago: University of Chicago Press, 2015); Stephen Prothero, *Why Liberals Win the Culture Wars (Even When They Lose Elections)* (New York: HarperOne, 2016); Francis Fukuyama, "The Decay of American Political Institutions." *The American Interest*, 9:3 (December 8, 2013). http://www.the-american-interest.com/2013/12/08/the-decay-of-american-political-institutions/.

7 Hannah Arendt, *The Promise of Politics* (New York: Schocken, 2007).

8 This issue is discussed at some length in David J. Dunn's excellent biography, *From Power Politics to Conflict Resolution: The Work of John W. Burton* (London and New York: Palgrave Macmillan, 2004), esp. 115 *et seq.*

9 John Burton, "Conflict Resolution as a Political Philosophy." *ICAR Working Paper No. 1* (Arlington, VA: George Mason University Institute for Conflict Analysis and Resolution, 1993), 22. http://scar.gmu.edu/wp_1_burton.pdf.

10 Ibid., 31.

11 Human Security Unit, United Nations Trust Fund for Human Security, "Human Security in Theory and Practice" (2004), 12. http://www.un.org/humansecurity/sites/www.un.org.humansecurity/files/humansecurity_in_theory_and_practice_english.pdf.

12 "State Security, Human Security, and the Problem of Complementarity," in Edwin Daniel Jacob, Ed., *Rethinking Security in the Twenty-First Century* (London and New York: Palgrave Macmillan, 2016).

13 Human Security Unit, United Nations Trust Fund for Human Security, "Human Security in Theory and Practice," *op. cit.,* 12.

14 Johan Galtung, *Transcend and Transform: An Introduction to Conflict Work* (London and New York: Routledge, 2004).

15 Alain Badiou and Marcel Gauchet, *What Is To Be Done? A Dialogue on Communism, Capitalism, and the Future of Democracy* (London: Polity Press, 2016).

16 See TRANSCEND Media Service at https://www.transcend.org/tms/. On ethical issues, see Daniel Rothbart and Karina V. Korostelina, *Why They Die: Civilian Devastation in Violent Conflict* (Ann Arbor, MI: University of Michigan Press, 2011), and the materials collected in Daniel Rothbart and Karina V. Korostelina, Eds., *Identity, Morality, and Threat: Studies in Violent Conflict* (Lanham, MD and Plymouth, UK: Lexington Books, 2006).

17 See Lester R. Kurtz, *Encyclopedia of Violence, Peace, and Conflict*, 2nd Edn. (Cambridge, MA: Academic Press, 2008); Johnny Mack, "Nonviolence as a Theory of Social Change and Human Development for the Peace and Conflict Field" (2015). Unpublished dissertation available from George Mason University School for Conflict Analysis and Resolution at scar.gmu.edu.

18 A good starting point for this discussion is Diane Enns, *The Violence of Victimhood* (University Park, PA: Pennsylvania State University Press, 2012).

19 See William F. Styron, *The Confessions of Nat Turner* (New York: Random House, 1967) and John Henrik Clarke, et al., Eds., *Styron's Nat Turner: Ten Black Writers Respond* (Boston: Beacon, 1968).

20 Wilhelm Reich, *The Mass Psychology of Fascism*, 3rd Edn. (New York: Farrar, Straus, and Giroux, 1980); Vamik Volkan, *Blind Trust: Large Groups and Their Leaders in Times of Crisis and Terror* (Charlottesville, VA: Pitchstone Press, 2004).

21 Wilhelm Reich, *Sex-pol: Essays, 1929–1934* (New York: Vintage, 1972).

22 "President Lyndon Johnson's Statement on the Watts Riot (1965)." http://www.historycentral.com/documents/LBJwatts.html.

23 These responses are discussed in Richard E. Rubenstein, *Rebels in Eden: Mass Political Violence in the United States* (Little Brown, 1970). See also Anthony M. Platt, *The Politics of Riot Commissions, 1917–1970* (Collier Books, 1971); Gerald Horne, *Fire This Time: The Watts Uprising and the 1960s* (Da Capo Press, 1997).

24 *Violence in the City—An End or a Beginning?: A Report by the Governor's Commission on the Los Angeles Riots* (University of Southern California, 1965). http://www.usc.edu/libraries/archives/cityinstress/mccone/contents.html.

25 See David O. Sears and John B. McConahay, "Participation in the Los Angeles Riot." *Social Policy*, 17:1 (Summer 1969), 3–20. http://www.ssgs.ucla.edu/sears/pubs/A024.pdf.

26 *Report of the National Advisory Commission on Civil Disorders* (Bantam Books, 1968). This report was criticized by some researchers for not being systemic/historical enough; in particular, for overemphasizing racial prejudice as a cause

of violence without sufficient appreciation of the relationship between institutionalized racism and oppression based on social class.

27 See National Commission on the Causes and Prevention of Violence, *Final Report: To Establish Justice, To Insure Domestic Tranquility* (U.S. GPO, 1969), and Commission Task Force reports including Hugh Davis Graham and Ted Robert Gurr, *Violence in America: Historical and Comparative Perspectives* (New York Times, 1969), and Jerome H. Skolnick, *The Politics of Protest*, 2nd Edn. (NYU Press, 2010).

## Bibliography

Arendt, Hannah, *The Promise of Politics* (New York: Schocken, 2007).

Avruch, Kevin, "Does Our Field Have a Centre? Thoughts from the Academy." *International Journal of Conflict Engagement and Resolution*, 1:1 (January 2013).

Badiou, Alain and Marcel Gauchet, *What Is To Be Done? A Dialogue on Communism, Capitalism, and the Future of Democracy* (London: Polity Press, 2016).

Burton, John, "Conflict Resolution as a Political Philosophy." *ICAR Working Paper No. 1* (Arlington, VA: George Mason University Institute for Conflict Analysis and Resolution, 1993), 22. http://scar.gmu.edu/wp_1_burton.pdf.

Clarke, John Henrik, et al., Eds., *Styron's Nat Turner: Ten Black Writers Respond* (Boston: Beacon, 1968).

Dunn, David J., *From Power Politics to Conflict Resolution: The Work of John W. Burton* (London and New York: Palgrave Macmillan, 2004).

Enns, Diane, *The Violence of Victimhood* (University Park, PA: Pennsylvania State University Press, 2012).

Galtung, Johan, *Transcend and Transform: An Introduction to Conflict Work* (London and New York: Routledge, 2004).

Graham, Hugh Davis and Ted Robert Gurr, *Violence in America: Historical and Comparative Perspectives* (New York Times, 1969).

Hartman, Andrew, *A War for the Soul of America: A History of the Culture Wars* (Chicago: University of Chicago Press, 2015).

Hartz, Louis, *The Liberal Tradition in America* (New York: Harvest Books, 1991).

Hunter, James Davison, *Culture Wars: The Struggle to Define America* (New York: Basic Books, 1991).

Fukuyama, Francis, "The Decay of American Political Institutions." *The American Interest*, 9:3 (December 8, 2013). http://www.the-american-interest.com/2013/12/08/the-decay-of-american-political-institutions/.

Horne, Gerald, *Fire This Time: The Watts Uprising and the 1960s* (Da Capo Press, 1997).

Governor's Commission on the Los Angeles Riots, *Violence in the City—An End or a Beginning?* (University of Southern California, 1965). http://www.usc.edu/libraries/archives/cityinstress/mccone/contents.html.

Johnson, Lyndon Baines, "President Lyndon Johnson's Statement on the Watts Riot (1965)." http://www.historycentral.com/documents/LBJwatts.html.

Kurtz, Lester R. *Encyclopedia of Violence, Peace, and Conflict*, 2nd Edn. (Cambridge, MA: Academic Press, 2008).

Mack, Johnny, "Nonviolence as a Theory of Social Change and Human Development for the Peace and Conflict Field" (2015). Unpublished dissertation available from George Mason University School for Conflict Analysis and Resolution at scar.gmu.edu.

National Advisory Commission on Civil Disorders, *Report of the National Advisory Commission on Civil Disorders* (New York: Bantam Books, 1968).

National Commission on the Causes and Prevention of Violence, *Final Report: To Establish Justice, To Insure Domestic Tranquility* (Washington, D.C.: U.S. GPO, 1969).

Nye, Joseph S. Jr., *Bound to Lead: The Changing Nature of American Power*, Rev. Edn. (New York: Basic Books, 1991).

Platt, Anthony M. *The Politics of Riot Commissions, 1917–1970* (Collier Books, 1971).

Prothero, Stephen, *Why Liberals Win the Culture Wars (Even When They Lose Elections)* (New York: HarperOne, 2016).

Ramsbotham, Oliver, et al., *Contemporary Conflict Resolution*, 4th Edn. (Cambridge, UK and Malden, MA: Polity Press, 2016).

Reich, Wilhelm, *Sex-pol: Essays, 1929–1934* (New York: Vintage, 1972).

——*The Mass Psychology of Fascism*, 3rd Edn. (New York: Farrar, Straus, and Giroux, 1980).

Rothbart, Daniel and Karina V. Korostelina, Eds., *Identity, Morality, and Threat: Studies in Violent Conflict* (Lanham, MD and Plymouth, UK: Lexington Books, 2006).

——*Why They Die: Civilian Devastation in Violent Conflict* (Ann Arbor, MI: University of Michigan Press, 2011).

Rubenstein, Richard E., *Rebels in Eden: Mass Political Violence in the United States* (Boston: Little Brown, 1970).

——"State Security, Human Security, and the Problem of Complementarity," in Edwin Daniel Jacob, Ed., *Rethinking Security in the Twenty-First Century* (London and New York: Palgrave Macmillan, 2016).

Sears, David O. and John B. McConahay, "Participation in the Los Angeles Riot." *Social Policy*, 17:1 (Summer 1969), 3–20. http://www.ssgs.ucla.edu/sears/pubs/A024.pdf.

Skolnick, Jerome H., *The Politics of Protest*, 2nd Edn. (NYU Press, 2010).

Styron, William F., *The Confessions of Nat Turner* (New York: Random House, 1967).

United Nations Trust Fund for Human Security, Human Security Unit, "Human Security in Theory and Practice" (2004), 12. http://www.un.org/humansecurity/sites/www.un.org.humansecurity/files/humansecurity_in_theory_and_practice_english.pdf.

U.S. Institute of Peace, "Iraq: Back in the Green Zone" (July 2, 2007) https://www.usip.org/publications/iraq-back-the-green-zone.

Vine, David, "The U.S. Probably Has More Foreign Military Bases than Any Other People, Nation, or Empire in History." *The Nation* (September 14, 2015). https://www.thenation.com/article/the-united-states-probably-has-more-foreign-military-bases-than-any-other-people-nation-or-empire-in-history/.

Volkan, Vamik, *Blind Trust: Large Groups and Their Leaders in Times of Crisis and Terror* (Charlottesville, VA: Pitchstone Press, 2004).

# INDEX

# Taylor & Francis eBooks

## Helping you to choose the right eBooks for your Library

Add Routledge titles to your library's digital collection today. Taylor and Francis ebooks contains over 50,000 titles in the Humanities, Social Sciences, Behavioural Sciences, Built Environment and Law.

**Choose from a range of subject packages or create your own!**

**Benefits for you**

- » Free MARC records
- » COUNTER-compliant usage statistics
- » Flexible purchase and pricing options
- » All titles DRM-free.

**Benefits for your user**

- » Off-site, anytime access via Athens or referring URL
- » Print or copy pages or chapters
- » Full content search
- » Bookmark, highlight and annotate text
- » Access to thousands of pages of quality research at the click of a button.

REQUEST YOUR
**FREE**
INSTITUTIONAL
TRIAL TODAY

**Free Trials Available**
We offer free trials to qualifying academic, corporate and government customers.

# eCollections – Choose from over 30 subject eCollections, including:

| | |
|---|---|
| Archaeology | Language Learning |
| Architecture | Law |
| Asian Studies | Literature |
| Business & Management | Media & Communication |
| Classical Studies | Middle East Studies |
| Construction | Music |
| Creative & Media Arts | Philosophy |
| Criminology & Criminal Justice | Planning |
| Economics | Politics |
| Education | Psychology & Mental Health |
| Energy | Religion |
| Engineering | Security |
| English Language & Linguistics | Social Work |
| Environment & Sustainability | Sociology |
| Geography | Sport |
| Health Studies | Theatre & Performance |
| History | Tourism, Hospitality & Events |

For more information, pricing enquiries or to order a free trial, please contact your local sales team:
www.tandfebooks.com/page/sales

 Routledge
Taylor & Francis Group

The home of
Routledge books

www.tandfebooks.com